About the authors

Malcolm Ritchie is Ikuko Osumi's 'deshi', or apprentice. He has previously worked as a teacher, labourer, librarian, ship's cook, and geriatric nurse. He was awarded a Literary Grant by the Arts Council for a book of experimental writing called *Transmissions*. Before going to Japan to work with Ikuko Osumi he trained in Vipassana meditation with a Thai meditation teacher.

Ikuko Osumi was born into an old samurai family. She received transmission of Seiki from her aunt in 1935, and was subsequently trained as a Seiki master by her. In 1966, she officially opened her own clinic in Tokyo.

D0034073

Also by Malcolm Ritchie
Transmissions (Plexus)

THE SHAMANIC HEALER:

The Healing World of Ikuko Osumi
and the Traditional Art of Seiki-Jutsu

By Ikuko Osumi and Malcolm Ritchie

HEALING ARTS PRESS
Rochester, Vermont

Healing Arts Press
One Park Street
Rochester, Vermont 05767

First US edition 1988.
British edition published in 1987 by Century Hutchinson Ltd., London, England.

Library of Congress Cataloging-in-Publication Data

Osumi, Ikuko.
  The shamanic healer.

  1. Mental healing.   2. Osumi, Ikuko.   I. Ritchie,
Malcolm.   II. Title.   III. Title: Seiki-jutsu.
RZ401.077 1988   615.8'52   87-34887
ISBN 0-89281-204-4

Printed and bound in the United States.

10 9 8 7 6 5 4 3 2 1

Healing Arts Press is a division of Inner Traditions International, Ltd.

Distributed to the book trade in the United States by Harper and Row Publishers, Inc.
Distributed to the book trade in Canada by Book Center, Inc., Montreal, Quebec
Distributed to the health food trade in Canada by Alive Books, Toronto and Vancouver

CONTENTS

We are surrounded by many beautiful things, but few real things. Real things are truth.

Ikuko Osumi

FOREWORD

It was about twenty years ago when I first met Mrs Osumi. At that time I was teaching anatomy at a school of Anma and massage where Mrs Osumi attended as a student in order to qualify for a certificate with which to practice as a therapist, as required under Japanese law. I also learned later that she wished to learn anatomy in order to be able to describe her patients' conditions to them more clearly.

When I first entered the classroom that day, twenty years ago, I saw a middle-aged female student wearing a kimono, sitting at the front of the class. Young students usually change their seats from class to class, but this student always sat in exactly the same seat and always listened to my lectures with such extreme eagerness that she immediately created a strong impression on me.

Mrs Osumi and I often talked together when she was a student, and because she was so especially interested in anatomy, our conversations were restricted mainly to the structure and functioning of the human body. She may have mentioned Seiki-jutsu to me at this time, but I have no memory of it.

One day, after she had graduated from the school, I was invited to her house where she told me about her work and her desire for the future. This was the first time I heard of Seiki-jutsu. She expressed her intention to study anatomy more deeply, not only theoretically, but by observing actual dissections of human cadavers.

Later she began to visit my laboratory at the university, where we began an intense study of anatomy together. Gradually her *deshi* came to join us and we soon developed into a study group. We met regularly at the university or at Mrs Osumi's house, where even some of her patients joined us. For myself, this became a chance to begin to study Seiki-jutsu.

I began my study of Seiki-jutsu without any preconceptions or judgements, simply through watching her giving treatment and receiving therapy myself.

Experiencing her way of thinking, her attitude and way of giving treatment, I started to reconsider, and eventually became critical of, contemporary medical treatment. What immediately impressed me about her treatment was the human relationship that was established between therapist and patient.

In contemporary medical treatment we tend to approach the cause, condition and process of sickness objectively, through the use of a sophisticated technology. Today there hardly exists any relationship between the doctor and the patient.

One of the words for 'treatment' in Japanese is *teate*, which literally means to put our hands on the part of the body where there is pain or sickness. The first step to any treatment should begin with this 'skinship' between the patient and the doctor (therapist).

Mrs Osumi believes that the essence of treatment is to become one with the body of the patient. In Seiki treatment she understands the patient's body as a whole, and when she gives treatment she knows the condition of the patient's body very deeply. It is her extraordinary concentration on her patients that encourages them and creates their deep trust in her.

I have been a patient of hers since I fell sick last year and have come to realize the vulnerability of the sick person. She will always come immediately to a very sick patient, regardless of whether it is day or night, weather conditions or distance. It is only her total devotion to her patients that makes this possible. So often during treatment she has told me, 'It is the patient's body that calls me.' And 'My hand is pulled by the sick part of the body.' There is also some very important advice of hers that I should remember as a patient: 'Don't look. Don't speak. Don't listen.' This means I should withdraw all my energy into myself, not socialize or even read or watch television. Even if things need to be attended to, or people have expectations of me, in my condition I must leave them until I have fully recovered. Only in this way can I obtain full benefit from my treatment and regain my energy without losing it and suffering a relapse.

Taking very seriously what she has said, I am now trying hard to look after my own condition in order to recover my health.

I hope that Mrs Osumi will continue her practice for as long as she has strength and train many good therapists.

Takeshi Hashimoto
Professor of Anatomy
Toho University Medical School

AUTHOR'S NOTE TO THE AMERICAN EDITION

The writing of this book was made part of my training and, therefore, became part of the confusing and difficult process which I underwent during that time. It was a period of personal crisis and, as the Chinese say of such occasions, one of 'danger and opportunity'.

I was given little or no conceptual description concerning the experiences I was undergoing. This caused me to try to grasp hold of things I thought I had learned in the past in order to provide some form or structure through which to understand my situation. However, this proved of little help or value under the circumstances and only exposed the shallowness of much of that earlier learning.

In the year that has passed since I finished writing this book and since its subsequent publication in Britain, I have come to realize how much of my personal struggle and confusion had been transmitted to the book itself. And, as I was also banned from resorting to any sources of reference outside my immediate environment and my own limited knowledge, this had resulted in some excesses and contradictions on my part. Most notably, a confusion, reflecting my own at the time, between a Western psychological approach and a Buddhist one.

I have tried to rectify these errors wherever possible for this edition, and any that I have overlooked or I am unaware of remain entirely my own responsibility. I realise that some unevenness still exists in the book, but have to allow it to remain as an echo of the conditions surrounding its writing.

Malcolm Ritchie
Tokyo
1987

INTRODUCTION

There were once people who lived profoundly on this planet, essentially without the selfconsciousness of doing so, and some survive precariously in a few isolated places today. They were people who lived in reciprocal, respectful relationship within ecosystems of which they recognized themselves a part and whose sacred nature they knew and understood. They lived lives in which the everyday activities of living were more akin to ritual or sacrament, paced by the rhythms of nature and linked to and in harmony with the greater movements of the cosmos – blending the sacred and the profane, past and future, time and timelessness, in the present moment. They were people who inherited an uninterrupted transmission of the knowledge of a way of being that stretched back to their distant ancestors. They knew the anatomy of the land in which they lived, dreamed its dreams, learned what it taught, and felt the same pulse stream of life flowing through the veins of the universe that they heard singing within their own bodies.

It is the lives and the beliefs of such people, who in the West until recently were considered as merely 'superstitious', 'primitive' or 'backward', which we are now beginning to realize were dynamic and vivid ways of experiencing and understanding the universe, ways that we have forgotten, and which were far more precious, far truer and far beyond anything our modern scientific belief systems or our pale interpretations of religion have been able to give or teach us.

1

In the West we have created a 'culture'[1] of anaesthesia and amnesia, a 'culture' that encourages us to stop feeling our bodies and minds and prevents us from experiencing and realizing ourselves as part of the universe, instead of existing as paranoid strangers within it, and divests us of the knowledge of our spiritual destinies – our true natures. This is a result of our having developed philosophies or descriptions of reality that are based on an egocentric dualistic rationalism. For the paths of innate wisdom and insight we have substituted the schools of acquisitive, second-hand knowledge, placing intellect over intuition and raising it to the centre point of human endeavour[2]. By so doing, we have disinherited ourselves of our own insight and of our wise ones, our Elders, the custodians of true knowledge of the Way and of those paths that could lead us, with all the self-evident and terrifying consequences.

We need to relearn and assimilate into our own lives what has survived of this ancient knowledge, in order to begin to heal ourselves, each other and the planet on which we live. In so doing we may also in some part, pay homage and respect to those peoples and their traditions and cultures that were banished and forbidden a place under the sun and the moon. Most often the denial of the right of existence of such peoples was (and still is) perpetrated by increasingly degenerate 'civilizing cultures' with ever impoverished descriptions of reality.

Now within our own moribund 'culture', devoured by the nihilism and malignant technologies of consumer consciousness, we are hearing the voices of people who have retained or rediscovered this knowledge. We are beginning to relearn and remember through these teachers, who, though many of them have roots which are nourished by the soils of various different cultures, are essentially of the same world spirit. These teachings, and our own dreams, analeptic memories, experiences and changing awarenesses, are opening us up to what we had 'forgotten', are bringing us to a turning point[3]. This turning point is the realization of a need to re-turn, which does not mean to regress, but to turn in the circle, to rejoin the dance of life once more – to turn away from the dead highways of a purely materialistic 'culture' to the living paths that lead in the direction of our common home.

*

This book is about a Japanese healer called Ikuko Osumi, whose way of living and being I believe bears witness to, and perpetuates, the old ways and is a reminder of what she would call our 'real selves'.

In September 1981 a chance meeting led me, a few weeks before my fortieth birthday, to commence the difficult training of a *deshi* or apprentice to this woman, who is both a gifted healer and teacher and the possessor of extraordinary shamanic powers.

Ikuko Osumi is master[4] of a way of healing that has all but disappeared in modern Japan. She is a master of Seiki-jutsu or the 'Art of Vital Life Force'. The original object of Seiki-jutsu was the transmission of this life force to a person in an unusual and particularly powerful way, and it would seem that, from this, individual masters developed their own techniques or methods for giving therapy.

This book is an attempt to describe something of the nature of Ikuko Osumi's Seiki-jutsu and the world of Ikuko Osumi herself. The idea of writing it originated when I was shown a manuscript in Japanese of what I was told was a transcript from tapes of Ikuko Osumi talking about Seiki-jutsu. At that time I understood it to be a manual of Seiki therapy and decided that, if it could be translated, I would try to find a publisher for the book in Britain. However, when the manuscript was finally translated two years later by Ikuko Osumi's daughter, it turned out to be a rather confused collection of reminiscences about her life, interspersed with incomplete case histories, and contained very little of the shamanic side of her nature. By now, however, the seeds of writing a book with her had been sown, and my wife Masako and I undertook our own series of recording sessions with her on Sunday evenings after the last patient had left her house.

Ikuko Osumi is an intuitive, which sometimes leads her into difficulties over conceptualizing certain aspects of her life and Seiki-jutsu. In fact, this was the first time that she had been seriously faced with describing either her life or her therapy. As she was so often to repeat during our interviews, 'I don't like to theorize or analyse.' Rather, she just acknowledges the naturalness of gifts and experiences that others might describe as 'supernatural'. It was this intuitive, spontaneous nature of hers, often augmented by flashes of clairvoyance, that made it very difficult to direct our interviews in accordance with any idea of structure, as she could only 'speak what is in my head'. The few times when we were able to guide the interviews in any specific direction were the occasions on which she opened the sessions by announcing, 'I have nothing in my head. It's completely empty.'

Finally, after several months, we had a large collection of tapes which, when they were transcribed and translated, proved to contain many repetitions, though later accounts sometimes included details omitted in the first telling. She had also discussed her cases of healing, but still in only a general way and, unfortunately, without the depth of detail that would justify their being treated as case histories, so we decided to leave most of them until such time as they could be properly recorded.

When she talked about her life, she did so in rather a fragmentary manner with little regard for chronological sequence and with many personal recollections about relations and acquaintances. When pieced together, the transcript needed a great deal of editing in order to create a short biography of Ikuko Osumi (pp. 21–35). The important areas dealing with Seiki-jutsu, her learning, psychic powers and therapy, I have placed in appropriate places in Part I where related subjects are dealt with.

Her descriptions were either extraordinary and filled with a beautiful poetic vision, or prosaic and dull and often very confusing. This being the case, I have allowed Part I to speak in her own words wherever possible, but have used my own knowledge and experience, limited as it is, wherever I felt that expansion, and the theorizing and analysing that she so rightly suspects, was necessary. Much of what I have written, for example, in the chapter on Seiki energy, will be familiar ground to many readers, but I felt it necessary to include this material for the increasing number of people who are becoming interested in this form of therapy but who have little or no experience or knowledge of it. Surprisingly I found that the

Part I

The Healing World of
Ikuko Osumi

Healing means to become your real self.
Ikuko Osumi

1

THE UNIVERSAL BREATH

From the research of the scientific avant-garde a radically 'new' vision of the universe is emerging which totally contradicts the Newtonian/Cartesian mechanistic and deterministic concept of the universe which has dominated Western consciousness for well over two hundred years. This 'new' description of the nature of the universe closely resembles and supports more ancient, and particularly oriental, traditional cosmologies and experiences of reality, which are based on mystical and meditative insights. Some of these philosophies are, by their very nature, no less empirical and analytical than contemporary theoretical physics, though based on a fundamentally different approach. Both visions describe the cosmos as an interacting and reciprocating energetic process, a macro/microcosmic, totally inclusive energy field – a universe that defies definition within the limited terms of our common dualistic frames of reference, and in which an observer cannot be considered as separate from what is under observation, but is seen as essentially part of it.[1]

The image which often occurs in some of the most ancient of these traditional descriptions of the universe is that of an 'ocean' of primordial energy which is both unmanifest and unconditioned, but at the same time given to manifesting in a multitude of ways and at various vibratory frequencies. That which is manifested is both imbued with and animated by this same energy, finally to return to it in its primordial, unmanifested state, as the source of all existence. That is to say, fundamentally there is no difference between this energy in its abstract unconditioned state and its manifested conditions; the manifested and conditioned and the unmanifested and unconditioned are both aspects of the one reality.[2]

To extend the analogy of an ocean perhaps rather crudely, it is as though in places its waters become frozen into lumps to form matter, and then these lumps melt back into the main body of the ocean, while freezing takes place in other areas to produce different 'solid pieces' of ocean. This process of freezing, melting and refreezing is continuous and infinite, constantly repeating itself over incalculable periods of time.[3]

The universe, then, is a harmonious whole, an organic continuum in which every 'thing' resonates with and reflects, and is itself reflected in, every other 'thing'. That is to say, it is a universe wherein fundamentally no one 'thing' can be considered in isolation from any other 'thing'; nor indeed can one 'thing' be truly described without describing every other 'thing'. While in ordinary states of dualistic consciousness we experience a universe of diversity and difference, in heightened states of awareness things are seen to share the same nature, to be the same. In other words, we live in a universe in which things are essentially both the same and different, two aspects of the same reality.[4]

We are part of a living, energetic universe in a perpetual flow of change and impermanence. This energy in its raw state is the life breath of all existence and manifests to form many different dimensional realms apart from the world in which we live. Although most of us are usually unaware of these other levels of existence, they nevertheless interpenetrate and reciprocate with our own world. No separation exists; there are no separate realities, except in our inability to apprehend, identify or know them. But there have always existed people in different cultures, and at various times, who possess the ability to cross the invisible bridges to the unseen, and who know how to control and work with this life-giving energy in its raw state.

This life force is by no means unfamiliar to us in the West. We have known about it since the earliest times, when we traced its terrestrial or telluric arteries as a network of meridians or ley lines across the land. We founded our sacred centres at certain places along these lines where the energy flow was at its most powerful or most accessible to being worked with by the shaman/priestesses and priests of our early shamanic cults, for spiritual, magical or therapeutic purposes. This energy has been given almost as many names as the cultures which recognized it and the disciplines that were developed for working with it.

The earliest recorded description of this energy appears in Chinese texts. Of these earliest writings, the *Huang-ti Nei Ching Su Wen (The Yellow Emperor's Classic of Internal Medicine)* deals specifically with this energy in relation to the human body and to healing. These texts describe thirty-two different forms of this life energy in the universe and gives it the name *ch'i*, which literally means 'breath', 'gas' or 'ether'. It describes *ch'i* as having two complementary and opposing aspects, which it names as *yang* or masculine, which corresponds to all the attributes associated with the 'masculine' in nature, and *yin* or feminine, which relates to all that is 'feminine'. The human body receives the masculine aspect from the universe or sky, while it receives the feminine aspect from the earth. Correspondingly the directional flow of *yang* energy in the human body is downwards, while the feminine is upwards. These two complementary, opposing aspects of *ch'i* or life force come together in the human body at a point in the lower belly or *hara*, roughly two inches below the navel and deep in the body's interior – a point called the *tan t'ien* (Chinese) or *tanden* (in Japanese). This area is sometimes referred to as the 'stove' or 'furnace', as it is here, at the energetic and gravitational centre of the body, that in certain disciplines this life energy can be transmuted into spiritual energy, literally creating physical heat.

Later, in Indian yogic texts, we find this same energy given the name *prana* and disciplines and techniques described for raising this energy in the human body in such a way that it flows through a subtle system of nerves or *nadis* up the spinal column, opening energy centres or *chakras* on its path and finally arousing the yogi's innate wisdom or cosmic consciousness.

In Japan this life energy is called *ki*, using the same Chinese character for *ch'i*, but pronouncing it differently. Many methods which embrace spiritual practices, healing and the martial arts have been developed for working with it. *Ki* as a word is an indispensable part of the Japanese language: all conditions affecting the environment, as well as the physical and psychological states of the human body and mind, are understood in terms of the constantly changing and different conditions of *ki*, and as such *ki* is at the deepest level of Japanese consciousness.

All living organisms exist reciprocally with the environment and are constantly exchanging the primordial energy or life force with the universe. When the flow of energy in an organism is restricted or becomes imbalanced, then the organism becomes sick. If the flow ceases altogether, then so does that individual life.

We are born with a natural complement of energy which we derive from each of our parents, though even this may be impaired or lost in the womb or during birth itself. It may also be lost later through sickness, accident or unwise living habits. Throughout our lives we continue to receive it in a variety of ways: from the air, through our food, from the earth and the environment generally. One important period when we receive it beneficially is during sleep. As we progress in age, however, our ability to absorb it is reduced, until such time when we can no longer maintain the life force within our bodies and return it to the universe.

Although this energy permeates every part of the human body, it flows in a much more concentrated form through specific pathways or meridians. The most sophisticated and thorough theory of the meridian system originates in the early Chinese text cited above and forms of therapy have been evolved for working in accordance with these principles. These therapies are concerned with working with these meridians in order to maintain the balanced flow of life energy throughout the body. This is done by using certain points called *tsubo*, where the flow of energy is most accessible to diagnosis and manipulation.[5] This theory and the techniques used today have been developed from what was originally an essentially intuitive way of healing, based on massage and touch, without reliance on any concept or theory – its methods arose naturally out of the body's own awareness and contact with itself and its neighbours. The most familiar of the many derivative healing systems that have come to the West from the East in recent times are acupuncture, *do-in*, shiatsu and yoga. And, of course, we have always had our own indigenous natural healers in the West who intuitively use this same energy.

One often comes across apparent contradictions existing between different schools or systems of therapy using the *ki* energy theory. It should be remembered that the earlier forms were never codified or systematized as an exact science. There is a tendency now to define these systems in just this way to the point where there is a danger of them straying far from their natural, intuitive, inspirational origins. They risk becoming reduced to rigidly defined systems more in keeping with Western rational consciousness with its emphasis on marketing, technology and formalized education systems, and in some cases they have been brought under the umbrella of an increasingly technologized medical science.

Recent research in Japan has not only shown that the ancient theory concerning the directional flow of this energy in the human body is correct, except under certain conditions, but also the actual speed of its flow through the meridians and between specific *tsubo* points has been measured in subjects who are 'meridian sensitive'.[6]

One of the ways in which this energy interacts with the environment is electromagnetically, and it is a simple matter to demonstrate that the human body emits an electrostatic field, using a staticmeter. Substantial differences in readings are obtained between people who are full of vitality and those who are in poor health. Of course, this planet also emits its own energy field in which our personal energy fields breathe, so to speak. Each moment we are unconsciously transmitting signals through this terrestrial energy field on frequencies of which we are usually unaware. Someone who has mastered the life energy in his or her own body can, however, through interaction with the earth's field, extend his or her own field over vast distances in concentrated and powerfully coherent patterns. This is done, for example, in what is called 'distance' or 'absent' healing, in which a patient may be on the opposite side of the world from the healer.

It is this same energy that Ikuko Osumi calls 'Seiki' – a word made up of the character for *ki* and a character meaning 'vital' or 'live'. And she is one of the few people who have retained the knowledge and received the training for working with this energy in an extraordinary and powerful way.[7]

While she is obviously aware of the *yin–yang* theory and a great deal of what is discussed above, she does not adhere to them as rigid concepts either in her teaching or within her own consciousness. Rather, her way is intuitive in both therapy and teaching, and, as she frequently says, she is wary of theories and analysis. Her own way was taught and developed with few words, much in the way in which Zen is transmitted, and that is how she generally teaches today, with little conceptual description, but by creating situations in which an individual's innate knowledge and insight can arise.

2

SHINTO, BUDDHISM AND THE DOCTRINE OF SUIJAKU

I have a very ancient Amida Buddha[1] in my family altar. One of Amida's tasks is to protect ships and also to act as a bridge between people. The hand the Amida holds out becomes extended to reach something or somebody. That is the effectiveness of the Amida. For example, if someone wants to get married, they visit the Amida. If the person they want is right for them, then the Amida will be like a ship to reach that person. The Amida is also protecting this book.

One of the Osumi family who owned this Amida image lived in Kyoto during a period of many wars. During these wars, in order to protect the image against fire, they wrapped it in oiled paper and hid it in the well, sometimes for several years. Inside the image are eighty ancestor spirits.

Ikuko Osumi

In order to give Ikuko Osumi's experience of the world, its religious and spiritual background and related cosmology, it is necessary to discuss briefly and in general terms the Shinto–Buddhist milieu which both forms and informs her life. Although these beliefs are not necessarily held as an organized, conscious philosophy by her, they are certainly the substance of the deep well of her being and give her life both coherence and direction.

The ground of her experience is found in the blending of two systems of belief – on the one hand, the early indigenous, shamanic religion of Shinto, which links the Japanese people to the spirits of their ancestors and the ancient gods and elemental energies of their land, and on the other, the later,

15

foreign introduction of Buddhism. It is the confluence of these two great spiritual traditions that has shaped the Japanese mind up to the present day.

In the first of these, Shinto, humankind is understood as living in a shared cosmos which is both sacred and mysterious, and the religion expresses a profound spiritual awareness of the divine power of which all natural phenomena are manifestations. The word *Shinto* literally means 'the Way of the *Kami*'. *Kami* is popularly translated as meaning 'a god', but its real meaning is more complex and includes the idea of spirit, deity or anything that displays transcendent qualities or gives off an other-worldly or numinous ambience. While all nature (of which human beings are part) is considered sacred and its mystery and beauty appreciated as a bridge between mundane human consciousness and the divine, it is only things which exhibit extraordinary or awesome qualities that are singled out for actual worship or veneration. These include both the animate and the inanimate in nature, such as rocks, winds, oceans, mountains, trees, waterfalls, animals and birds, and also the spirits of ancestors and any man or woman who in his or her life possessed qualities of high spiritual attainment or who personified such qualities as great bravery or even the capacity for evil. The remains of such people are enshrined, usually in the area associated with their lives or deeds, and their support, protection or intervention sought in time of trouble or hardship.

That which is associated with or identified as a *kami* may either be understood as 'containing' or providing an abode for the *kami* or its actual form be seen as a manifestation of the *kami* itself. At one time, if one wished for dialogue with a particular *kami*, one employed the services of a medium whom the *kami* could be persuaded to possess or enter temporarily for that purpose. At the present time, however, there are very few shamanic mediums in Japan who still retain this ability.

As well as families, villages and clans, all crafts and professions fall under the tutelage or protection of particular *kami* and shrines for them are kept in workshops, offices, factories and shops. There are also large communal shrines located in the city or countryside dedicated to these individual *kami*

Up to the end of the Second World War the imperial family was considered to be directly descended from the highest *kami* or gods, and the emperor to be descended from the *kami* or sun goddess Amaterasu Omikami and to be a *kami* or living god himself. We find a similar belief held in the early history of our own European cultures with respect to royal or imperial lineage.

Early Shinto understood the purpose or mission of human life to be that of acting on behalf of the *kami*, and its cosmology described three realms. The highest of these was called The Plain of High Heaven and was populated by superior male and female *kami* or gods. The second, middle realm consisted of this world of human, animate and inanimate beings; and the third and lowest realm was an underworld of malevolent and evil spirits. Later this hierarchical order was reduced and simplified to just one realm or heaven called Takamagahara, in which the spirits of the dead and all *kami*, both superior and inferior, coexist.

Kami or spirits often cause trouble for human beings for various reasons, and there are still many shrines, temples and shamanic practitioners who regard them as one of the main causes of sickness and misfortune and who specialize in methods of healing based on exorcism. Ikuko Osumi rarely sees this kind of spirit activity as the main cause of illness, but in certain instances as a contributory or aggravating influence which takes advantage of a patient's weekend condition.

Buddhism and the Doctrine of Suijaku

When Buddhism first spread to Japan there was a great deal of resistance to the introduction of 'foreign gods', but by the Nara period (710–81) several schools of Mahayana Buddhism[2] had become firmly established. This had been made possible by the creation of a convenient doctrine called *suijaku*,[3] which was designed to form a religious alliance between Shinto and Buddhism. For the followers of Shinto, it explained the Buddha and Buddhist deities as other forms of *kami*, while for Buddhists it described the *kami* as manifestations of the Cosmic Buddha or guardians of the Dharma.[4] Such was the climate of conciliation and reciprocation resulting from this doctrine, and both belief systems coexisted so harmoniously, that the shrines of Shinto and the temples of Buddhism shared the same compounds. While the *kami* could assume guardianship of the Buddhist temples, it was understood that the Shinto shrines came under the protection of the Buddha.

The two main sects of Mahayana Buddhism which became associated with Shinto at the outset were the Tantric sects of Shingon and Tendai, and it was during the Nara period that there occurred a syncretic fusion of these exoteric schools and Shinto in the form of shamanic Buddhism and the rise of the cult called Shugendo – 'the Way of the Mountain'. The priests of this sect were ordained Buddhists who underwent spiritual training deep in the mountains. This involved severe austerities and difficult initiations, finally enduing them with the shamanic powers of clairvoyance, exorcism, healing and mastery over fire and extreme cold. These priests, who would be attached to a particular sacred mountain which they understood as a living mandala and gateway to the other world, were called *yamabushi*, and the remnants of some branches of this ascetic shamanic cult are still extant today, though in a much reduced form. It is such a Buddhist shaman–priest that we shall meet later in the form of Ikuko Osumi's ancestor and tutelary spirit, Eizon Hoin.

The central teaching of Buddhism which is common to all schools and sects, though their ways of expressing it may differ, is the doctrine known as the Four Noble Truths. This doctrine describes the condition that characterizes the state of human existence and the way to transcend it, and it is considered to be the core of the historical Buddha Gautama's enlightenment. In it, the human condition is seen as one of unsatisfactoriness and suffering due to our basic ignorance of the true nature of existence as being one of continual change and impermanence. Our illusion about the nature of reality causes our lives to be centred around attachment to the idea of a permanent and separate individual self and we constantly attempt to hold onto the things which endorse and reinforce this false understanding. Based on this, our attitudes and perceptions are supported by and in turn support a dualistic, discriminating, conditioned and perpetually conditioning consciousness, which leads to actions that can only result in unhappiness and delusion. It is due to the nature of these repeated actions, or conditioned habitual patterns of behaviour, that we are trapped in a perpetual cycle of birth and death as they are governed by the laws of cause and effect, or karma.[5]

The last of the teachings of the Four Noble Truths points to a way to salvation called the Eightfold Path, which is a prescription for the final transcendence of dualistic consciousness through the discipline of meditation and correct living. The realization and experience of the essential non-self nature and oneness of the universe — Nirvana — results in the extinction of all karma-forming, conditioned behaviour and liberates us from the need for continued successive reincarnations on the Wheel of Birth and Death.

Buddhist cosmology describes five or sometimes six realms into which the dead may be reborn according to the karma which has been accumulated during a lifetime. These various realms consist of hot and cold hells at the lowest level, rising up through the realms of hungry ghosts or *preta*, beasts, and *asuras* or titans, the world of human beings, and finally the celestial realms or heavens of various orders. None of these realms is considered as a permanent state, as one will be spiritually promoted or relegated according to the law of karma and must eventually attain liberation and transcend all these states, including the most blissful, as they are all conditioned and therefore illusory.[6]

In the Meiji period (1868–1912) the Japanese Government downgraded Buddhism and anulled the doctrine of *Suijaku* in order to set the stage for transforming Shinto into a state religion around which a nationalistic and imperialistic consciousness could be fostered. Even so, Shinto and Buddhism still remain fused or 'confused' in the minds of many Japanese, and they find no difficulty in avowing faith in both beliefs, while often not really being able to make any clear distinction between them. Generally, in a house one will find both a Shinto house shrine and a Buddhist family altar. And while Shinto is concerned with worship of the ancestors, their spirits are now usually to be found residing within the Buddhist family altar at such times as O-Bon, the festival of the dead, when the ancestral spirits gather at the family home.

This is probably due to the fact that, before the advent of Buddhism, Shinto priests had nothing to do with funerals or funeral rites as their duties were solely concerned with serving the *kami*. Death and burial were the duty of individual families and all rites and arrangements were carried out by them. However, after the introduction of Buddhism and at the time of the Tokugawa period (1603–1868) it was required that all dead must receive Buddhist rites. And so it would seem that as the burial of the dead was carried out by Buddhist priests, the spirits of the dead became associated with the Buddhist temple and hence, with the Buddhist family altar at home, while the Shinto house shrine is now reserved for worship of the household and tutelary *kami*.

In a small back room of Ikuko Osumi's house are kept her Shinto house shrine, her Buddhist family altar and a small shrine to her ancestor, Eizon Hoin, who is revered as a *kami*. Outside her house, on top of a rock, stands a very beautiful old Shinto *inari* shrine, traditionally the guardian of a village or family group. These shrines and altars are attended to daily with offerings of incense, food and water, especially at the relevant festivals.

3

THE STORY OF IKUKO OSUMI

I have always thought that difficulty or hardship was my way.[1]

Ikuko Osumi

Ikuko Osumi was born in 1918 into an old samurai family called Katagiri, in the coastal village of Shiogama, near Sendai, Miyagi Prefecture. As a small child she lived in the house of her grandfather who was effectively the local lord of the manor, a politician who owned the local fishing fleet as well as several large rice fields. It was the Katagiri family on whom the livelihoods of the local people depended. She enjoyed a close relationship with her grandfather, who taught her how to read Chinese poetry and instructed her in Kenbu or Kendo dancing. But even as a small child she says she was struck by the contrast between the lifestyle of her family, whose lives revolved around the genteel pursuits of poetry, painting and writing political speeches, and the lives of the local people, who spent all their time working physically in the fields or at sea fishing.

From the age of four or five she was taken by her grandmother on regular visits to Mount Maki, where the remains of a famous Katagiri ancestor, a seventeenth-century Buddhist priest called Eizon Hoin, are enshrined. It was during this period, when she was five years old, that she had an experience which was to prove to be her introduction to a lifelong relationship with her ancestor as tutelary spirit and to presage the future direction of her life.

It is common for people of a shamanic calling to be introduced to their guardian spirit by undergoing some kind of

21

interior experience such as a powerful dream, vision or mantic journey to another realm. However, in Ikuko Osumi's case this experience seems to have occurred in waking consciousness or 'external' reality.

'In one corner of the garden was a shrine on top of a mound. My grandmother told me that there was a white snake which lived near the shrine and that it had lived there for generations and supported and protected the Katagiri family, though no one had actually ever seen it. Only its cast-off skins were found each year and collected by my grandmother, who used pieces of the skin for bandaging wounds and as a very good cure for warts. She would put rice out in front of the shrine each morning and, by the evening, all the rice would have disappeared.

'One day I was playing with a ball and it happened to roll in the direction of the shrine. When I went to fetch it. I suddenly saw the white snake in front of me. It looked very exhausted. It raised its head and looked at me and began to speak! It told me that it could not support the family any longer. "You have to do it. I want to ask you."'

During this period of her life, as a young child, she was already in possession of psychic or extranormal powers as described by her aged great aunt, who held a dental practice in Shiogama.

'She was not at all an ordinary child. She didn't speak like ordinary children and she always knew in advance when there was going to be a birth or sickness in the village, and would see a ghost on the eve of a death. Sometimes when she heard a child cry she would say, "That child is going to be ill" or "That child is going to die. Someone should go and attend to it." And the next morning the child would either be sick or die, according to whatever she had predicted.'

It was apparently not uncommon during this time for the local people to come and seek her advice concerning decisions which had to be made or problems which were troubling them.

'I remember the villagers always treated me with great kindness and respect when I was a child. When I went into the village, the people would say, "Ah, here comes Katagiri's grand-daughter," and bow to me. I always wanted to return their kindness by becoming a doctor so that I could help them. There were no doctors in the area at that time, which is why so many of them became sick and died.'

One of her most powerful childhood memories is the death of her father when she was six years old. By this time her grandfather had lost his position as a politician and had sold off most of his land and property in order to build a harbour for the fishing fleet in Shiogama, which was subsequently destroyed by a tidal wave. The family had become bankrupt and half the house had been rented out, with the result that her father, who was sick with tuberculosis, had to lie in an annexe with those who were caring for him. She was forbidden to visit him, but crept in when his nurses had gone for their meals. 'At these times my father would hold my hands between his own thin, bony hands and say, "Ikuko, you have to go to America or London to study and come back to help the villagers."'

This is the strongest memory she has of her father; in contrast she has almost no memory of her mother during this time. This may be the result of her repressing any memory of her mother because of later developments which affected their relationship. In fact, after the death of her father, her mother moved out of the house and returned to her own family.[2]

Her grandfather, whose health was also failing, had moved away and Ikuko Osumi was left alone with her grandmother in the old house, which was up for sale. 'One day my grandmother took a very sharp knife and pressed it against my breast saying, "You can die at any moment! This old house is going to other people and the family is declining because we have no money. So you must go and work for other people."'

There is a common Japanese expression which says that, once you have accepted the transcience and uncertainty of life, you can undertake any task or bear any burden.

The next period of her life seems to have been marked by a succession of moves from one house to another, from one relation or family friend to another, and by contradictory messages about her absent mother. On the other hand, she was given the image of a perfect mother who would one day take her back to live with her when the time was right, and, on the other, she was told that she wasn't going to join her, 'because she is staying with other people and it's not a good idea for you to join her.' In reality, unbeknown to her, a second marriage was already being arranged for her mother.

'I remember, after my father's death, I stayed very briefly with an aunt and uncle who had no children. One night I cooked the rice and was looking out of a small window in the kitchen which had no glass, only wooden slats that you could slide back and forth so that you could see outside if you wanted to. Between the slats I could see the very pure moon, a very cold moon, and I could hear the moon telling me, "*Gambarei! Gambarei!*" encouraging me. So whenever I had extreme difficulty I always remembered the moon encouraging me.

'I have always thought that difficulty or hardship was my way. I always thought that any kind of difficulty would be useful for my future.'

For a time she lived happily, but frugally, together with her grandmother and an aunt only a little older than herself, relying now and then on the pawnshop to supplement their meagre resources. One day she thought to herself, I was born into the Katagiri family with a very famous ancestor, but as long as I stay here, the whole family will die out. She made up her mind to go to Tokyo, and finally it was arranged. She was now about fourteen years old and, although she had not had any contact with her mother during this period, she still preserved an ideal image of her and believed that one day she would join her.

During this whole period and her first years in Tokyo she seems to have had few of the kinds of psychic experience that she had as a young child. Whether this was due to her insecurity at this time and the shock of having lost both her parents, or to her own supression or blocking of these faculties in an atmosphere which would most certainly have become increasingly hostile to any such expression in a young woman of her class, or to a combination of these is difficult to determine.

In Tokyo she lived with a childless aunt and uncle whose family name was Hayashibe. It was here that she was to learn finally of her mother's remarriage, the effect of which was traumatic and finally led to a breakdown. All her dreams and the ideal image of her mother were shattered and her projected future destroyed. Now, the contrast between her life in the country and her present situation with her very socially active aunt and uncle in the city became sharply contrasted in everything she experienced around her. She suddenly found herself defined as an uneducated country girl, and in her frequent contacts with her cousins, all of whom attended prestigious Japanese schools, she felt inferior and an outsider, becoming withdrawn and introverted. The only time she found comfort was in the company of her aunt's elderly mother, with whom she felt secure, while her relationship with the domestic staff was such that, while her plight engendered a certain amount of sympathy, she was frequently taken advantage of and made the scapegoat for their own mistakes and shortcomings.

A major problem was that her aunt had no idea how to relate to a teenage girl and even less ideas as to how she should be educated. Whenever Ikuko Osumi asked about her education, her aunt's usual response was to appear too busy to discuss it. Finally her aunt decided that she should be educated at home in subjects that would befit her social status and prepare her for marriage. However, she proved to be such an unwilling or incapable student that her tutors resigned one after the other and she acquired a reputation for being unteachable, selfish and fickle.

Her general condition worsened, complicated as it must have been by her reaching sexual maturity and possibly developing an ambivalence towards her own femininity due to the shock of her mother's apparent rejection of her. This in turn may have caused her to reject either consciously or unconsciously, the curriculum for domestic subjects she was supposed to study in order to prepare her for her own marriage, which, she says herself, she neither expected nor desired. Finally her plight was so obvious that it was arranged for her to visit various healers, shamans, hot springs and herbal baths, as well as, at one stage, a Western medical doctor, but to no avail.

At this point, although nothing had been mentioned about it previously, her aunt had obviously decided to 'give' her Seiki.

Her aunt had always been sickly and weak since childhood, but had received Seiki as a young woman from an acquaintance of her mother, a man who had been trained by a master of Seiki-jutsu and who had a dojo[3] in the Tokyo suburb of Hongo. From that time on her health steadily improved until she became an energetic and robust woman and received some training herself in the transmitting of Seiki. She 'gave' Seiki to several people, including a priest of the Shugendo sect attached to Mount Ontake, who was a healer and exorcist.

From this time on and without her realizing it, her aunt was to become her teacher. It is strange that, although she became her teacher and actually led Ikuko Osumi onto the path of Seiki-jutsu, it seems that she actively tried to dissuade her from becoming involved in it. Nevertheless, it was through her aunt's subtle and invisible teaching, a teaching in the main by example and presence, that Ikuko Osumi came to master Seiki-jutsu and fulfil the request of the white snake[4] by redeeming her family, not materially, but by restoring the tradition of caring and supporting others which was begun by her ancestor Eizon Hoin. Just as a seed needs no theory in order to grow into a tree, so she needed little or no conceptual or theoretical teaching in order to master Seiki-jutsu, and it is in this spirit that she continues to teach today.

For some time she had been receiving regular treatment from a shaman–healer to her head and back, and it is obvious to her now that this treatment was designed to prepare her body for receiving Seiki.

One day her aunt noticed that her body was ready and decided to give her Seiki. She has virtually no memory of how her aunt gave her Seiki or what her own reaction was at this time. She had no knowledge of or particular interest in Seiki-jutsu at this stage, and was certainly unaware of its potential for self-healing. All she remembers is that one day her aunt told her to go upstairs and sit on a small stool. She says that she now realizes how difficult it must have been for her aunt to have arrived at this decision, since her own husband objected to Seiki-jutsu and only had faith in modern Western medicines.

Some time after she received Seiki, her aunt taught her the exercises necessary for developing it in order to heal herself. Through this daily routine of exercises, Seiki-jutsu slowly but steadily began to establish a subtle but firm influence on her life.

One experience which helped bring Seiki-jutsu and healing to a central place in her consciousness was the death of her aunt's mother and her own experience of spontaneously trying to heal her. After the old woman's death, she realized that this experience had created a very strong intention within her to become a healer. With the old woman's death, the shape of her life had altered and she was able to see the course that her past life had taken and how the shock of her mother's remarriage and dismissal of her had caused her sickness. She also realized that the Western medicines and injections she had received had exacerbated her condition. She began to think about the effects that these medicines had had within her own family and to question what it means to be human, and how as human beings we can best maintain healthy bodies. She thought that in most cases Western medicines were 'dynamite for the body'. She decided to seek no more treatment or remedies and to concentrate solely on her Seiki exercises. Within three months of regular exercise her condition had improved.

With the marked improvement in her health and her resulting ability to perform the tasks that were expected of her, her standing in the household improved and her confidence began to grow.

At the age of twenty-two a marriage was arranged for her, to a relation of her aunt, a man called Osumi whom she had already met on several occasions. She had not considered marriage for herself and her whole life now was oriented in the direction of Seiki-jutsu, even though one family member had criticized her ambition because Seiki-jutsu was 'classical Edo

healing and stinks of the earth!' She was very relieved, therefore, to discover that her prospective husband was not only
interested in Seiki-jutsu but encouraged her to study it.

In 1939 she became pregnant with her daughter and immediately after her husband was inducted into the army.
Although she was still living in her aunt and uncle's house, she
was left alone to continue her studies of Seiki-jutsu and to
appreciate the stability and peacefulnes which had now entered her life. On one occasion during this period her mother
suddenly came and visited her, but both found there was
nothing in common in their lives and had no real communica-
tion.

On one of the few times when her husband came home on
leave in 1942 she became pregnant with her son and two years
later, when bombing raids on Tokyo had become frequent and
heavy, she and her children were evacuated to Minegishi in
Ibaragi Prefecture. Here she was back in the countryside, and
because of the war it was impossible for her to engage any
domestic help. This meant a sudden, drastic change in the
lifestyle she had grown accustomed to in Tokyo. She had to
climb the mountain daily to gather firewood and till her own
garden to grow the vegetables that they needed. She felt very
happy living in this way and being involved with the local
people. However, she soon became ill because she was unused
to such an extremely physical life. For two or three days she
was unable to get up from her bed and was too ill even to look
after her children, but after asking for her Seiki stool to be
brought to the house from where it was stored, she was able to
recover. It was during her recovery that she spent a period of a
hundred days exclusively devoted to her exercises on the stool
and it was here that she began to learn about the nature of the
human body (see p. 53). After this she began giving treatment
to the local people who came to visit her.

One day just before the end of the war she received a letter
telling her that her husband had been killed in action.
'Although it may sound unfeeling, I have to say that my
husband's appearance was timely, as was his disappearance. If
he hadn't been killed in the war, he would probably have taken

over my uncle's business and I should never have become the therapist I am today. Even though our life together was very short, I appreciated him.

'When I heard of his death, I went up the mountain to collect wood. I had to lie on my back in order to hoist the bundle of wood onto my shoulders. When I stood up, I was facing the sea, which, in spite of everything, made me feel very peaceful. I felt that I wasn't alone. That I was supported by Eizon Hoin and my aunt and uncle.'

On returning to Tokyo she found that her sister-in-law, who was studying pharmacology and had always criticized Ikuko Osumi for being interested in Seiki-jutsu, had fallen ill. This sister-in-law had always looked down on her as a country girl and on Seiki-jutsu as being unscientific and of no value. Now she refused to take Ikuko Osumi's advice not to take the strong medicines which she was being prescribed by the three specialists who were attending her for what was understood by them to be three different and unrelated conditions, and her health deteriorated rapidly. Later she confided to Ikuko Osumi that she had been wrong to put all her faith in modern medicines and apologized for being critical of Seiki-jutsu.

'Very late one night, while I was doing my exercises, my sister-in-law suddenly appeared in front of me in a kind of vision. Her face looked waxy and sweaty and her breathing was irregular. I rushed up to her room and found her in exactly the state in which I had seen her in my vision. I saw that she was dying and ran for the doctor. When we returned to the house, she was already in her last moments. Before she died she said to me, "Iku-chan, I'm terribly sorry. I thought you would die before me!" She was only twenty-four.'

Since her return to Tokyo, her life had become so busy that she had no time to continue her search for knowledge of Seiki-jutsu, and she began to realize and appreciate the value of the hundred days which she had spent sitting on her stool in the countryside without any distractions. It was this period that was to form the foundation for her own Seiki therapy later on. Her main purpose at this point, though, was to learn how to transmit Seiki to other people. This her aunt adamantly refused to teach her, telling her she must master it herself.

Her uncle's health had by now slowly deteriorated and a nephew, who was a Zen priest, wanted to introduce him to a Seiki-jutsu master who had healed the head monk of Gokokuji Temple after he had been told by his doctors that he only had a few months to live. The monk had survived for a further ten years after receiving Seiki treatment. Her uncle, who, as already mentioned, was a great advocate of modern Western medicine, refused the offer, but as soon as Ikuko Osumi heard about this Seiki master, whose name was Kaneko, she wanted to visit him. At first, due to the strict restrictions which her aunt had laid on her, she was forbidden to go to visit this man, but finally her aunt relented and gave her the address; she even accompanied her on the journey.

When they arrived at the Seiki master's house they were met by a *deshi* who informed them that the master was on his deathbed. When she asked the *deshi* where she could get more information about Seiki-jutsu, he explained that very few people had the knowledge any more and directed her to visit the leader of a 'new religion' and a university lecturer. He explained that they represented the two directions that knowledge of Seiki-jutsu had taken in recent years. She visited these people and several shaman, but none of them could tell her anything about Seiki-jutsu. Finally she realized that she was 'searching for the point of the arrow instead of sharpening it myself.'

For several years each summer after her uncle's death she stayed by the sea or in the mountains with her children. It was here that a second phase in her learning process took place, by observing the natural environment around her. This period had a profound affect on her, so that two or three years later, unknown to her, she had reached the point of knowing intuitively how to transmit Seiki.

One day a cousin came to visit her and her aunt. He had been seriously ill for some time and had come to ask her aunt if she would give him Seiki. Instead, her aunt told Ikuko Osumi that she should give him Seiki (see p. 42). With a sudden powerful surge of confidence she felt that she was capable of transmitting Seiki to her cousin, and taking him upstairs to the room in which the Seiki stool was kept, and after some considerable time, she was successful.

This marked her graduation from a training of which she had up to this time been unaware. Indeed, she had been in the paradoxical position of looking for a Seiki master while already being the *deshi* of a master in the form of her own aunt.

At the end of her life, her aunt insisted that Ikuko Osumi should qualify as a professional massage therapist so that she could legally open her own clinic and practice Seiki therapy. On the very day she returned from having submitted her application to take the exam, her aunt died.

Ikuko Osumi passed the massage exam and started giving treatment the next day. On 10 March 1966, at the age of fifty, she officially opened her house as a clinic. When her daughter, who had been studying in Europe for several years, returned to the house, she did not recognize her mother. She seemed transformed. Physically she had grown very large, and it was only by her voice that her daughter was able to recognize her.

Because of the variety of psychic powers which she possesses, apart from her power of healing, several people have tried to create a religion around her.[5] In fact, had she remained completely within her own traditional cultural milieu, it would have entailed her either building a new shrine to her ancestor, Eizon Hoin, or taking up residence in the existing temple and operating from within its precincts. It is typical of Ikuko Osumi that she has chosen to remain in the house of the woman who became her guardian and ultimately her teacher and avoids any obvious religiosity.

All her patients have been introduced by word of mouth. They are composed mainly of what used to be samurai class and aristocracy, though since the war the hereditary class system technically no longer exists. They form the professional class in Japan, which includes university teachers, musicians, politicians, company directors, architects, writers and one or two medical doctors and their wives. There are also from time to time several foreign patients who either live and work in

Japan or who, on some occasions, come to Japan and stay in her house in order to receive treatment. Two regular foreign patients, one an American professor of English, and the other an American captain with Japan Airlines, have been patients for over ten yeas. They were the first foreigners to receive Seiki.

Two *deshi* who appear frequently throughout the book are Mr Okajima, her first *deshi* and now her assistant who also teaches, and Mr Sato. Both have been with her for over ten years.

So many places where Ikuko Osumi looked for knowledge on the path of Seiki-jutsu had already closed. It is through the genius and selfless devotion of this woman that a dynamic way of healing has survived which otherwise almost certainly would have disappeared.

'Even though my life has been chaotic and difficult, the more the difficulties, the more I acquired the energy to withstand them. I always imagined that by the time that I reached fifty people would come to me for advice about their lives. So whatever my own condition, I tried to become involved. Everybody has ancestors and I was particularly conscious of mine. I always knew that Eizon Hoin was supporting and protecting me.'

The Story of Eizon Hoin (translated from the Makiyama Shrine pamphlet by the kind permission of Morio Sakuratani, priest of Makiyama Shrine)

Eizon Hoin[6] was born into the great samurai family of Katagiri. His grandfather was Katsumoto Katagiri, the famous vassal of Hideyoshi Toyotomi, who controlled Japan in the sixteenth century.

When Hideyoshi was defeated by Ieyasu Tokugawa, who established the Tokugawa Shogunate in Edo (present-day Tokyo), Eizon Hoin, who had wandered about the country in order to escape the war, eventually settled in Manganji Temple in Miyagi Prefecture.

In 1641 he was appointed by the clan lord of that area to

restore the shrine on the sacred mountain Makiyama. The
shrine had originally been founded 1700 years previously, on
the orders of the empress at the time, in order to support that
area and its people, but had since fallen into disrepair and
neglect. After accomplishing this task, Eizon Hoin began to
preach to the local people and became very respected by both
the clan lord as well as by the people.

During this time the mouth of the local Kitagami river had
become badly silted up with mud and was dangerous and
almost unnavigable for shipping. This had been a serious
problem for many years and, although the authorities did their
best to clear it from time to time, their efforts were unsuccess-
ful. At last the clan lord decided that it was a task that was
beyond human powers and ordered Eizon Hoin to erect a
shrine at the mouth of the river and beg for the help of the *kami*
of Makiyama.

For three nights and four days Eizon Hoin prayed at the
altar and at the end of the fourth day there was a great storm
with heavy rains which caused such severe flooding that the
entire river mouth was completely cleared of mud, making it
possible for even the larest ships to enter the river.

The clan lord was so full of admiration for Eizon Hoin that
he decided to honour him with a gift of land. The local lord
who administered that immediate area, however, was extremely jealous that Eizon should receive such a valuable piece
of land and, as the transaction had to pass through his hands,
he exchanged the land for a piece of inferior property before
Eizon Hoin was informed of the clan lord's gift.

Eizon Hoin, who knew nothing of this deception, thanked
the clan lord and devoted himself to his work for the local
people and the Makiyama Shrine. On hearing of his extraordinary devotion, the local lord became even more jealous and
ordered his officers to take away the land that belonged to the
shrine. On hearing of this, Eizon Hoin got so angry that he
took legal action in order to protect the shrine's land. However, the local officials, who were under the influence of the
local lord, rejected his complaint.

Meanwhile someone informed Eizon Hoin that the land
which had been presented to him by the clan lord had been

exchanged for another, inferior piece of land before he had received it. When he understood the full extent of the local lord's injustice towards him, he angrily made up his mind that the local lord should not be allowed to succeed in his dishonest deeds. He decided to appeal to the clan lord, but first his appeal had to be approved by the local lord, so it was naturally rejected.

He made several more attempts, but without success. Instea, he was falsely accused of misdemeanours by the local lord himself to hide his own crimes. When these charges were made public, the local people refused to support Eizon Hoin, even though they knew he was innocent, out of fear of the local lord. The people even stopped visiting Makiyama Shrine, which they had been in the habit of visiting in order to pay their respects to Eizon Hoin. One man, however, remained loyal and continued to visit the shrine. Eizon Hoin was deeply impressed by this man and secretly made him a talisman and told him to place it on the beam in his house to protect him from misfortunes such as fire and difficult childbirth in his family. In fact, some time later, when fire destroyed the whole village, only this man's house was left untouched.

Eventually Eizon Hoin was tried on false charges and sentenced to lifelong exile on a distant island. There he prayed day and night to be able to prove his innocence. Three years later, in 1681, after asking the people around him to bury him upside down, 'He stared at the sky and died, keeping back tears.'

In spite of his request, the people buried him in the ordinary way, because they were afraid of being punished by the authorities. But afterwards many misfortunes befell those who had buried him without carrying out his request, culminating in each of them dying from a very high fever. Also the people of the island found they were unable to catch the fish on which they depended and had difficulty surviving. Eventually they realized that these misfortunes might be connected with their denial of Eizon Hoin's wishes, so they decided to dig up his body and have it reinterred upside down, as he had asked. After this, life on the island was able to return to normal.

Some time after the death of Eizon Hoin, the local lord at Makiyama and his entire family died under very strange circumstances, causing the whole family bloodline to be wiped out. Many mysterious legends arose concerning Eizon Hoin, and fifty years later an amnesty enabled his case to be reopened at the request of the local people and his innocence established. He was then reburied at Makiyama[7] and the present shrine was dedicated to him. Since then he has been worshipped as a *kami* who protects the weak, maintains justice and guards against fire and difficult childbirth.

4

'GIVING' SEIKI

Truly speaking, the place teaches me, 'Here is the place.' I can almost hear those words.

Ikuko Osumi

Central to Ikuko Osumi's practice of Seiki-jutsu is the ability to bring together the different aspects of Seiki and transmit it to a person in such a way that, once received, it is retained within the body of that person for the duration of his or her life. Through a discipline of daily exercises, the Seiki that has been received can then be developed for self-healing, for healing others and for one's own spiritual evolution. Receiving Seiki in this way is not to be confused with Seiki therapy, which is dealt with later.

Seiki can only be transmitted or 'given' at certain specific places where, and at times when, the optimum flow of Seiki is available. It is there that it is most amenable to being harnessed and worked with in its purest and most concentrated form. Ikuko Osumi is particularly sensitive to these places, and it is on such a spot that a specially designed stool, shaped like a triangular box with a flattened apex, is placed on which the person who is to receive the Seiki sits. These places are where Ikuko Osumi says, 'I can feel some special line of Seiki comes in from the universe.'

She sometimes refers to these lines as being like a 'road' or a 'river', as follows: 'I think that a Seiki line is very broad, but the place where I put the stool is the very centre of that line. If you think of a very wide river with both its bank curving and irregular, the middle of that river is very stable and deep.

'In my house there is only one room in which I can give Seiki. This room is called *san-jo* or three-mat room, where I feel a special line of Seiki comes in from the universe. A few metres away there may be another line, as there are so many all over the world, but until about fifteen years ago this was the only place where I had given Seiki. All good things are drawn to that line. I feel the line comes down from the sky and along the ground like an *obi*[1] round the earth. I've felt these lines in every country that I've visited. For example, in Paris and London I can feel many places, even in hotels, where I can give Seiki. A Seiki line falls in a very specific place and I never need to look for that spot, I just place the stool exactly in that place.

'When I'm near a Seiki line, I just feel it. Something makes me feel it. If I say "I" feel, it's because something makes me feel. There are many Seiki lines like roads on the earth, in the same way that there are many places where we can find water, where we can dig a well. Finding a Seiki line is something like that.

'My uncle was very good at finding the right spot where there was natural gas. He would hold some kind of stick and suddenly say, "This is the place." Someone else I knew could find the exact spot of a hot spring in exactly the same way. My feeling is that there are so many stars in the sky that relate to some place in the earth, and so it is like this with Seiki lines.

'We have an old children's story in Japan about a very honest old man who had a clever dog. The dog would sometimes start scratching the earth and telling his master, "Dig here. Dig here." And when the old man dug there, he found lots of money. The dog might have been taught or told by something under the ground in certain places. For me, it is like this. Something teaches me. I am taught by the place. I know that I can't say that "I" know it. Truly speaking, the place teaches me, "Here is the place." I can almost hear those words.'

Timing in the giving of Seiki is of prime importance, and the period during which the optimum flow of Seiki is available and the precise moment when it can be transmitted are recognized intuitively by Ikuko Osumi. 'To me, giving Seiki is a very natural relationship between myself and the person who wants to receive it. To me, it's the same as the relationship between the sun and the moon. I feel there is a special connection between myself and the people I give Seiki to. I sometimes think it is also like a kind of line. This line is calling or teaching me.

'The thing that first gave me confidence to give Seiki was the thought, Ah, I've got all the elements of the universe inside my own body. And whenever I'm about to give Seiki, I always feel the rhythm and the timing of the sea.

'The time when I decide that Seiki should be given is what you would call intuitive, I just get a feeling that it's the right time. One of my *deshi* pointed out to me one day that whenever he checked the newspaper after we had given Seiki, it was always at high tide, but I never use timetables. I don't like to theorize or analyse the relationship between Seiki and the tide, sun and moon, but just to acknowledge the natural relationship between these things. For example, the sun is always in the sky, but it is often covered by cloud. If the sky is cloudy at the time that we give Seiki, the sun always shines through afterwards.'

This is a very strange phenomenon that occurs if Seiki is given when weather conditions are very bad and even when the cloud coverage is total. The sun always breaks through either just before Seiki is given or directly afterwards. When asked about it, Ikuko Osumi will only say, 'The sun shines as a result. I have no other idea about it. I always feel stable and confident when I'm going to give Seiki. The sun may shine as a result of my confidence.'

At present when she gives Seiki in her home she is accompanied by Mr Okajima and Mr Sato. After a date has been decided upon for giving Seiki to someone, preparation for that day begins as much as three months in advance. At this early stage it is necessary for everyone involved to restrict their lives so that they may concentrate purely on Seiki practice and avoid all socializing outside the house. This even includes weddings or funerals that may occur within their own families during this period. These restrictions are observed in order that they may be free of any distractions, to accumulate and concentrate Seiki in their own bodies. If one of them has to attend to some business outside the house, then all will go in order to maintain the psycho-energetic unit formed between them and to prevent their Seiki from becoming scattered.

One week before giving Seiki Ikuko Osumi asks all patients whose conditions are stable to suspend their treatment until after the event. This is in order that they use as little of their energy as possible in the last few days, while establishing the Seiki in their own bodies through a special form of Seiki exercise and a regimen of frequent and large amounts of nutritious food. Ikuko Osumi says that it is essential to accumulate Seiki in the body in this way, and to concentrate it until it has become 'very thick', if Seiki is to be given successfully.

'A Seiki therapist's condition should be ten tenths, not even the smallest minus, in fact a little bit of a plus. A little more than one; one plus.

'On that day, from the morning, this house is filled with Seiki and the atmosphere in the house is pure white, like a holy atmosphere. Our bodies are so full of Seiki that when we go to say something, it's as if, before words, Seiki is falling out of our mouths. When I'm ready to go upstairs to *san-jo*, as soon as my foot is on the first step I'm completely empty [i.e. in a concentrated state of no-thought].

'If the weather is cold, I usually start to warm up the room the day before we give Seiki. The temperature of the room also depends on the condition of the person. The temperature should not be too hot or too cold. It's important to have the right temperature when the room is full of Seiki. If it is too cold, we can't manage. The right stable temperature is very important.

'Before receiving Seiki, the patient is given an ordinary, general treatment on a *futon*.[2] Afterwards, when I ask the patient to move from the treatment room into *san-jo*, I can already feel how long it will take to give Seiki. To receive Seiki, some patients don't need a lot of preparation. It depends on their condition, age and lifestyle as to how they are prepared for receiving Seiki.

'The main purpose for giving Seiki is that, through their lives, most people have lost the original or proper amount of Seiki that they should have in their bodies. Most people only have nine tenths, eight tenths, seven tenths, and so on. The purpose of giving Seiki is to fill them up. Ten tenths equals one, but when a person is given Seiki they receive one plus something. That means, for example, that if a cedar tree was very sickly and was to receive Seiki, it would become a real cedar tree.'

The person to receive Seiki is seated on the stool set exactly on the place where a Seiki line falls. 'Even if the stool is on the right spot, Seiki cannot be received without a giver. Equally, if everyone is prepared, but the stool is in the wrong place, then Seiki cannot be given.

'For receiving Seiki, the condition of the sacrum is crucial.[3] If you think of an animal when it reaches out for food, it's not just its eyes that are involved in reaching out for it, but also its tail.

'Seiki enters the body through the top of the head, at the point of the hair whorl, and is caught by the sacrum while at the same time filling the whole body. If the sacrum is very hard and tense, Seiki cannot enter the spine, which means that it cannot be received. This is why it is important to give therapy beforehand, in order to open up a way for Seiki.

'When I used to give Seiki on my own, I would place my hand on top of the person's head and at the same time place my knee against their sacrum in order to help catch it. Sometimes, on my own, it used to take me about two hours to give Seiki, but nowadays I work with Okajima and Sato so we can share these parts and the whole procedure takes about fifteen minutes.

'Usually, after giving Seiki on my own, my heart was weak and I would have to go to the toilet for a pee every half an hour or so. I used to eat nine umeboshi[4] afterwards, and the next day I would eat seven and so on, until the number was reduced. After giving Seiki, my eyes were so weak that I couldn't see properly. This was one reason why I decided to train deshi. Sometimes it took me months to recover.'

While the person is seated on the stool, Ikuko Osumi can feel the heavy flow of Seiki, and she and her assistants set about attracting and gathering Seiki to that place. This is done by using the Seiki already accumulated in their bodies and sometimes by spontaneously creating sudden loud noises: banging the walls, clapping and loud *kiai*.[5] The resulting vibratory activity attracts and also activates the Seiki in the atmosphere; if there is anyone in the immediate vicinity of the room to which Seiki is being attracted, then Seiki will be drawn from his or her body, as happened recently to a woman who was seated in a room directly beneath the room to which Seiki was being attracted.[6]

This whole business is performed without plan or arrangement, but instinctively. 'I have my eyes closed and I'm like the conductor of an orchestra. Okajima and Sato don't need to watch me. We are three in one; it's like dancing. I never try to attract Seiki strongly, it just comes to me naturally. The person's body tells me when it's time to give Seiki to them, just as when a fruit is ripe, it is ready to fall to the ground. At this moment I feel that it is Eizon Hoin who is teaching and supporting me.'

Throughout this operation all those involved have been maintaining a condition of 'emptiness', a one-pointed state of no-thought, in which body and mind are brought into harmonious unity, while breathing deeply into the belly or *hara*. As the process of attracting Seiki progresses, the mass of energy that is gathered is controlled and manipulated by using the Seiki that has been accumulated in their own bodies, particularly with the Seiki coming from their hands. This is why the preparation period is so vital and the reason why, without it, Seiki cannot be transmitted. It is important to stress here that at no time does the mass of Seiki that has been attracted to that place pass through their own bodies. Their own bodies are already filled with Seiki and the amassed Seiki remains outside them and is controlled in such a way that it only enters the body of the person who is to receive it. Ikuko Osumi says, 'When the Seiki comes together, there's not even a hair's breadth between it.'

At a given moment, which, as she says, she knows intuitively, she places her hand on the receiver's head, covering the hair whorl, which 'is the main point that wants to receive Seiki.' Often, but depending on circumstances, this action is accompanied by a loud *kiai* or series of *kiai*. At this moment Seiki enters the person's body through the head, while at the same time the whole body is enveloped in this potent charge of primordial energy. If for some reason the first attempt fails, it must be repeated immediately.

At the actual moment–point of transmission, her hand becomes attached to the receiver's head 'like a magnet', until the person has received the amount of Seiki that his or her body requires for its future wellbeing. The moments during which Seiki is received are often accompanied by a gentle rocking of the person's body back and forth, and after it is completed Ikuko Osumi's hand naturally separates from the head.

'Up to the point when my hand separates, everything is just a natural rhythm without thinking or anything. Whenever I have given Seiki, my appreciation and joy are always the same. After I've finished I thank Eizon Hoin in my body, everything in the universe, everybody in the house and the patient, because I could give Seiki.'

Five Cases of Giving Seiki

CASE 1

'For a long time I had been waiting for my aunt to teach me how to give Seiki to others. Since my uncle had died, I had arranged things in order to give my aunt and me space to be together so that I could question her about the giving of Seiki. Every time I approached the subject, though, her response was always the same: "It doesn't please me as long as you have the idea of being taught how to give Seiki. If you are truly interested in doing so, you will have to master it on your own."

'During this time I thought a lot about Seiki every waking minute, thinking about how it could be given. One day one of my cousins came to see me about receiving Seiki from my aunt. He had great difficulty in walking and was suffering from an illness that had been diagnosed by the hospital as heart disease. He always carried a lot of medicine with him because he couldn't sleep. In the course of our conversation he said that he was intent on recovering from his illness and we talked for some time about Seiki therapy and being given Seiki. He knew that both my aunt and I had recovered through receiving Seiki and he asked my aunt if she would give it to him. She turned to me and to my surprise said, 'You should give him Seiki.' The moment that she said this, I immediately felt that I could in fact give Seiki. My cousin asked me if he should stop taking his medicine and I told him, "You had better not change anything yet." In fact, after a few days, he did stop taking his medicine and stayed with us for a few weeks while I gave him therapy in order to prepare a way in his body for Seiki.

'When the day arrived, my aunt remained downstairs sitting beside the *hibachi*[7] while my cousin and I went upstairs to *san-jo*. It took me about two hours to reach the point where I could give him Seiki. When I felt the time was right I placed my hand on his head, and his head and my hand stuck together like magnets. His body started to move backwards and forwards and my hand followed his movements. When he had received the Seiki he needed, my hand came away from his head and his movement became independent of me. I asked him if his movement was spontaneous and he said that it was. "I feel as though I'm floating on the clouds!" he said.

'I was very excited and told him, "I thought I could give you Seiki." I ran downstairs to my aunt and asked her to come upstairs. When she saw my cousin moving on the stool, she said, "Yes, that's Seiki. You've finally got it. Well done! This is what I've taught you!"

'I suddenly knew that while my aunt had never taught me in any obvious way, just being with her had been the real teaching.

'My cousin has enjoyed good health since and often mentions to me, when I see him, how Seiki has helped his life.'

CASE 2

'For some reason I had always given Seiki on a Sunday, but in Malcolm's case I decided it should be on a Saturday. I felt strongly that it should be given at about 5 o'clock in the afternoon, that 4 or 6 o'clock would be no good.

'It was a big challenge for me. I had never given a *deshi* Seiki so early in his training and I had never given Seiki on a Saturday, but I was really in a hurry to give him Seiki.

'Someone said to me, "You don't need to give Seiki to a man you don't know. How do you know he will return here after he goes back to Britain to sort out his business?" But at that time I felt that I must give him Seiki because he had given up all his past life to come to Japan to learn Seiki-jutsu and he depended on it, so I really thought I should give it to him even if the others were against me.

'In some ways it looked impossible, as the house was in the middle of being renovated and altered, but it was a beautiful day with the sun in the sky and birds singing and a gentle breeze. It had rained the day before, so the air was beautifully clean and clear. At first the house was filled with carpenters, but afterwards we discovered that they had suddenly moved to the half-finished part of the house. Even though we were in a tiny three-mat room, I felt as though we were in some heavenly place. I felt as though we were in some huge vast place deep in the mountains. Suddenly afterwards I realized we were surrounded by mess and building materials and remembered that it had taken Miss Misako three days to clear the room for giving Seiki.

'When I had first gone upstairs, I went up so easily and quickly. But when I came back to reality, it took me a long time to come back down the stairs![8]

'The disappearance of the carpenters at the crucial moment is, for me, the same thing as the appearance of the sun at the right time when the sky is covered by cloud.

'When I decide to give Seiki, it is really definite, and I was so happy after we succeeded that we celebrated when we returned to the apartment we were living in temporarily. We ate *sukiyaki*[9] and seafood and drank beer and *saké*. Then I gave gifts of money to three of my *deshi* and I gave Malcolm a watch.'

CASE 3

'I remember another case though, when I couldn't give Seiki. In this case, the person who was to receive it had just become engaged and was due to meet her fiancé later that evening after receiving Seiki. Previous to arriving at my house she had had her hair set and didn't want it disturbed. She was overexcited and couldn't settle down at all. In fact, the whole situation was too disturbing for me, so that I gave up trying to give it to her on that occasion.

'Afterwards I advised her, "When you're married you can be with that man for the rest of your life. For Seiki, we need a very specific time and preparation, so you should postpone your marriage day and concentrate on receiving Seiki." She agreed, and I succeeded in giving her Seiki the second time, before her marriage.'

CASE 4

'I'll never forget Mr Kilcullin's son's case. The day that Mr and Mrs Kilcullin arrived at my house with their son, it was snowing heavily. It had been difficult for them to reach Tokyo from where they were living, and when they arrived they left their son with me while they went somewhere else. By the time we had given their son Seiki the snow had stopped and the sun was shining brilliantly. It's just natural, so I don't like any kind of theory.

'In terms of the natural world, I just feel that the sun helps me give Seiki. But sun, rain, snow, wind, all these are important for life, even though we may prefer sunny weather to typhoons because our bodies and minds feel relaxed. Here in Japan it is said that when we have snow, several insects that are harmful to rice are killed. This is why rice from the "snowy country" is better than that from other areas. All things in nature are important.'

CASE 5

The act of transmitting Seiki requires enormous strength, and this is one reason why the life and training of Seiki therapists is so disciplined.

'My aunt, from her own experience, warned me not to do "such an extraordinary thing as to give Seiki to other people."

She told me that, when she gave Seiki, her right arm and hand became purple, and that it was necessary for the person giving Seiki to "die for a moment". She told me that she had to stay in bed for at least a month after giving someone Seiki and that it was too much for a human being!'

It should be pointed out that Ikuko Osumi's aunt's life was that of a gentlewoman and not a Seiki master, and although she had mastered Seiki, she did not work as a therapist.

The reason for the resulting exhaustion after giving Seiki is due to the fact that those involved have used up a great deal of the Seiki in their own bodies in the effort required for attracting and controlling the powerful flow of external Seiki.

Here Ikuko Osumi describes how she became ill after giving Seiki to a very aged and sick woman.

'The eighty-year-old mother of one of my patients had been diagnosed by her doctor as suffering from stomach cancer and had been given only about a month to live. Even at this late stage, and under seemingly impossible conditions, the whole family were very determined that she should receive Seiki, as this was a wish that the old lady had expressed on hearing that the reason for my own good health and strength was due to having received Seiki.

'While I was considering the possibility of giving her Seiki, I suddenly had the strong feeling that, if I did so, I myself would fall sick.

'Okajima and I travelled to her house carrying a Seiki stool with us. When we were inside the house, I felt that the only place where a Seiki line fell was beside the family altar, so that's where we placed the stool.

'The old lady was so thin and frail that it looked impossible for her even to sit on the stool, but the enthusiastic support of her whole family and her own strong desire to receive Seiki made it possible for Seiki to be given.

'Almost immediately afterwards I felt blood coming from my uterus. This bleeding lasted for a whole week and stopped only when I put on my sleeping kimono, but as soon as I changed to go downstairs in the morning, it would start again. It made it impossible for me to give therapy, so that I was forced to close my doors and rest for ten days, and it was a full two months before I fully recovered. I remember thinking to myself, Ah, this is what my aunt warned me about!

'The old lady lived for seven more years after receiving Seiki, and even began to give treatment to other members of her family, often asking me for advice from time to time.'

5

SEIKI EXERCISES (*TAISO*)

I asked questions and they were answered on the stool.
                                    Ikuko Osumi

Receiving Seiki does not mean that we are suddenly made impervious to sickness. The story that Ikuko Osumi tells in the previous is a case in point – if we overextend ourselves, naturally we become tired and ill. Although, having received Seiki, our capacity is that much greater than it was previously, we still have to know our limitations very well and work within them. We are human beings with conditioned minds and physical bodies which reflect that conditioning, and it is the nature of this human life that we experience discomfort and illness at times. But through having been given Seiki we are much less prone to conditions that result in serious illness, and by working with conditions and states that have arisen, usually through our own carelessness, we learn to understand how they arise and lead our lives more wisely.

Having been given Seiki does not mean that there is suddenly a miraculous transformation of our state of being. It is more like having been given a seed which once we have planted it, we must nurture and provide the conditions necessary for its growth and development. The need for discipline and commitment is essential in this respect as, after the initial transmission, it takes three years of regular daily exercises for the received Seiki to become properly active and it often takes ten years for it to reach maturity. Ikuko Osumi says that, by developing our Seiki and bringing it to maturity, we become our 'real selves', growing to our full potential as human beings and at the same time extending the span of our lives.

Essential for performing these daily Seiki exercises is the state of 'emptiness' or no-thought. A simple method for achieving this state is to breathe from the belly and concentrate one's awareness on the breath at a point roughly two inches below the navel. When sensations and feelings arise in the body one can 'breath into' these places, while at the same time shifting one's attention to them and keeping awareness of the quality of the feeling without discriminating 'good' or 'bad'. When thoughts arise, attention can be brought back immediately to the breathing and body awareness. The whole of one's exercise is really performed as meditation.

These exercises are carried out while sitting on a Seiki stool. After relaxing for a few moments and emptying one's mind, both hands are placed on the chest and, while exhaling, the hands brush down the torso, along the thighs to the knees, then, as one inhales, the hands leave the knees in a wide circle back to the shoulders, then move down the chest to repeat the cycle perhaps half a dozen times.

Next, after a pause, the inner corner of each eyeball is gently pressed with the middle or second finger of each hand. This alerts the autonomic nervous system through the optic nerve and the motor nerve, which responds with movements that are in harmony with the condition of the body at that time. The most common of these is the rocking movement already mentioned in the description of receiving Seiki. While these movements are taking place, Seiki is directed to those parts of the body that are diseased or tired and need healing.

Initially, for some people, immediately after having received Seiki, there may be no spontaneous movement for a period of some months; for others, instead of a rocking movement the torso may swing in a circular movement to right or left.

These spontaneous movements are followed by a programme of learned exercises which exercise every part of the body. If one experiences no spontaneous movement initially, then one will simply follow whatever exercise programme is appropriate to one's condition at the time.

The length of time taken by these exercises will obviously vary according to one's condition and therefore will vary from day to day, as will the type of movement experienced. Sometimes the movement may only last for ten minutes or so if one's condition is very good, or it may last as long as an hour, as it did occasionally when I was very sick.

As these exercises develop, so too does one's body awareness. There comes a growing sensitivity to the energy flows and to the needs of different areas of the body, and this means that one can actively work on these areas with one's hand during the exercises. This is really an extrasensitive extension of the natural and unconscious way in which we rub, scratch or strike parts of the body which need attention or energy. Ikuko Osumi refers to this as the body 'calling', and she is a master at hearing the 'call' from the body of a patient.

Often, when we begin to pay attention to our bodies in this way, we begin to feel slightly ill or uneasy. This vague negative feeling is our first real perception of body conditions which may have been present for some time, but of which we have been unconscious until now. They are conditions of imbalance within our bodies which have gone unnoticed in our normal day-to-day distracted state. This growing awareness of our body states deepens our understanding of how the body and mind are affected by different emotional and physical experiences and environmental changes from day to day and, indeed, often during the course of just an hour.

The quality and feeling-tone of the spontaneous movements in Seiki exercises are very different from the spontaneous movements that result from the sudden release of energy which has been blocked or held within the body's masculature. The movements in Seiki exercise have a strong, positive, concentrated feeling, in contrast to the scattered, agitated quality that most often accompanies the release of hitherto blocked energy, though this kind of energy release also occurs at times.

Part of the exercises involves several *kiai* which in effect concentrate a great deal of Seiki in the *hara* and then discharge it throughout the whole body. In my own experience this brings a sensation of heat like a subtle fire, often accompanied by a buzzing or tingling electrical sensation up the back and along the arms and into the fingertips.

Ikuko Osumi says that, although she was born with psychic abilities, they were sharpened through doing her Seiki exercises. 'Because of Seiki-jutsu, I can be empty.' It is by being 'empty' that the body can express itself as wisdom, heal itself as its own medicine and resonate with the universe as an integral part of it. Thinking very subtly disturbs the energy flow within the body and the reciprocal exchange of Seiki with the universe – in a sense it cuts off from the environment perhaps like a radio which short-circuits. 'Emptiness' or *mu-shin* (literally, 'no-mind') could be said to be the heart of Seiki-jutsu.

Ikuko Osumi says that it is often during these exercises that she receives some of her psychic experiences or insights. It is by performing these daily exercises that 'We push out what we don't need from the body and replace it with what we need from the universe.'

These exercises are completed by lying on the floor in a position called *dainoji*, in which the body, with legs spread wide and arms outstretched to either side, forms the Chinese character *dainoji*, which means 'big' or 'great'. After stretching the whole body and then relaxing, one breathes deeply into the *hara*, alternating the inhalations and exhalations between nose and mouth for between five and fifteen minutes.

Seiki exercises were a very important part of life in Ikuko Osumi's aunt's house, to the point of being a ritual that seems to have had priority over all other activities.

'Our *taiso* was a kind of solemn ceremony for us. We changed our kimono and *tabi*[1] and, according to the season, we wore different kimono made from different materials. We put a carpet on the *tatami*[2] and placed the stool on top of it, and my aunt put a lovely cover made from some kind of grass on top of the stool.

'Since there was only one stool, my aunt and I had to share it, and it was natural that my aunt should do her *taiso* first, while I waited downstairs until she signalled that she was finished. I felt that it was my duty to keep as far away from her as possible while she did her *taiso*, in order not to disturb her.

'One day I decided to wait behind the *shoji*[3] of the room in which she was doing her *taiso*. When she finished and came out she was very surprised to see me and said, "Ah, you were waiting there!" Then she gave me the warmest smile that I had ever seen on her face.

'I think this moment was crucial for me in my learning of Seiki-jutsu. It occurred to me that this was the first sign that she had noticed of my eagerness for learning. I think she had misunderstood my keeping a distance from her while she was doing her *taiso*, seeing it as a lack of interest, and felt disappointed after all the effort and sacrifice she had put into giving me Seiki.

'My *taiso* on that day was very good and, from that point on, the relationship between my aunt and myself became much closer. She began to give me advice about my body and how I should approach my *taiso*. She taught me the importance of emptying my mind when I sat on the stool and of generally developing a strong belief in my recovery. I began to understand what she meant when she said that we should do *taiso* for itself, without any idea of a reason or goal, that we should do it for its own sake. That this was the only way that we could break the wall and reach the truth of Seiki-jutsu.

'My aunt's discipline was such that she refused to answer the telephone if she was doing her taiso, and when her mother was gravely ill with heart and kidney disease, my aunt told the maids and myself not to call her if she was on the stool, even if her mother's condition was critical. She said that she and her mother had talked about it and made the agreement that, even if her mother was dying, we were to call the doctor, but not my aunt if she was doing her *taiso*. The understanding was that *taiso* should never be stopped or interrupted. Such was the relationship between them that they could reach this kind of arrangement, and while my aunt's behaviour towards her mother may seem unfeeling, in fact their relationship was one of great warmth.

'From this point my whole life revolved around my Seiki *taiso*, which I started to do three times a day. When I was sitting on the stool, I felt that all that was bad in my body was flowing out and something energetic and alive was flowing in.

I felt like the pictures I had seen of Fudo-myo-o[4] surrounded by flames.'

Years later, during the Second World War, when she and her two children had been evacuated to the countryside from Tokyo, Ikuko Osumi became very ill, and, after several years' hiatus in doing her regular *taiso* because of her marriage and looking after her family, she suddenly knew that this was the only way in which she could heal herself. This period of re-establishing her Seiki *taiso* was to prove crucial for her future, both in helping her to learn about her body and to develop her own form of Seiki therapy.

'Although, for the first three days, sitting on the stool had been very difficult and there had been no apparent movement, in fact inside I could feel the faintest stirring. And though this movement seemed inside my body only, by sitting in *zazen* on the stool I was able to change that tiny unseen movement until it developed and flowed out through my body as the rocking movement of Seiki *taiso*.

'After these three days I was able to wash rice and cook for my children again and realized that I had no idea how they had survived up to that time!

'Through my *taiso* I learned that when we are ill we must push out all the tiredness from our bodies in order to take in new energy. I felt that if my body didn't move on the stool at first, then that was natural for my body at that time. I left everything naturally to my body.

'I began to do my *taiso* daily again, after quite a long break from doing it after my marriage and having my children. I kept the stool in a room which faced a path which led to the mountain. It was such a peaceful place to sit and do my *taiso*, in spite of the fact of the war, with all the rice fields filled with the shoots of the young plants. I felt as though I was absorbing all the good energy of the universe when I sat there each day.

'This was another important time in my development of Seiki-jutsu. Without any knowledge of anatomy, I began to learn very deeply about the body and how it works in relation to its surroundings. How certain movements relate to certain organs and nerves and the relationship between all of these things. When somewhere felt painful, it appealed to some other part of the body to heal it, and I could feel that so well. I could concentrate on my body until it became as though it were made of glass and I could see all its functioning. At these times I became totally unaware of any of the sounds of the world around me. It was as if I was in another realm. My movement on the stool wouldn't stop until I had understood its meaning completely. These investigations easily lasted for two or three hours a day. I asked questions and they were answered on the stool. Sitting on the stool taught me the reasons why I had become ill. How everything that had happened to me in my past and present had causes and how whatever I was doing now affected my future.

'When I did finally come to learn anatomy, it just endorsed what I had already learned during this period, facing the mountain.'

6

SEIKI THERAPY (*RYOHO*)

When I respond to the body's calling, the calling and myself
become one.

Ikuko Osumi

There can be said to be at present two main approaches to
treating sickness. One is a dualistic approach, wherein the
roles of patient and therapist are clearly defined, and the other
a 'one-being' therapy, as Ikuko Osumi calls hers, in which the
dualistic relationship between patient and therapist is transcended during therapy. There are also various combinations of
these two extremes.

In the first approach the patient is acted on, so to speak, as a
passive object and therapy is generally concerned with returning the patient to a state which was considered to be healthy
before the appearance of any obvious symptoms. That is to
say, a restoring of the status quo, without any change or
learning on any meaningful level. It is a way of treating illness
which is not designed to upset or inconvenience the ego (the
conditioned self) any more than inevitably happens when one
is ill. Such therapy too often denies the patient responsibility
for, and knowledge of, his or her own condition and the
treatment he or she is receiving.

There are other forms of healing which belong to the second
approach in which the patient becomes an essential and active
part of the healing process and heals him/herself with the
assistance of the therapist. This approach usually requires a
certain discipline on the part of the patient, a self-inquiry and

awareness that often results in a change in the orientation of that person's life.

Our bodies and our minds are like living archaeologies in that they contain all our past conditioning experiences, and this is why true healing comes from insight into one's own nature. This is why illness itself is so important in this respect.

Each illness, each crisis, is an opportunity for learning, a chance for change. As the nature of conditioned consciousness is itself sickness (in the Buddhist sense), many illnesses reflect something of the nature of what is ailing at the root. Our tendency is always to see illness, or a 'negative' compulsive pattern of behaviour, as weakness, as something that must be hidden or fought and conquered, instead of something to be entered into in a positive relationship, so that the potential strength and wisdom that are held within it are revealed. If we look at sickness correctly, we have to pay attention to ourselves and reflect upon our past behaviour, something we may hitherto have disregarded. Ikuko Osumi in her therapy always encourages a patient to see how a particular condition has arisen and what it was that led to it.

Illness and what it is 'saying' or leading us to learn, coupled with a therapy that encourages this learning process, are transcending and transforming. Real healing of this kind requires time, patience and perseverence – the rhythm time of nature, not the instant time of technology.

In Seiki therapy one of the most important things we have to learn, both as patients and as therapists, is to develop patience, not only in therapy but throughout our lives. Ikuko Osumi refers to the people who receive her therapy as *kanja* – a Japanese word that is equivalent to the English word 'patient'. Many people writing about so-called alternative therapies seem shy of using the word 'patient', perhaps because of its association with conventional medicine. But 'patient' is a very good word, meaning as it does 'having or showing patience'.

The Japanese word *konki*, which literally means 'root *ki*' or the energy that is contained in the root of a tree, also contains the meanings of both 'patience' and 'perseverence'. Ikuko Osumi stresses the need for a Seiki therapist to develop *konki*.

'A therapist must develop *konki* through Seiki-jutsu. *Konki* achieves the impossible and is developed by doing the unseen, by staying steadfastly with one's work, rather than spending time out in the world enjoying oneself. It means keeping a strong discipline, something people find difficult and complain about these days. It is like the roots of a tree: they are never seen and they never see the sun, but receive it through the leaves and support the whole tree.

'A therapist should combine *konki* with devotion and bring these to single-minded concentration on the patient. As soon as I receive a call from a patient, I concentrate solely on that patient as I prepare to make my visit.

'About ten years ago I went to visit a patient who suffered from cancer and who lived on the outskirts of Tokyo. It was snowing heavily. In those days I always wore a kimono and travelled by public transport. The patient's family came to meet me at the station, expecting, they told me later, to find me wearing gumboots, but we missed each other. By the time I arrived at their house they had already returned and were all surprised to find that, not only was I not wearing gumboots, but I hadn't even got my *tabi* wet! I hadn't thought about getting wet as my mind was completely occupied with the patient and her condition.

'I remember an ancient Chinese proverb which says, "One mind can even penetrate a rock."[1] This strong mind makes it possible for us to walk in the rain without getting wet or walk across fire without burning our feet.'

The discipline of Seiki-jutsu is reflected in both the behaviour in and the appearance of the treatment rooms.

'The colours should be neutral, and the light and sound should be minimal, in order to create as stable an environment as possible. The temperature should be adjusted to each patient's individual condition and, obviously, according to the time of year. For some patients the temperature may need to be changed several times within an hour.'

Seiki treatment is generally given while a patient is lying down on a traditional Japanese sleeping mat or *futon*, though there are occasions when a patient may be asked to kneel or sit.

The patient is dressed in a cotton sleeping kimono or cotton pyjamas and the *futon* is prepared in a formal way, with a cotton undersheet and cotton towelling overblanket, on top of which is placed a quilt. At the head is a firm pillow filled with the shells of soba seeds. Ikuko Osumi stresses the need for warmth in Seiki treatment, so the nature of the blanket and/or absence of the quilt depends on the season. In the winter, for example, an electric blanket is placed beneath the undersheet.

Usually treatment is carried out through the towelling blanket, though there are times when this may be removed and treatment given either through the kimono or directly onto the skin. The reasons for this are various and depend on the situation and the way of working of individual therapists.

The manner in which therapy is given by Ikuko Osumi today has developed over many years and is different from the way in which she originally gave therapy when she worked on her own.

'My only purpose in the beginning was to give Seiki. First I needed to prepare a way in the person's body. In doing this, so often I found that the person was suffering from some problem or other and I would heal them. Eventually I was healing illness more than giving Seiki and I realized that I wanted to master this healing so that I could heal any illness.

'When I first started my clinic I worked very differently from the way we work today. The patient would sit on the *futon* and wait for me to come into the room, so that when I came in we greeted each other very formally before I took the patient's pulse. At that time I didn't make the patients lie down on the *futon*. They would sit *seiza*[2] and I would treat them with a lot of *kiai*, sometimes touching certain places but sometimes without touching the body at all. Then I would ask them to turn round and I would treat their backs in the same way. Sometimes then I would ask the patient to lie down on the *futon*.

'When I greeted the patient I told myself, "This is the only chance to give my best treatment," even though I knew I would be seeing the patient the next day or the day after.

'When I started to train *deshi*, in order not to waste time I stopped that kind of formal greeting, and now I start with the patient already lying in the *futon*, as the *deshi* starts giving therapy before I come into the room.'

Ikuko Osumi says that the main cause of illness is the accumulation of tiredness, and the task of Seiki therapy, in common with Seiki exercises, is to 'push out this tiredness'. She explains that this tiredness is due to the overuse of nerves and body functioning resulting from unwise ways of living and working, our reactions to climate and our psychological disposition.

The therapy is massaged-based, but includes many techniques found in other oriental therapies. 'A therapist's body can create an almost endless variety of techniques according to a patient's condition.'

These techniques are similar to acupuncture when the fingernails are used in a particular way, to moxibustion when places on the patient's body are heated by blowing hot air into them through a cloth, and Shiatsu when points on the body are pressed with the thumb. On occasions the body is also moved into certain positions and treated by slapping, rocking and pulling. Certain changes in diet and way of life may be recommended and also particular exercises.

As will be obvious, Seiki therapy treats the patient holistically and understands the human body as energetic and mutable, as undergoing constant change in reciprocal relationship with its environment. It recognizes the interdependent relationship between all functions of the body and mind and works on a system of correspondences which at times coincides with, and at other times differs from, the meridian/*tsubo* systems used in other oriental therapies.

In my own experience Seiki therapy is capable of producing profound changes in both body and mind or psyche. And there are times during powerful or strong treatment when it works in the same manner as the deep-massage therapy developed by Ida Rolf in America.

While a whole system of points or *tsubo* is used, Ikuko Osumi rarely refers to *tsubo* as such and certainly does not consider that these points occupy fixed positions within a rigidly defined system, which would allow a deterministic type of therapy in which one could diagnose and treat specific *tsubo* for a particular condition.

When asked directly about *tsubo* she will only say, 'The whole body is *tsubo*.' She makes the very important observation that the points are constantly changing position according to the patient's condition. This movement is due to the presence of excessive tension or the lack of natural tension in nerves and local muscles, fascia and veins, and so on. She says, 'In some patients the change may only be a hair's breadth. Nothing is fixed in the human body. The body is alive.'

While, generally speaking, the correspondences between parts of the body and certain organs and organic and nervous functioning are the same for everyone, there are times when certain of these correspondences may differ from one person to another according to their particular physical and psychological type or condition at the time of treatment.

While, of course, there exists a conceptual body of knowledge gained from experience and observation, a real 'body of knowledge' is revealed during therapy arising from the conditions created by a 'one being' or 'one body' treatment. It is this symbiotic 'one body' situation which allows what is innately known and what is also intuited moment to moment by the therapist to arise simultaneously. That is to say, the real ground of Seiki therapy remains intuitive and the conceptual knowledge remains secondary to the therapist's intuitive actions at the patient's side. This often means that the course of a treatment may be quite unexpected in relation to any prior conceptual diagnosis of a patient's condition.

When Ikuko Osumi works on a patient, she responds to what she describes as 'the patient's body calling'. That is to say, she works on the patient's body in much the same way as a dowser works over the land. Similarly, as she herself recognizes the place at which a Seiki line falls on the earth, the energy in her body responds to the conditions of energy in different parts of the patient's body. Without touching the patient's body, she can detect intuitively where there exists an excess of energy due to a blockage or stagnation and where there is too little.

'When I respond to the body's calling, the calling and myself become one. It is this calling which also gives me the confidence to give Seiki. When I am giving therapy, I am not thinking about the patient's condition, only responding to the calling. Seiki treatment depends upon the response to, and guiding by, the calling from the patient's body, but it is very important for the therapist to know the anatomy of the body and how it functions. This also helps make the therapist full of confidence.'

When she says 'the calling and myself become one', she is referring to the all-important state of 'emptiness' or *mu-shin* which was mentioned earlier. It is this state which she first became familiar with through her aunt and the Zen art of *cha-no-yu* or the tea ceremony. She often emphasizes the importance of therapist's bringing an 'attitude' of the tea ceremony into the treatment room. This is called *ichigo ichie* and means to carry out one's work – making the tea, or in this case giving therapy – with one's whole being, as though this is the only time in one's life when one will perform this act. This attitude or way of doing something is a natural result of the state of *mu-shin* and means that dualistic relationships are transcended so that one brings one's whole life, the entire universe, to this one point. In other words, *one is that which one is doing*.[3] This is the real meaning of 'one-being treatment', and it is this aspect of healing which is expanded later when we discuss timing in relation to therapy.

During therapy a patient is often given a more powerful and concentrated charge of Seiki than flows normally from the body of the therapist to the patient. The method for producing Seiki in this way is similar in some respects to the way in which Seiki is transmitted to a person as an endowment. It differs in that the charge is not so powerful; nor is it given in a place where a Seiki line falls or at any special time. Also frequently the Seiki comes through the therapist's own body, except under certain conditions. It is similar in the way in which it is given through *kiai*. In these cases Seiki is given to those areas on the body where it is needed: that is to say, it is administered locally in relation to a specific organ, nerve or function, although on occasions it is given to the whole body.

Kiai cannot be the result of a decision or idea but must be made spontaneously; it will vary in expression and nature according to how and where on the body it is given. It may be almost silent and without any particular movement or it may be very loud and accompanied by a great deal of activity. At such times Ikuko Osumi works herself into a state of angerless fury which produces a heavy charge of Seiki accompanied by a sensation of heat.

There are other times when she does not give Seiki directly through her own body but attracts it from the immediate surrounding atmosphere. This is done often by a *deshi* clapping his or her hands or slapping a fan over the area where Ikuko Osumi is going to give Seiki. She says that when her hand comes down to touch the patient's body, Seiki is even released from the air trapped between her hand and the blanket covering the body.

There is also a way in which she uses *kiai* without touching the patient's body at all. This is done by bringing the right hand, with palm open and fingers pointing at the spot on the patient, to within a few inches above the intended area and giving *kiai*. I have also seen her give Seiki with *kiai* in this way, but from a distance of quite a few feet, often as she enters a treatment room. She says, 'I can't help giving Seiki. My *kiai* is like the natural world. Like the way all creatures are influenced by the moon.'

Diagnosis in Ikuko Osumi's practice is carried out or determined in a variety of ways, although she has often divined the patient's illness psychically before any formal diagnosis and often before the patient has even arrived at her clinic!

In common with other oriental therapies, diagnosis can be made through observation of the patient's appearance, tone of voice, smell, way of moving, body shape, tactile quality on contact, and so forth.

Two important methods of diagnosis are from the pulse and the condition of the spine. From both these the condition of all the organs can be determined. 'When I read the pulse, for me it's an accurate confirmation of what I already know is the patient's condition.'

Here is a diagnosis she made of my father-in-law's condition after he became her patient, having been diagnosed as suffering from cancer of the liver and given 'about two months to live' by his hospital:

'When I took his pulse, I knew that his heart was in excellent condition and very strong. His body told me that the lower part of his right lung suffered a little from cancer that had transferred from his liver.

'His body told me that the original cause of his sickness was due to his right lung. He is a man who has used his brain a great deal and has also been through periods of extreme anxiety and worry.[4] When we use our brains a lot they demand a great deal of freshly oxygenated blood which often causes the lungs to become very tired. As the brain is demanding so much blood it takes a long time for blood to reach the stomach and the digestive system and this has an adverse affect on the liver. In fact, through tiredness of the brain, the autonomic nervous system becomes unbalanced.

'The poor condition of his liver created the skin disease.[5] The ointments he has been using were absorbed by his skin and passed into his blood and through his liver, creating a vicious circle which has finally led to his cancer.

'The harder he worked at his business, the more he needed to take fishing trips in order to relax. The cold in the fishing boats affected his liver again as well as his kidneys.

'Because his digestive system wasn't functioning properly, he wasn't getting proper nourishment from his food, no matter how good it was.

'His left eye is very bad from using the left side of his brain so much, and his sight in that eye is very poor.

'If he could have had a good rest at home at the onset of the symptoms of skin disease, he could have healed himself. Staying at home, he would have urinated more frequently than in the office and pushed out his sickness. Even if he had only worked every other day and on the off day stayed at home to have a long relaxed breakfast and talked with his wife, he would have produced more saliva and the hormones that produce proper digestion. That kind of relaxed life would have saved him from becoming seriously ill.

'Now his kidneys are bad. He can't filter blood, so that he is urinating away what could have been energy, and also his excreta are full of nutrition that hasn't been absorbed by his body. His right kidney pipe is very fat from passing nutritious things with the water. His left kidney is very tense. The right one is affected because it's next to his liver and the left one is tense because his stomach is enlarged.

'The nerve that runs from his brain to his nose and from his nose to his throat is very tense. This causes difficulty in breathing which has also helped affect his lungs. Giving therapy to his nose has healed the nerves in his face and those running into his brain, relaxing the whole nervous system in the brain, causing the pituitary to activate the thyroid. The vagus nerves which run across the throat become tired through speaking all day at his office and affect his thyroid, and this also affects his left eye. When the brain is tired, the pituitary gland doesn't work properly and therefore the thyroid doesn't function well. It's the hormone which the thyroid secretes that controls the rate at which we use the energy we get from food.

'A most important part of healing in a situation like this is the support of the family.'

It appears that Ikuko Osumi is capable of healing every kind of sickness. She says that since she began practising she has never failed to heal anyone who has remained as a patient for the full term of treatment, which in many cases means following her instructions on the way in which one should be living one's life as an essential part of the therapy. This is particularly true in the case of very sick patients.

The time it takes to heal a patient obviously varies according to his or her condition, but also depends greatly on the patient's own disposition and whether the immediate environment is supportive or not. Of two patients suffering the same sickness, one may be healed much faster than the other. Also, while perhaps three or four patients are suffering from the same illness, the way of treating them may be quite different in each case, owing to the fact that the cause of the illness and the psychological disposition of the individual patient may be different in each case. Usually, in the case of serious illness, she gives three years for full recovery. I know of quite a number of patients who have recovered in this time, having been declared incurable by hospitals. They have remained loyal patients and receive treatment once or twice a week in order to maintain their health, as, of course, the main purpose of any therapy should be preventative.

Sometimes we have the naive expectation that we will immediately get better as soon as we start receiving therapy, and certainly this can happen. However, there are two points to be made about recovery. One, the effects of Seiki therapy are cumulative and we may not begin to feel the benefit until after several treatments. And, two, the symptoms we are initially suffering or are aware of may only be the superficial expression of a much more complicated and deeper condition, so that, as treatment proceeds, other symptoms become apparent on the path to recovery; in fact, they act as signposts in the direction of that recovery.

Another important aspect of Ikuko Osumi's attitude in her relationship to her patients is what in Japanese is called *shunen* or 'devotion'. 'The patient is sacred to me. The whole basis of my life is to be devoted to human beings to help them develop their potential. When we are born, I believe we are born with a particular mission or purpose. It is this that gives meaning and dignity to life. When I can heal someone who could not move some part of their body, or could not walk, or could not eat, when they are restored to health, that is my great joy. Then, when they have recovered their health, they have to develop their own potential as human beings.'

Shunen is a natural response, without intention; rather it is the expression of whole being or 'egoless ego'.

As has already been stated, Seiki therapy is a 'one-being therapy', transcending the dualistic relationship between patient and therapist, and essential for this condition is the state of 'emptiness' or 'non-ego' on the part of the therapist. This is a meditative state in which the therapist becomes one with the body–mind condition of the patient. It is a condition of knowing oneness with the other that every master of Seiki-jutsu must attain. If we are 'empty', then we can be 'filled', but by something other than our usual egocentric attachments and conceptual thinking. If we can be 'empty' without preference or opinion, then the universe speaks to us; the things that are 'right' for us, or that in a real sense *are us* 'come to us' and reveal our path. This is as true in therapy as it is in our lives generally.

Timing is of prime importance in Seiki therapy. Indeed, it should play a part in our lives generally but is little understood. The ego perceives time as something separate from itself and most often in opposition; it turns time into an adversary.

In Ikuko Osumi's therapy there are three main levels of timing involved, and often they appear to merge. The egoless state of 'emptiness' just mentioned relates directly to time and timing.

When a therapist is in a state of 'emptiness' during therapy, then whatever actions she or he makes will be spontaneous, in complete harmony with the situation or conditions of that moment and everything will proceed naturally. There is no separation, no interference from the ego. This way of being one with the environment, or acting at one with time, is referred to in Chinese Taoism as *wu-wei* or 'non-action', that is, an action which is not based on nor proceeds from the ego's desire or conceptualizing, but action without intention. It is an intuitive action or a *being-action*, and not a *re-action* to information or ideas, which on the normal level of dualistic consciousness we call 'action'. This spontaneous way of acting means that a pattern of treatment may be, as has been said previously, contrary to 'ordinary' expectations.

An old teacher of mine, John Layard, the anthropologist and psychotherapist, used to say, 'What is needed is not common sense, but uncommon sense.' It is in this kind of one-being therapy that 'uncommon' or intuitive sense arises.

Another level of Ikuko Osumi's sense and understanding of timing comes from her years of observing the natural rhythms of nature in the environment around her, her awareness of the ceaseless motion of change and impermanence in all conditions. This law she knows intimately when it is related to the conditions of the human body and mind. She constantly tries to draw the patient's attention to awareness of timing through his or her own body and the way in which it reacts and responds to the environment.

A very important part of her sense of timing which is related to the condition of 'emptiness' is her psychic powers which enable her, as she says, to 'see through time'. It is this ability that often allows her to see into a patient's past and future, and this obviously introduces a very important dimension into her healing art.

7

'NOT ME – NOT IKUKO OSUMI'

I never think of the spirit world, only of Eizon Hoin. Spirits or ghosts just appear to me. I don't ask them to come, they just come.

Ikuko Osumi

Ikuko Osumi's clairvoyance frequently causes her to speak out, often to her surprise and when she would rather not have done so. She sometimes draws a distinction between her ordinary self and this 'other' side of herself, by prefacing some of her out-speakings with, 'Not me – not Ikuko Osumi. I think my mouth is going to open and say . . .' And once, after one of these out-speakings, she said, 'If Ikuko Osumi had said that, it might have been a mistake!' There is usually a difference in quality between the way in which 'Not Ikuko Osumi' express-es herself and her general appearance and energy and the 'ordinary' Ikuko Osumi. This is most notable of course, but for different reasons, during times of actual spirit possession.

She cannot say much about how or why she had psychic experiences and feels no reason to question or provide theories about them; she simply accepts them as they are, as part of her life. They have been part of her life since she was a child and frequently saw 'ghosts'.[1]

'When I was young, the man who lived next door loved orchids and often came into our garden to look at my uncle's. One evening I went to close the entrance gate, when I saw our neighbour standing in our garden beside the stone lantern. He was wearing a kimono and *haori*.[2] I could hear a noise, 'gasa-gasa-gasa', like dry bamboo leaves rustling. I knew that at that time he was very sick and that he shouldn't have been out in the garden, so I told my aunt. She said it was very serious and went

68

straight next door and found that he was in the last moments of his life.

'Another time I heard my dressmaking teacher's father, who always used to walk with a stick, even in the house. I heard his footsteps and the tapping of his cane coming along the corridor of our house. I felt that something was wrong, so I phoned my teacher and found that her father was on the point of dying.

'I never think of the spirit world, only of Eizon Hoin. Spirits or ghosts just appear to me. I don't ask them to come, they just come. In recent years I've been avoiding people coming to see me as what you might call a medium, so that they could find something out about their future or get advice, because when people come to me ask about these things, sometimes dead people come into my body. My body is taken and my voice changes. Sometimes, when someone asks me something, that person's dead grandmother or grandfather or even a child comes into me so enthusiastically with what they have to say that they make me roll up my sleeves or bang the chair with my fist! Afterwards I'm so exhausted because, for that kind of business, I'm not talking, it's not me. Sometimes I have to explain why I have said something because it is not me, not Ikuko Osumi. The spirit makes me say whatever it is, so I have to explain afterwards.

'In therapy, if I say, "Ah, this bit is a little hard, your liver or heart, or whatever, is tired," usually the patient can feel it, so they easily understand what I'm talking about. But with my clairvoyance, if you want to call it that, people can't see, so I really have to try to make them understand.'

Recently I had occasion to sit and talk with Ikuko Osumi about something that had been concerning me. 'A few days later she told me that while we had been talking she had seen my grandfather standing between my wife Masako and myself. She said, 'At first I thought it was Hagiwara-san's [Masako's] grandfather. Then I looked closer and was surprised to see that he was a foreigner! But his skin and hair colouring[3] were exactly the same as Hagiwara-san's. In fact, he looked like her. Then I realized it was your grandfather. He is very happy about your situation now.'

The most convincing thing about this, for me, is the fact that I in no way resembled my grandfather physically, being tall, with medium-brown hair, pale complexion and blue-grey eyes. My grandfather, a Scot of short Celtic stature, was so dark that he was often taken for a foreigner.

I thought that maybe she had divined this image from my own memory of him, until I realized that he had had white hair from the time that I was born and that even my father, when questioned, had no memory of his black hair as he had turned white prematurely.

Sometimes not just conditions involving the patient in this world, but those prevailing in the world of spirit are given consideration in her therapy. During treatment she will often see and have dialogue with the ghosts of ancestors or guardian spirits of one kind or another. The two main functions served by these apparitions seem to be, on the one hand, to help support the patient and to intercede on the patient's behalf and, on the other, to try to take the patient or to 'eat' him or her, that is, to bring about his or her death (see p. 193).

On other occasions these spirits or visions, which she also experiences at times, give her important information concerning the past, present or future conditions surrounding the patient. There were several such stories in the original manuscript, but she later withdrew them because she no longer knew how to contact the patients involved. Very often and for various reasons, they remained ignorant of this aspect, mainly because of their own inability to accept such a dimension in their healing process. She feels a strong loyalty to her patients and would not publish anything without their knowledge and consent.

I once asked her if she had ever had to retrieve the 'soul' of a patient which had for one reason or another left that person's body, in the traditional manner of shamanic healing. She replied that there had been a few situations in which she had had to do this, and that it 'happens with certain kinds of patients', but would not elaborate further.

In the case of serious illness, she knows, regardless of hospital prognosis, whether she can heal a person or not by seeing the condition of their Seiki. In a person who is dying, she can see what she calls his or her 'death face'. She sees the person as he or she will look as a corpse. This image she sees as though superimposed as she looks at the patient. She describes two such cases:

'I once visited the house of a woman who was about to leave Japan to go to Europe on business. As soon as I entered her house I felt that the atmosphere around her was like that on the night before a funeral party. I advised her not to go to Europe. "If you go to Europe, you will definitely develop cancer," I told her. She didn't listen to my advice and went to Europe. But a few months after she returned she developed cancer as I told her she would.

'Another time, a relative of mine from Nagoya was going on an expedition to climb Everest. He stayed in my house for one night before he left with the other members from Haneda airport. Immediately he arrived at my house I saw that he didn't have much Seiki left in his body and I realized that he would die on Everest. I prepared a beautiful dinner for him with *tai*⁴ fish, and before he left the next morning a *deshi*, Misako-san, and I, prepared red beans and rice and other nutritious food for him to take on his flight.

'Later I heard that, just after they reached the top of Everest and were on their way back down to the base camp, the man in front of him looked back and couldn't see him. He had disappeared.

'In situations like this, when I see the face of the person for the first time, I see their death face. Actually I see their whole body as a corpse.

'When a patient has been told by a doctor that there is no chance of recovery, if I feel that the patient can recover and they agree to accept my treatment, then they do. There are other times when I feel it is impossible for the patient to recover. On these occasions, when I go to visit the patient I can see the Seiki flying out of the house. At such times I know there is no chance of recovery. The body is negative. There have been times like this when the doctor has said that a patient will definitely recover, but even so I have felt that it was impossible. When I have been called in to give treatment, I have seen the Seiki flying out like a bird. That is when I have been called too late.'

In some cases, she takes into account not only a patient's physical and psychological condition and his or her relationship to family, job and so forth, but often includes the topography of the house and surrounding district. Recently, for example, one patient was advised to enter his house by the back door for a few weeks during the course of his treatment, because to enter his front door, due to its position in relation to the street, entailed making several left turns which she considered to be detrimental to his recovery.

Sometimes her treatment includes the house or nearby land in the sense that they too are given therapy (exorcism) to rid them of malevolent spirits or energies. There is a Japanese expression which speaks of the 'face' of a house or land. It is these 'faces', too, which she is able to read.

With respect to this side of her healing art, we should remember that we live in reciprocal, interdependent relationship with the environment, interacting with it and it with us, often in obvious ways, but more often in many invisible and subtle ways which we are not conscious of. To use Ikuko Osumi's term, we 'support' certain things or conditions and are in turn 'supported' by them. In a real sense we are the environment; there is no separation between it and ourselves, even though our conditioned, discriminating ego consciousness would have us believe otherwise, although, of course, knowing this conceptually is naturally different from experiencing it.[5] And whatever actions we make, no matter how apparently insignificant, contain or express the very essence of our relationship to the universe on all levels, in that moment-time of action. It is because of this that certain people are able to 'read' or divine conditions or influences appertaining to an individual's life, from the simple throwing of coins, bones or yarrow stalks or the shuffling of cards, and so on.

This faculty of being able to 'read' the 'face' of a house or a piece of land enables Ikuko Osumi to know (just as she knows in the case of a patient's body) where there exists a 'plus' or a 'minus' of energy, as she refers to them. These plus or minus areas of energy can either feed us – give us energy – or siphon energy from us in various ways. She will often see a dark shadow or a light over land where the energy is negative or positive just as she often does around the part of a person's body which is diseased.

In some situations in negative areas, it is as though the environmental energy field has become imprinted or contaminated, that is to say, patterned by the strong psychoenergetic charge of an individual or an event involving a collective trauma of one kind or another, which sets up a 'memory' in the local energy field. This is equally true of areas where there has been a powerful positive charge, for example, the energy experience on the sites once occupied by saints or where 'miracles' have been performed. Although there are also many other areas connected with actual ghosts or spirits, many places with powerful positive or negative energy to not owe their origins to human involvement at all, but simply arise from the natural energy states of the earth.

Some people are very sensitive to these areas and are able to understand them, while others are sensitive to them without understanding them; most people, however, are totally unaware of the existence of such conditions. And there is a variety of reasons why some of us may be strongly attracted to or repelled by such places, sometimes to our benefit and at others to our detriment. For example, the 'memory' in some places may coincide on some level with a repressed trauma or psychological tendency of which we are unconscious, and in extreme cases this may cause us to re-enact the drama which is held within the 'memory' of a place. Sometimes such a place may release repressed or 'forgotten' memories and their attendant emotions, while at the same time bringing to the attention or consciousness of that person the trauma or history held within the environment of that location. Just as the human body can render up repressed memories and experiences, its pictures, emotions and ambiences, so too can the land.

There were individuals in early communities who always knew which areas were right for establishing a village, a house or a temple, apart from the practical considerations. They knew which areas were energetically right or wrong according to a function, an individual's nature or the collective energy of the tribe or clan. The art/science that evolved from this intuitive ability is called geomancy (*feng-shui* in the East). Geomancy seeks to place individuals or communities in areas which are in harmony with their own energies and needs, where they can best relate to the local environment and resonate with the universe, like an organ in a healthy body. This art/science is still practised in various parts of the world today.

Very often we are attracted to a place and feel that it is the 'right spot' for us because it reflects and endorses our fantasies and images of ourselves, while perhaps leading us to deny something fundamental concerning our true nature and potential, whereas the true 'right spot' may, on the other hand, seem uncomfortable or even inhospitable until we have learned to accept, to open up to and harmonize with it at a deeper level.

This faculty which allows Ikuko Osumi to be able to 'read' the land is psychically extended to the reading of maps or plans of houses. From these she is able not only to divine the energetic conditions and its historical past and the type of people that live in a specific area, but also to predict future events that will take place in, or affect, it.

The earth 'calls' her to a place in the same way that a patient's body will 'call' her to a particular part; when she answers that 'calling' she is 'taught' what is there. When a map or a plan is spread before her, it will 'call' her in just this way. 'In the same way I can see where a Seiki line is on the drawing of a plan of a house. And I can feel what the energy is like underneath the land in an area, whether it is stable or unstable, when I look at a map.

'One day Mr Kilcullin came to visit me after he and his family had left Japan and returned to America, to live in California. He showed me a plan of his new house to see what I thought of it. As I looked at it, I had a strong feeling that there was a Seiki line that passed through one of the rooms. Then I could see that line when I looked at the plan.

'About a year later Okajima and I travelled to California in order to give Seiki to Mr Kilcullin's wife. As soon as we entered his house I felt that I was being pulled towards a place in exactly the room in which I had seen a line on the plan a year earlier. The room was a dining room and the line fell just below a picture, which was where we gave Seiki to Mrs Kilcullin the next day.

'Once someone came and asked me whether or not they should build a house on a piece of land. At that time I thought that that particular year would be a good time for them to do so. What I didn't know was that they had already built it and moved in! When I looked at the map, though, I could see that a well had originally stood on the land, and I saw a body had been thrown into it many years previously. Now it turned out that this house had already been built over the well and I could see that a grandson or someone would fall from the building in the future.'

On one occasion,[6] when we were staying with Ikuko Osumi in her apartment at the foot of Mount Fuji in order to read through the first draft of this book, I drew a very rough map of Britain in order to explain to her the alignment theory of ancient sacred sites. As I proceeded to explain these alignments I realized she was not listening to me. She was waving her hand across part of the British Isles saying, 'Dame! Dame!'[7] The energy underneath this part is very unstable. It's very beautiful and a nice place to visit, but if you live here, you won't do anything. You will be attracted to too many things. This place will sink into the sea and disappear some time.'

Then she moved across my map pointing out other areas that would be bad for us and areas that would be all right. Sometimes she added details, some of which, to my knowledge, were certainly correct. 'This area is very bad. Too many people have died here. This city will develop in the east in the coming years. This place over here, though, is sinking.'

Suddenly she jabbed her forefinger at an area of great natural beauty. 'Wonderful!' she exclaimed. 'The sun is rising here. The energy of this place is next to my own house. Once this area was a place of great activity and wealth. Many very intelligent people live around this area, but the people who settle here don't want to work very much. A cup of tea will last all afternoon. People give up easily, saying, "It's all right, it's my life, I can do what I want with it." I feel the divorce rate is very high here. But this place will be very good for you and you will be very successful. It's a strange thing to say, but this area is calling you like a body.'

After a period of a great deal of work I had become very tired and ill. One day during treatment Ikuko Osumi told me that we must move out of our sitting room. This sitting room had bothered her when we had first moved into the house and it had been the room in which the previous owner, an old woman, had spent most of her time (see p. 121). She explained that the area where a chest of drawers was now standing had once been the place where the old woman had kept her Buddhist family altar and where she had said prayers each day to her ancestors. This I knew to be true. She explained that this area was now energetically 'minus' and that it was taking my energy. 'You must move out. That room is only for objects now, not for human beings.'

For Ikuko Osumi the inanimate world is often imbued with vitality and life as certain objects either have absorbed, or are expressions of, energy that has come from their makers or their owners. These inanimate objects may also 'support' or assist our lives in some way; or they may be negative influences and actually create a threat to our wellbeing. Living things, too, often assume similar roles in our lives. Quite a number of patients are advised to dispose of, or preserve, certain objects in their houses or gardens. She will sometimes advise someone not to cut down a tree or move a rock, because it is 'supporting' them, or to restore some object that has been broken. As with the interdependent relationship between the organs of the body, if a particular organ becomes diseased or is removed, it creates an imbalance that threatens the welfare of the rest, so, if something negative is introduced into the system, it must be 'pushed out' or healed (in this case removed or purified). Under certain circumstances, to add or subtract or re-arrange something may be to upset or restore, depending on the situation, the energetic unity of an area or place, by blocking, freeing or otherwise changing the flow and balance of energy of that place. In Shinto terms it may mean to interfere with the *kami* or deity of that area. Ikuko Osumi says that some patients actually come to realize this relationship and how it has affected their lives.

Here are five stories concerning inanimate objects and one concerning a tree in relation to this phenomenon.

'My uncle used to love collecting very old swords. Eventually he sold all of them except two or three very special ones. After he died, we still kept these swords in the house and my aunt told me that the finest of them had killed many people. 'Some years ago, whenever I went upstairs to close the amado[8] in the evenings and look out at Mount Fuji, I heard a terrible banging sound coming from inside the cupboard in loku-jo,[9] like something trying to get out. Suddenly I felt very strongly that it was the sword wanting to see blood again,[10] so I thought we should get rid of it.

'It happened that my uncle's youngest brother had always wanted that sword, and when he heard that I was going to sell it he came and begged me to give it to him. I told him that he couldn't have it, because if he did take it something bad would happen to him within half a year. He just laughed at me and insisted that he should have it. Finally, realizing I had to protect my patients, I relented and sent my son to his house with the sword. He was delighted and came to thank me with a huge smile on his face. Six months after receiving the sword, he fell ill and died.

'After that I thought I had better protect the rest of the family and asked his son to return the sword to me, telling him that it really should belong to my uncle's family. In the end I sold it to an antiques dealer who had bought a lot of things from our family in the past. As long as the connection between the sword and our family was broken, the sword was safe. Because of his kindness in the past, I sold him the sword at a good price although it was very valuable.'

The following story is about a broken object that needed restoring:

'Okajima and I arrived too early to visit a patient one day, so we decided to take a short walk around the area. We came across an inari shrine within the compound of Sumiyoshi-jinja. I remembered that my dressmaking teacher's mother was born to this shrine,[11] so I decided I should like to tell her that I had visited it.

'Just as we entered the area of the shrine, I felt as though I was being pulled back very strongly by something. I turned back in the direction of the pulling and it led me to two stone foxes standing on either side of the main gate. When I looked at them carefully, I noticed that one of them had a broken nose. I handed some money to Okajima and asked him to give it to the priest in order that he could repair the broken nose of the fox. When Okajima returned from the shrine office, I told him that if the priest failed to repair the nose, he would die very suddenly.

'Two weeks later we returned to the shrine and found that the fox's nose still hadn't been repaired. One day, a few months after this, we happened to notice a large obituary in the newspaper which announced the priest's sudden death.'

This story involves an inanimate object that became an agent through which Ikuko Osumi was able to gain knowledge of my condition and progress during the early period of writing this book:

'My aunt and I were travelling in Nagano Prefecture when we happened to visit an antiques shop. Soon after entering the shop I felt, through a very strong pulling, that there was something underneath the floor where the boards were obviously loose. I felt pulled very strongly to that spot. The antiques dealer noticed me peering down at the floor and came over to ask what the matter was. When I explained that I felt that there was something underneath the floor, he pulled up the boards and was very surprised to find a small shrine containing an image of Michizane Sugawara.[12] It had been lost for a long time, so he was very glad to see it. When I looked at it, it appeared to me to be shining, so I told him I wanted to buy it. He said that he had no idea how it had got there and that he would give it to me. However, I gave him some money and in return he gave me three very good *saké* cups. Since then I have always kept the image of Michizane Sugawara on a shelf in my room.

'When Malcolm started working on the book, I thought that I would lend the shrine to him for his desk, so that it could guard and encourage him. But when I came to take it from the shelf, I felt it say that Malcolm didn't need it, and that he could manage on his own, so I didn't give it to him.

'I feel almost every day that it wants to be moved, even a few inches, so I move it. I really feel it is guarding us, especially Malcolm, and I can tell by the position of his right hand, in which he holds a brush [for calligraphy], whether Malcolm is doing well or not, or having a rest. The other day I noticed that Michizane Sugawara was looking very strange and I was worried if Malcolm was all right.'

A patient told me later that, on that day, Ikuko Osumi had pointed at the image of Michizane Sugawara and said, 'That's Malcolm. Today he's not feeling very good!'

It happened that on that particular day I was feeling very bad and experiencing a lot of difficulty.

One day, during a period of sickness, Ikuko Osumi came to visit me at our house and was sitting by my *futon*. 'You must remove that scroll,' she said, indicating a scroll which hung in our *tokonoma*,[13] depicting a Bodhisattva. She turned to Masako. 'That scroll is taking Malcolm's energy. That is why I suggested that you sleep facing away from the *tokonoma* when you first moved into the house' (see p. 121). She explained that the painter of the scroll was suffering much grief when he painted it and that the grief was transmitted to the image. At the time my lungs were very weak, and emotionally and psychologically the lungs relate to withheld or unexpressed grief, which I certainly knew was one of my problems. The scroll was to be taken down and carefully rolled up. It was not discarded, but placed in a drawer until my condition was healed.

Here is a story concerning a living 'object', in this case, a tree:

'One day I received a phone call from a teacher of batik. Since her husband had died, she had converted the first floor of her house into a self-contained flat to let to foreigners. For the first three years she had had a tenant who was the head secretary at the Indonesian Embassy. After he left, she tried to get another tenant, but no one came through the agent, so she phoned me and asked me what she should do.

'Instantly, as she explained this on the phone to me, I felt that one of the trees in her garden was bound with wire and couldn't grow properly. I could see that it was rusty old wire and I told her so, and that she must find it and free it. She and her maid looked all over the garden for the tree, but couldn't find it. She phoned me back to say that I must have made a mistake. But I still had that very strong feeling and told her to look again. Now, they had thought that when I said "tree" I meant a big tree, so they looked again very carefully. This time they found a small tree bound just as I had described, with old rusty wire. Apparently the next-door neighbours had moved their house slightly, and at that time the carpenters must have wound the wire around the tree for some reason and then, after they had finished working, cut it and left it. That tree had a very strong life force and it was protecting that house, but it had been ignored and damaged.

'Immediately they found the tree they removed the wire and she put special fertilizer at its roots. Two days later she got a very famous baseball player as a tenant.'

Each thing has its true place and function in the universe, where it can resonate and harmonize with every other thing. If something does not function properly, we say it is 'out of order', i.e. something is 'out of place'. Our planet is being put increasingly 'out of order', while constantly trying to rebalance its energies, to heal itself, as does the human body.

8

TRAINING (*SHUGYO*)

If you come to me thinking I am a *kami*, you might find an ordinary human being and find many bad things about me. If you come to me thinking I am a human being, then you might find something extraordinary. A *deshi* must struggle with me and take what is good.

Ikuko Osumi

As will be understood from this general introduction to Seiki-jutsu, a *deshi*'s training is no easy matter and cannot be undertaken lightly. It requires total dedication and no small sacrifice. Over the years there have been many *deshi*, some with little formal education and others newly graduated from university, who, having read about Ikuko Osumi in newspaper articles or magazines, decided to train with her. However, to date only two *deshi* have remained to complete their training, the others having left after a few months.

In the West, if we wish to learn something, then we expect a particular structure to the learning situation. We know that there will be a certain place, time for learning, and a specific subject. We expect that any questions or queries we might have will be answered and, of course, we know that there will exist a carefully defined teacher–pupil relationship. However, in a traditional Japanese training situation (of which there are increasingly fewer these days), it might sometimes seem to a *deshi* that none of the above applies. There is, naturally, a teacher–pupil relationship, but it is not defined in quite the same way.

In the West we learn to acquire knowledge or a skill in something. In Japan traditionally one is taught to master

81

something, which means, in fact, that by way of mastering that thing one must master oneself, and by so doing *become* what it is that one originally set out to master. The difference between Western and traditional oriental teaching is similar to the difference between Western medical treatment and traditional oriental methods of healing, namely, in Western teaching very little change in any real sense is required on the part of the pupil, whereas in the oriental approach the need for change is implicit. A comparison which might be used to reflect this can be made between the meaning of the Latin word *educare*, from which we derive the word 'education' and which means 'to bring out', and what education seems to have come to mean today, that is, 'forcing in'!

Generally speaking, the Western method is to teach actively and conceptually, whereas the traditional oriental way is to create situations in which the intuitive knowledge of the pupil may be led to arise. It is the difference between teaching and 'non-teaching': in the latter a pupil must become of one mind with the teacher, that is, the teaching is addressed to the pupil's whole being. Ideally a pupil in the oriental situation must learn to 'kill' him/herself – to have no opinion, no history, no ego. In Japan it is said that you must 'steal' technique from your teacher. Later you must reach a point that transcends technique altogether.

For the first year or so a *deshi*'s life is very rigid and centres around a strict and exhausting domestic routine. This domestic routine has the effect of centring and earthing a *deshi* and preparing the body and mind for the next stage of training, although the *deshi* inevitably feels that training has not begun yet and may frequently ask to be taught something!

It is interesting to note that Skeat gives one of the meanings of 'routine' as 'a small path'. And anyone familiar with Zen literature will realize that this 'small path' or 'way' plays no small part in the history of *satori*.[1] Unfortunately in our technologized world today the virtues of 'a small way' are overlooked, neglected and misunderstood. In fact, it is a path to be avoided at all costs – and those costs may be greater than we realize as we delegate natural human functioning to machines. With the right mindful attitude, routine transcends the mundane and a 'small path' merges into a 'big way'.

After this period, when it has been decided that a *deshi* has reached a certain stage, he or she will be allowed to enter the treatment rooms, initially to watch treatment being given and later, slowly, to begin actual training treatment on patients. During this period few if any questions will be answered and the *deshi* is left alone to learn by observation and experience – a wordless teaching in which the *deshi* is sometimes admonished with the words 'Seiki will teach you.' From this point on the training of each *deshi* may be different, according to the nature and development of each individual.

When it is recognized that a *deshi* has attained a certain level, he or she may be given some conceptual description of what it is that he or she has been doing or learning. In my own experience this creates an 'Aha!' situation, in which you are made aware that you had already realized it on an intuitive level. At this point questions may still remain unanswered or may be answered directly. At other times Ikuko Osumi can be very evasive, and trying to pin her down is like swordplay with the wind!

This whole period of training has exhaustion as its ground tension. A *deshi* is taken to the point of exhaustion and then encouraged to go beyond it. This either creates a kind of 'second breath' and the birth of a new and greater strength, or results in the *deshi* leaving, or, as in my own case, collapsing! (The reasons for which are explained in Part II 'A *Deshi*'s Tale'.)

One of the things stressed in Seiki-jutsu training is the importance of *fu shiki* or 'don't know' – that is, in retaining what in Zen is called *shoshin* or 'beginner's mind'. This means keeping our initial attitude, our original spirit; not getting stuck at any point by believing that we have accomplished or 'know something', but remaining completely open and fresh. It is a way of relating to learning and life spontaneously, which leads to direct understanding. Ikuko Osumi, now in her sixties, says that her therapy is constantly changing, always developing, that she is always surprised.

Another equally important element in training is the need to learn the importance of what in Japanese is called 'facing a wall'. This, as it implies, means to face extreme difficulties and the need for 'going through' whereby we achieve transformative energy.

In my own training and its attendant difficulties I have been constantly reminded that these periods are essential in the making of a Seiki therapist by my other teacher, Okajima-sensei, frequently saying to me, 'I hope you have many walls to face!' Whenever I hear this phrase, I get the image of a Sōtō Zen monk in *zazen* – he literally faces a wall externally, while facing the great wall of his conditioned self within.

The essential way of learning is through one's own body, and it might be said that for some therapists it is essential to experience what might be called an 'initiatory sickness'. But this is true of any path of learning which is by way of self-knowing.

Slowly a *deshi* begins to realize that everything in his or her life is teaching; that there is no separation between training sessions, free time, bathing, eating, etc.; no difference between the easy, flowing times and the difficult situations which result in 'facing a wall'.

Ikuko Osumi lives on an instinctual, intuitive level, which means that if she feels something, or something suddenly occurs to her, she must act in accordance with whatever it is, at that moment. This often means a complete change of plans at very short notice and may lead to still more alterations within the following minutes or hours. She herself says, 'The day's programme, the things which are to be done, the order of the patients and who will give therapy to whom, exists, but doesn't exist!'

From a training point of view, Ikuko Osumi, with her gentle but very firm nature, and Mr Okajima, with his open, fiery energy, naturally complement each other like the moon and the sun.

Training in Seiki-jutsu cannot be obtained through any course or manual, but only in an intensive living situation, such as exists in Ikuko Osumi's house.

A Deshi's Day

The following description of a *deshi*'s day at Ikuko Osumi's house is based on my own experience during the first few months of my training; it may differ in detail according to the constantly changing situation. All the basic colours of the interior of her house are neutral, whites and off-whites. But the colours of certain of the furnishings – the curtains, cushions, tablecloths, pictures and pottery – are changed according to the season. In autumn, for example, the predominant colours will be brown, reds and yellows, and these will be matched by pictures depicting activities or plants relating to that season and vases containing twigs of trees and grasses of autumn. Each season the interior of the house reflects the changes in the environment outside.

Ikuko Osumi's house is still run in the traditional Japanese way, which entails plenty of work for a *deshi*. In the morning the junior *deshi* rises first and opens up the house. *Amado* are pulled back, the front and back doors unlocked, fires lit if the season demands, and water put to boil. As the household rises, another *deshi* will begin cooking breakfast, while the treatment rooms are cleaned and *futon* laid ready for patients. Each *deshi* will have his or her routine until 7.30, when the training session begins. This means giving training treatment to Ikuko Osumi and sometimes as many as three *deshi* at a time are involved in this. After training sessions, the *genkan*[2] must be swept and washed, the road outside the house swept, the garden tidied and hosed with water, the downstairs waiting room and toilet cleaned, until breakfast at 9 o'clock.

Patients begin to arrive from 9.30 onwards. When there is a large number of patients breakfast may be very early, and home visits to patients and the arrival of patients may start at 8 o'clock or earlier.

Treatment continues throughout the day, with a break of about twenty minutes for lunch. This sometimes may be as late as 3 o'clock at extremely busy times and taken in rotation, until the last patient leaves at about 7 o'clock in the evening. Then there is a break for supper, after which visits to housebound patients are made.

Deshi will be allowed to visit house-bound patients with
their teachers only after they have reached a certain point in
their training. Up to that time they will remain in the house and
be employed doing the day's washing, washing up after supper, ironing, changing linen, taking telephone calls and generally preparing the house for night. Those who have left to give
home treatment will return at midnight or often later. This
routine is carried on six days a week, and on Sundays as well if
there are many sick patients.

As can be seen, the life in Ikuko Osumi's house is one of total
devotion to healing, and their energy and strength a testimony
to Seiki-jutsu itself and their own discipline. In the West this
kind of sacrifice is difficult for most people to understand. It is
the difference between healing as a profession and healing as a
way of life.

Part II

A *Deshi*'s Tale

The body is more precious than a wishing gem.

Milarepa[1]

A *deshi* must be of one mind and one body with me.

Ikuko Osumi

On the last night that I slept on the Isle or Arran, where I had been living and to which I had returned briefly to store my few belongings before finally leaving for Japan, I had a powerful dream. I was told that I was 'going away to die', and I was shown a box made of pine, like a square coffin. (In fact, three years later, I was to see identical boxes at a Japanese crematorium; they are used to hold the ashes of the dead.) Inside the box I saw a scroll that I was told was my 'will'. At the time I understood the dream to predict some dying of ego or conditioned self, which might, I hoped, be expected under the circumstances. What I did not know was that the dream augered more than a psychological dying. The following years were to bring me to a physical and psychological crisis and to a confrontation with actual death that was to change my life.

The following narrative covers the first eighteen months or so of my life as a *deshi*. It is drawn from extensive journals and diaries which both my wife Masako and I kept during this period. These included recordings of Ikuko Osumi's talks and images and impressions which I had written down during the different states that I experienced while my own healing and learning progressed. I constantly cross-referred to Masako's

89

accounts in order to make mine as factually accurate as possible; nor have I manipulated any part for the sake of storytelling, save the addition of the images mentioned above, in order to 'decorate' the text. One problem I encountered when I came to write up this account was how to deal with the number of coincidences or synchronous events and patterns that emerged, and which led me later to new insights into my healing process, without their appearing either invented or contrived. Initially I cut some of them from the earlier drafts for this very reason, but finally decided that they should rightfully be returned to the text.

As a *deshi* I was not privy to the conceptual nature of Seiki therapy at this stage in my training, as it was considered a barrier to the development of my own intuition. With respect to this, I have not described either the conceptual side of diagnosis or the correspondences on the human body in relation to nervous and organic functioning in any depth. I have included one or two dreams, simply because I happen to have recorded them, without any real attempt to analyse them actively.

Reading the story myself now, I am struck by my own stupidity and by my constant fighting with my teacher, which reflects of course, my ego's resistance to changes that threatened it. It was a strange time and I found myself in a situation in which I seemed progressively to 'forget' all that I thought I had learned; it produced great confusion, great anxiety and great doubt. It was a time in which all the conflicts and contradictions of my life, which over the years of working with myself I had become familiar with in varying degrees, now seemed to come together at this one point in time and to become sharply defined, so that I saw them in a painfully clear light.

My fear for my condition at the time caused me to grasp hold of myself like a drowning man clutching at an empty reed, so that at times I found myself trying to deal with the situation from a Western psychological approach, interpreting and actively trying to analyse and 'work out' what was happening in the states that I was experiencing. This created attachment to and ego-identification with these experiences, thereby deepening my confusion and suffering, and giving rise to what Osumi-sensei often referred to as my head being 'away' from my body. At other times I found myself relating in a Buddhist way, by 'letting go' and not trying to 'do' anything with what was arising, but allowing it space to express itself. In this way but without any effort on my part, a certain amount of insight into what was happening naturally arose.

However, the mixing of these two approaches, which resulted from my own confused state, often caused me still greater confusion, and it was not until I realized what I was doing that things began to resolve themselves.[2] (This confusion is reflected in the story as I picked it up from my notebooks.) I fluctuated between periods of apparent harmony and tranquillity and terrifying feelings of disconnectedness and separation; a kind of *bardo*[3] in which I no longer felt or looked like 'myself'.

Life as a *deshi* is extremely restricted and during the time allowed for writing the first draft of this book these restrictions were rigorously enforced. Because of something she had seen concerning my nature, Ikuko Osumi told me, 'The book is part of your training. You must complete it within a hundred days. If you fail to do so, you will get stuck at a certain level and not progress. You must accomplish this to get beyond this level. If you have a problem, you must solve it at your desk. You mustn't go out for a walk. If you do, you will have an accident with a car!'

Many times I decided that it was an impossible task to accomplish in the time, and on several occasions I almost told her that I would have to abandon it. Strangely, as I proceeded with the book, many difficulties concerning my condition and learning seemed to resolve themselves. A few months after completing it, however, I realized that the whole book needed reorganizing and expanding. At this point my own condition worsened and I became very ill for the second time. On recovering, I finished the book and again noticed that, as it progressed, so my own condition and circumstances also improved. I became strongly aware that the book had 'become' my body, that it was as though I was writing or 'righting' myself.

In 'A *Deshi*'s Tale' I refer to Ikuko Osumi as 'Osumi-sensei or simply as 'Sensei', an honorific meaning 'teacher', and it is as such thet, as her *deshi*, Masako and I must address her. Also in this part of the book I have dropped the use of the English gender prefixes for Japanese names in favour of the Japanese neuter suffix of 'san'.

It is obvious to me now, when reading the text, that I have not mentioned Masako nearly enough, as she is a constant inspiration and healing presence. I should also like to say that neither Masako nor I make any claims with respect to healing.

1

I was due to go and live in New York where I intended to study Shiatsu. Before moving, however, I decided to take a short holiday in Japan as kind of buffer between the idyll of the Scottish west coast and the abrasivenes of Brooklyn. Some-where in my mind, though, I half entertained what on the face of it, for a man about to reach his fortieth birthday, was the ridiculous fantasy of finding a teacher in Japan who would train me in return for my doing work of some kind, as I had little money.

A week before leaving for Japan, I met a Japanese woman called Masako Hagiwara, who was studying in London. Our meeting was brief as she was in the process of packing in order to leave for Tokyo herself the following day. During our conversation I mentioned my interest in Shiatsu and she told me about a healer called Ikuko Osumi with whom she had been a patient for a number of years and who had healed her of a very serious illness. This healer apparently practised a form of therapy called Seiki-jutsu which, in certain cases, involved some kind of transmission of energy. Once received by a person, this energy could, through a certain discipline, trans-form that person's life.

We arranged casually for us to meet when I arrived in Tokyo and I thought no more about it. I did not even feel particularly interested in the healer she had mentioned and certainly made no connection with my absurd fantasy, which seemed to have been totally eclipsed now by the imminence of my move to New York.

This brief meeting, however, was to prove to be the most important half hour of my life!

2

The French architect with whom I had been sitting during the flight from Paris, suggested I accompany him from the airport into Tokyo, where he worked, as taxis could be difficult for foreigners and that he himself was used to them and spoke Japanese. I gratefully accepted his offer and, after reaching his destination, he directed the taxi to take me to my hotel.

After checking in and having a meal, I went to bed early to try to regain some of my lost sleep. As I lay reviewing my financial situation, I suddenly realized that my trip to Japan was a mistake. Japan was far too expensive and I had very little money left. I decided I had better book a flight to New York the following morning, then remembered that I had promised to phone Masako Hagiwara on my arrival. I decided I would phone her first thing after breakfast and tell her of my change of plan.

The next morning on my way from the dining room I stopped to buy some postcards from a revolving stand in the foyer and then returned to my room to phone her.

'Welcome to Japan!' she said brightly. 'I'm sorry about the rain. It's not much different from when we met in London last.'

I thanked her for her welcome and said that I thought the rain was rather pleasant. Then I went on to explain that I had found that I could not afford to stay much longer than a day in Japan after all, and that I was going to try to book a flight to New York that day.

'Oh, that's a pity', she replied. 'But before you do anything, I would like to see you. I have something to tell you. May I meet you at your hotel at about eleven?'

'Yes, all right,' I agreed, and told her the name and address of the hotel. 'There's a lounge on the second floor. I'll meet you there and we can have coffee.'

I put my clothes of the previous evening into a bag and went downstairs to the lounge. I sat at a table by the window overlooking a narrow street and began to write some post-cards. After the fourth card my attention was attracted by a woman with her dog in the street below.

The woman appeared to be in her fifties and was wearing an exquisite kimono. She was stooping to the pavement and, with the apparent mindfulness of the tea ceremony, with a pair of chopsticks was lifting her dog's turds from where they had dropped and placing them delicately into a polythene bag.

I was totally absorbed in watching this extraordinary ritual and did not hear Masako walk up behind me. She tapped me on the shoulder and, after we had greeted each other and she had sat down, I asked her about the scene I had just witnessed. She laughed. 'The law forbids the fouling of pavements by dogs in Tokyo,' she said with mock solemnity, and our laughter was interrupted by a waiter.

While Masako spoke to the waiter, I looked at her face. It had struck me on our first meeting in London that she did not look at all Japanese in the classical sense. She looked to me more Yunnan Chinese or Tibetan with her dark skin and high cheekbones. What had most impressed me on that first meeting was an aura of quiet nobility that seemed to emanate from her.

The waiter left the table and she turned to me with an excited expression on her face. 'I have something to tell you,' she said, grinning. 'I visited Osumi sensei last week. She's the healer I told you about in London. I told her all about you and how you were wanting to study Shiatsu. Well, she told me to ask an American patient, Mr Kilcullin, who is a Japan Airline's captain, if he thought a foreigner could train in Seiki-jutsu. He said yes, and that Osumi-sensei is the only person to train with. She wants us to have dinner with her tonight so that she can meet you.' She looked at me with a large grin on her face.

I had completely forgotten about my fantasy of finding a teacher in Japan and was suspended in a moment of indecision. It was probably too late now to book a flight to New York that day and a visit to this woman's house for dinner in no way entailed any commitment from me. Anyway, it would be very interesting in itself. We arranged a time for Masako to call at my hotel, and she went off to her research work which she was doing towards her MA in London.

The rest of the day I spent on an expedition to find a temple called Tokai-ji which had been founded in the seventeenth century by a Zen monk called Takuan. The invention of pickled radish (*takuan*) is attributed to him and after whom it was named. Finally, after many wrong turnings, I discovered the temple a short distance from Shinagawa railway station. It was crowded in, as so many temples in Tokyo are these days, by cliffs of ferro-concrete. After visiting the temple and its small garden for an hour or so, I returned to my hotel, tired, but with a sense of anticipation for my meeting with the healer that evening.

3

The small crowded bus shook its way through busy narrow streets. It had been raining again and the windows of the bus shimmered now and then as they were swept by the headlights of cars emerging from side streets.

Finally we reached our destination and walked for about a quarter of a mile, huddled beneath an umbrella. We seemed to be in a very quiet residential area. In the darkness I was aware that the air smelled as though it had passed through trees and shrubs of some kind.

Suddenly Masako stopped in front of a wooden door in a high wall and a bell sounded somewhere beyond it. There was the sound of footsteps and the door slid to one side with a rumble. A man slightly shorter than myself and probably about the same age stood bowing in the dim glow of a lamp. He indicated that we should follow him as he turned and walked ahead of us up a flight of stone steps in the direction of the house which appeared as a dark shadow above us.

When we entered the *genkan*,[4] where we removed our shoes, replacing them with the slippers that were laid out for us, a woman I took to be Osumi-sensei, the healer, was standing before us in the hallway. She smiled and bowed very low, muttering something in Japanese, repeating it several times. Then she shook our hands, obviously very pleased to see Masako. She was short and round, with a body which, while it looked as though it would be soft to touch, nevertheless gave the impression of a very solid rock. She wore spectacles and her hair was cut fairly short. She had on a white coat over a blouse and cardigan with a white cotton scarf tied loosely round her neck. She kept smiling and bowing as she ushered us into a traditional *tatami*-mat room at one end of the house.

We were motioned to sit on the floor around a large circular lacquered table which was laid with small dishes of various types of vegetables and fish. Osumi-sensei sat between us and talked to Masako, now and then turning to me and bowing her head slightly. I had no idea what they were saying, but bowed in return and watched as the man who had opened the gate carried in more plates of food and bottles of beer and *saké* from a back kitchen.

We began to eat and drink, and Masako explained certain dishes to me and how to eat them. While we ate we talked, Masako now and then interpreting or asking questions for Osumi-sensei.

I do not remember a great deal of the conversation, but I do remember that I seemed to be having an uncomfortable reaction, either to the house or to Osumi-sensei. My body state was fluctuating from hot to cold, from fatigue to wakefulness. At times I wanted to laugh out loud and at others I was possessed by a strange sense of fear; at one point I felt as though I wanted to terminate the dinner altogether and return to my hotel.

Then I noticed Osumi-sensei was looking at me with a serious expression on her face. Then, turning to Masako, she said something which Masako repeated to me in English.

'She says your lungs are very bad.' It was true that my lungs had begun to trouble me recently and I had had several bouts of flu which I felt were psychosomatic as they occurred each time I visited New York. As a baby I had suffered bronchial pneumonia and frequent bronchitis, and in my twenties viral pneumonia, but in recent years my lungs seemed to have improved until lately.

Masako again started to interpret something that Osumi-sensei was saying. 'To learn Seiki-jutsu is very difficult, but I feel I can teach you in three years.⁵ It will be very hard for you. To begin with you will have to do just ordinary domestic work, washing up, ironing, sweeping floors and that kind of thing. You won't receive any payment to begin with, but you will be paid a little as your training progresses. Meanwhile you will live here and I will take care of all your needs. I can arrange for you to have Japanese lessons maybe three times a week. A *deshi* must be of one mind and one body with me.'

Osumi-sensei was looking at me as though trying to gauge my reaction. Then she called the man we had first met into the room. He came in and knelt opposite us at the table. He had a thin, good-humoured face and his hair was beginning to turn grey in places. Masako explained that he was a *deshi* or apprentice. She said that Osumi-sensei had asked him to explain the difficulties of trying to train in Seiki-jutsu to me. He did this partly in English and partly through Masako.

'I don't know how long I shall be able to remain here. The life is so difficult. I have to work from early in the morning till very late at night with hardly any break. Mostly I'm just working in the house here and waiting on the patients, although I also have to do the shopping and sometimes cooking too. I don't get taught very much at present and I'm sometimes asked by Osumi-sensei and Okajima-sensei to do things which are physically impossible!'

I asked Masako who Okajima-sensei was, and she told me that he was Osumi-sensei's first *deshi*, who had come to her when he was dying from a liver disease, and that she had healed him and trained him, and he was now her assistant. I looked back at the *deshi* and wondered about the nature of the things which were 'physically impossible'.

Osumi-sensei was giggling. 'You see, it's very difficult. This is not a temple, but we still have a very strong discipline.'

The *deshi* finished with, 'I hope you decide to come, and come soon and help give me some strength to carry on.'

I looked at him. Suddenly he looked exhausted and there had been a tension of anger or frustration in his voice. He bowed, got up and left the room, presumably to carry on with whatever his burden was at that hour. I was surprised by the honesty with which he had expressed his negativity in front of his teacher.

I too was feeling exhausted now and noticed that Osumi-sensei was looking at me again. She asked me to think over what she had said and what I had heard from her *deshi*. I said that I would, though I knew that the decision was already made; it might even have been made before we had come to the house.

'Would you like to stay the night here?' she asked. 'You are very tired.'

'Yes, I would, very much,' I replied. The thought of going all the way back to my hotel only increased my weariness.

The *deshi* phoned for a taxi for Masako and when it arrived we saw her to the gate. It had stopped raining and a warm wind brushed invisible trees and grasses around the house.

That night I slept in the smallest room in the house, called *san-jo* or 'three-mat room', as the size of rooms in a Japanese house is determined by the number of *tatami* mats which compose the floor space. I must have fallen asleep very quickly, for the next minute it seemed I was awakened by the *deshi*, who had opened the *karakami*[6] and was kneeling and bowing at the threshold.

'Get up now,' he said in English and, sliding the *karakami* shut, went downstairs.

I lay in the *futon* for a few minutes remembering an extraordinary dream in which I saw, or remembered seeing, just one image very vividly, a huge hay wagon filled with a mountain of grain. It felt to me like a very auspicious dream and I got up filled with energy.

I folded the *futon* and blankets and put on my clothes. Downstairs I splashed my face with water and then waited in the hallway, wondering where I should go and hoping the *deshi* would soon appear. The front door was open and the light that came into the *genkan* was filtered with the green of the trees in the garden. Outside, on top of a large rock, stood a very old and beautiful shrine which I later learned was an *inari* shrine – a guardian shrine for the house. Suddenly there was a movement behind me and the *deshi* appeared. He led me into a sitting room furnished in 1930s Western style. It had an almost colonial air about it, with large armchairs arranged around a low table. He explained in English that this was where the patients waited for their treatment. He then explained some of his duties by going through the motions of cleaning and moving the furniture about, carefully replacing each item with meticulous precision and emphasizing the importance of this by drawing alignments and positions with his fingers. After making sure that I understood that everything had its special place and order, he looked at his watch. 'Come,' he said, and motioned me to follow him. He showed me into a small room adjacent to the room he had just left.

This room was cluttered with all kinds of objects from animal ornaments to bottles of *saké*, piles of ironed and unironed clothes, a small red television set, books and several small chests of drawers that looked as though they might contain herbs or sewing materials. High on the wall near the ceiling was a Shinto house shrine and, standing opposite it, on top of a chest of drawers, was a crowded Buddhist family altar. Next to it was a small shrine with, hanging above it, a scroll bearing the image of what looked like an old monk. I was later to learn that this was the shrine of Osumi-sensei's ancestor, a seventeenth-century monk who apparently possessed miraculous powers, and who, she says, helps her in her work. I sat on the floor in the midst of these assorted furnishings and became aware of the sounds and smells of breakfast being prepared in the kitchen.

An attractive girl with a halo of frizzy hair suddenly put her head round the door and said in fluent English, 'Hello, I'm another Masako. I'm Sensei's daughter. Did you sleep all right?'

I stood up and explained I had slept very well and introduced myself.

'I'm just making breakfast, it won't be long. Why don't you come into the kitchen?' She turned and I followed her across the passage.

The kitchen was small, but large enough to accommodate a table and chairs as well as the usual kitchen equipment. I sat down and we asked each other questions about our lives and what we were doing. I learned from this Masako that she had lived in Europe for eight years, that she was a weaver and had a studio in the city somewhere.

Just then a noise behind me made me look down to see a cat crawling out from under a blanket placed over a cardboard box. Masako Osumi explained that the cat was sick. At that moment Osumi-sensei appeared, picked up the cat and put it into my lap, placing my hands firmly around its body. While she and her daughter and the *deshi*, who had reappeared, were involved in breakfast preparations, I held onto the cat, which felt to be very sick. In fact, it felt to me as though it was dying, which I learned much later it subsequently did.

Breakfast was enormous and, apart from the many Japanese dishes, there were bacon and eggs. I could only eat half of what I was offered and after breakfast we all went and sat in the small room with the shrines to drink coffee, while Osumi-sensei lit incense and, clapping her hands together, bowed to each shrine in turn.

'My mother wants to know what year you were born in,' Masako Osumi said after some conversation between her and her mother.

'Nineteen-forty,' I said.

'Ah, the same year as me,' she replied to my amazement. 'We were both born in the Year of the Dragon and so was Masako Hagiwara. My mother says next year will be a good year for you.'

There was someone at the front door, and the *deshi*, who had been sitting quietly with us, now and then fetching things for Osumi-sensei, went to answer it. It was Masako Hagiwara and she came in and joined us for coffee.

Soon Osumi-sensei had christened the two Masako's

'Tokyo Masako' and 'London Masako' with a great deal of giggling and placing her hand over her mouth in the traditional Japanese manner.

After we had finished our coffee Masako Hagiwara said it was time for her treatment and that Osumi-sensei had invited me to watch. We went upstairs into a room next to the one in which I had slept that night. Masako lay on the *futon* in her pyjamas and was covered by a towelling blanket. Osumi-sensei worked quietly, first on her back and then on the front of her body. Now and then she made comments about her condition, saying that her spine was much better now than when she had last seen her. I watched her hands. They did not seem to move in any methodical way as far as I could see, but worked on different parts of Masako's body almost at random. Sometimes she worked very delicately and minutely and at other times with a heaviness and strength that was like kneading stiff clay. Now and then she would pick up a limb and shake it. She finished by placing a cloth on Masako's body and blowing into it in two places, one at the base of her spine and the other between her shoulderblades.

Finally, when the treatment was over, Masako said that Osumi-sensei wanted to see her *taiso*. This was apparently a form of exercise which she was given after receiving Seiki. It appeared that Osumi-sensei had transmitted some form of energy to Masako some years previously and that, in order that she could develop this energy, she had to perform a set of exercises daily. I still was not clear quite as to the nature of this therapy, but knew that it must be a way of working with *ki*.

A strangely designed stool was brought out from a corner of the room. It resembled a triangular-shaped wooden box, broad at its base and tapering towards the top, which consisted of a flat seat. On it Masako sat quiet and still for a few moments. Osumi-sensei watched her intently. There was silence. Saliva clicked in someone's mouth. Then Masako seemed to press her closed eyelids lightly with the tips of her fingers. She explained that this would initiate a spontaneous rocking movement and that Seiki energy would spread to those parts of her body that were tired or needed healing.

She began to rock backwards and forwards, slowly at first and then with increasingly deeper bows forward and backwards, so that when she fell forwards her long hair brushed the floor and completely covered her face. The house was silent except for the creaking of the stool and the plat! plat! of her hair threshing the *tatami*.

After a time the rocking slowly began to subside until it finally stopped and she sat motionless again. Her right hand went up to her face, to a point near her nose and she pressed it for a while.

'My body is telling me that this point needs attention,' she said.

Next she performed a series of exercises which I realized worked on each meridian or energy line of the body and also included all its joints, the places where the body bends. It was a total body-work system, much like some forms of yoga, but done while sitting on the stool. It also included several *kiai* exercises which superficially looked like something from one of the martial arts.

Osumi-sensei then said that she wanted to teach Masako some new movements and sat on the stool herself. I suddenly noticed that she was wearing a pair of very strange trousers that looked like a cross between silk jodhpurs and pantaloons. Much later I was to see her wearing these whenever she did her own *taiso*.

These new exercises seemed mainly concerned with leg movements. After she had demonstrated them, she made Masako repeat them until she was satisfied that she would remember them when she had returned to London.

Before we left we were invited to have lunch, which we ate in the waiting room. As we were eating, a man I had not seen before appeared in the kitchen doorway. He was introduced to me as Okajima-sensei, Osumi-sensei's assistant. While we continued eating, he spoke to Masako, obviously asking her questions about her life in London. He gave the impression of an easy naturalness and seemed to possess a good earthy quality.

As we prepared to leave, Osumi-sensei reappeared. She asked me if I thought I wanted to come and learn to master

Seiki. Still without any real idea as to what Seiki-jutsu and its related healing method was, I knew that there was no question of my going to live in New York. I knew this without having properly examined my reasons or feelings, and heard myself telling her through Masako that I had every intention of doing so. She took my right hand between both of hers and held it for a few seconds. Then she said something and bowed. Masako turned to me. 'She says you must come back as quickly as you can.'

Masako Osumi and the *deshi* walked us to the gate and stood waving until we had turned the corner of the road.

4

After parting from Masako at a station near my hotel, I went up to my room and lay down on the bed. I was feeling very tired. Then I suddenly recalled my absurd fantasy about finding a teacher in Japan who would teach me in return for working. Simultaneously with remembering this, laughter began to break from my belly until it filled my whole body and I was shaking helplessly on the bed. It was totally unexpected and brought with it a powerful feeling of some kind of affirmation from deep inside me.

On waking from a short sleep I realized that I had to return to Britain in order to arrange for the appropriate visa and to tell my daughter about my new arrangements.

At this point I was slowly becoming aware of something that I preferred to try to ignore or not to believe. During the time I had been watching Masako's treatment and *taiso* and again later, as she emerged from a subway station for our final meeting before I left for Britain and she returned to London, I had the most powerful premonition that our lives were becoming inextricably fused in a way that went beyond any of my previous experiences of relationships with women. It gave me an unsettling feeling, as I knew that something in my life was going to go through a change that was beyond my imagination or even desire at that time.

At Masako's suggestion, I spent my last day in Kamakura as I had expressed a need to see the sea. As it happened, I left the train one station too early and ended up in country lanes dotted with temples and shrines and did not reach the sea at all. However, it was exactly what I needed and I spent a long time sitting in the sun in the garden of one of the temples, just allowing the previous day's events to become focused and assimilated.

After some time an old woman came and sat on a wooden bench a few feet away from me. She seemed oblivious of my presence, totally absorbed in some other world, like someone rehearsing for ghosthood. Now and then her hands fluttered around her face as though trying to remove a nonexistent veil. Her hands were thin and pale, like bird bones miming a flight they could barely remember. She muttered something intermittently to herself or some invisible companion in conversational tones and eventually trudged off towards the main building of the temple with a folded parasol clutched in her right hand. I watched her until she had disappeared in the direction of the graveyard, then I started back to the station.

5

When I arrived in Britain I met my daughter and told her what I was going to do and how long I would be away. At that time I imagined I might be able to have occasional holidays during which I could see her. Parting from her was like every parting from her, and left me with the usual mixture of guilt and anguish at not having been a proper father to her.

I travelled up to Scotland to sort out some final matters and see a few close friends on Arran. I left the island for London with a deep feeling of sadness.

In London I stayed with two old friends whose generosity at several points in my life had exceeded more than I could have expected, even from them, and who again, now, did everything in their power to help me sort out my affairs, entertained people who dropped by to see me and were generally supportive of my decision.

Once or twice I saw Masako, who was helping me arrange for a visa. We discovered, to our amazement, that her lodgings were only a few doors away from my friends' flat where I usually stayed when I was in London.

Finally my application for a cultural visa was turned down and I decided to take my chance with a tourist visa by renewing it periodically until I managed to work something out.

My last night I stayed with my sister, who drove me to the airport in the morning. Masako arrived minutes before I was due to board. She wished me luck and gave me a list of people who were patients of Osumi-sensei and who spoke English. She also handed me a collection of cards with simple phrases in English and Japanese written on them. We embraced and I went through to the departure lounge.

6

When I returned to Japan, Osumi-sensei and the entire household had moved to a small apartment perched above a busy expressway. This move had been necessary due to repairs and renovation being carried out on Osumi-sensei's old house.

The next four months were like a baptism. Smells, tastes, sights and sounds were all new and intriguing and, coupled with my inability to communicate, it was very much like being a baby. Consequently, apart from the long working hours, I became very tired just trying to understand and assimilate each day. I used my phrasebook when it was useful and developed the art of mime to a degree that usually solicited hysterical laughter and utter incomprehension. However, I began to learn very quickly the domestic rituals I was taught. I learned how to roast the tea; how to place a teacup properly in front of a patient; which way to face pots, pans and kettles when they were not in use; how to prepare certain vegetable and fruit juices; where and how to place slippers for the patients' convenience; how to prepare *futon* and a thousand other domestic tasks. The *deshi* whom Masako and I had originally met at the old house had left, so I was on my own in my work, being the lowest *deshi* in the hierarchical structure of a traditional training situation.

One morning I was informed through Sensei's daughter Masako that I was not to receive Japanese lessons after all. I was to put all my energy into learning Seiki-jutsu. At first I was dismayed by this news as I could not imagine how I was going to learn without being able to speak and understand Japanese. However, Sensei insisted that I would be able to learn without taking Japanese lessons.

As the weeks progressed I slowly began to pick up a few domestic Japanese words, and when I had a problem, Masako Osumi, who came to the apartments at weekends, always assisted me.

7

Between my early-morning chores and breakfast I was given training sessions. This meant working on Osumi-sensei while Okajima-sensei watched and occasionally corrected me. Very often he did this by suddenly shouting at me and moving me out of the way, working himself in the area I had been working on to show me how it should be done. These were rare moments of active teaching at this time.

Sometimes I received a treatment myself, usually from a *deshi* called Sato-san. As he was my senior brother *deshi* I was supposed to wait on him, as I did on my two teachers. However, he rarely allowed me to do so and usually preferred to fetch things for himself. I admired Sato-san and watched him closely. He had the disposition and character of a good monk, with apparently infinite patience and equanimity. Perhaps there was something, in my ignorance of Japanese, that I was not seeing, but what I did see provided a good model. He treated me as an equal and often helped me in my work, covering up for me on more than one occasion when I had failed to do something.

Soon I was called in to watch treatment on patients. It was then that I realized that this was no ordinary therapy and that Osumi-sensei was no ordinary therapist. I quickly realized her shamanic power. In contrast to the first few weeks, when I was given a certain amount of time to relax, my life now was becoming more and more intense. There was little time now for me to stare idly from the windows of the apartment down onto the old wooden houses with their beautiful traditional tiled roofs and wonder about the interiors and what kind of life went on within them. Now the only time I had to relax was when everyone had gone to visit patients at night and I was left alone to work. At these times I would sing loudly and recite poetry to myself with histrionic fervour. These nightly theatricals were an essential valve for the pressure exerted by the crucible of silence in which I found myself due to my inability to express myself verbally at times when it was often very necessary to do so. This, added to the strain of trying to understand simple commands, which were often changed three or four times within a period of five minutes, and attempting to grasp the rudiments of a difficult therapy, was beginning to exhaust me.

'I want you to cut off completely from the outside world,' Sensei had told me one Sunday morning through her daughter Masako. 'I don't want you to lose energy writing letters. It doesn't matter what your friends think. It doesn't matter if they think you've gone mad or died in Japan.'

At first I felt annoyed. I was writing quite a lot of letters as I felt I needed contact with certain friends during this difficult period. In fact, it was a long time before I was able to dispense with my need for letter writing and I was to learn a very severe lesson from it.

This brought about the first indication of a feeling that was to develop over the months, namely that my life was being taken away from my control, or imagined control; at times I was to feel almost manipulated by Osumi-sensei.

I knew I was becoming very tired. I could no longer rise early enough to meditate before starting work and was too exhausted by the end of the day to do so. Now, though, some of the people whose names Masako Hagiwara had given me were beginning to come for therapy. This created a very different space and texture to my life as I was allowed to sit and talk to them after their treatment.

8

One of these patients was Burton Foreman, an interesting and amusing American professor of English at a prestigious women's college in Tokyo. Burt had been in Japan for thirty years, having originally arrived as an American soldier at the end of the war. He returned to Japan after taking his master's degree to teach English and assist in the establishment of language schools for that purpose. During his long residence in Japan he had accumulated a hilarious repertoir of extraordinary stories about his experiences.

He had been a patient of Osumi-sensei's for over ten years and it was she who had healed him of a heart condition which had threatened his life. He was the first foreigner to receive Seiki as a patient at a time when Osumi-sensei actually doubted that a foreigner could receive it! When I asked him about Seiki, though, his knowledge of it seemed rather vague.

Burt told me one day of an incident concerning the shamanic side of Sensei's nature. Some years ago he had been presented with a very fine black carp. He had kept it in an aquarium until it had grown so large that it could no longer turn round; it seemed doomed to spend the rest of its life facing one end of its cramped quarters.

During one summer holiday Burt decided to build a pond for the carp in the small garden behind his house. On starting the preliminary excavation, he discovered just beneath the surface a waterpipe that would effectively cut straight across the middle of the proposed pond. A neighbour suggested that he build two ponds, one on either side of the pipe. Acting on his neighbour's advice, he commenced digging two ponds. However, when he was excavating the pond on the right of the pipe he unearthed a large ceramic pot wedged between the offending pipe and a cistern to which the pipe was connected. He spent a long time and great effort in attempting to dislodge the pot, but to no avail. Finally he decided to smash it with his spade and use the resulting sherds for building up the side of the pond to the left of the pipe. As he was doing this he was suddenly struck by a kind of paralysis. He went into the house and lay down to rest for a while. After a couple of hours he felt a little better, though his body was still stiff and felt very strange. He telephoned Osumi-sensei and described his condition. She told him to come to her house immediately.

Burt, with some effort, was removing his shoes in the *genkan* when Osumi-sensei appeared and, looking at him, said, 'What have you been doing?' He explained that he was digging a pond.

'I've told you before that this is not the time of year to do that kind of thing,' she said, and asked him to go upstairs to one of the treatment rooms.

Later Osumi-sensei came in and began to give him a gentle treatment. After working on his back for some period of time, she stopped abruptly. 'What's wrong with the left side of your pond?' she asked.

Burt felt a little puzzled by her question and told her how he was making two ponds and how he had broken the pot he had unearthed and was building the pieces of pottery into the pond on the left.

'Get up!' she shouted. Burt was quite shocked and frightened by the tone of her voice and the expression on her face. 'Get up, dress and come downstairs!'

Burt stumbled into his clothes and went downstairs to the waiting room. There was a bottle of *saké* and a paper bag in the centre of the table. Osumi-sensei entered from the kitchen. 'The pot you broke was a burial urn. Tokyo is built over many graveyards where temples have been demolished. That is why your body is sick. You must go home immediately and sprinkle this salt, which I have put into a bag for you, and this *saké* in the area where you broke the urn. Then for the rest of the week, each day, I want you to go into your garden and show a good smiling face in the direction of the place where the urn stood.'

Feeling not a little uneasy, Burt went home. He went straight into the garden and rather shyly, wondering what his neighbours would think if they saw him, did as instructed. Quite suddenly, while he was sprinkling the *saké*, the stiffness and strange feeling left his body. He was amazed. Fortunately his neighbours, far from thinking his actions odd, understood the situation completely.

9

While serving tea one afternoon to an English-speaking patient, I learned that Osumi-sensei had forecast, some months earlier, at the time of my first visit to her, that Masako Hagiwara and I were going to marry. This news at first I accepted with amusement, assuming she must have misunderstood our relationship. But I slowly began to remember my own strong premonition.

Three or four days later I was summoned from giving a training treatment to answer a telephone call. It was Masako Hagiwara calling from London.

'I suddenly have to talk to you,' she said. 'I'm coming to Tokyo to talk about our future.' I felt a strange shock.

'That's very odd,' I replied. 'I just heard only two or three days ago about some crazy fantasy Osumi-sensei has about us getting married!' I laughed.

'I've just spoken with Sensei and she will give you time off so that we can meet.' She told me the date and time of her arrival and that I had been given permission to meet her at the airport. And, to my amazement, that evening I was told I was going to be given a week's holiday starting from the time I was to meet Masako!

I felt like a rider whose horse has just bolted. It was getting difficult to stay in the saddle! Again, in my worst moments I began to feel that Osumi-sensei was inventing a kind of fiction of my life in accordance with which some suggestible part of myself had agreed to act. Much later I was to learn that she was not the author, but a catalyst or mediator – a kind of psychic go-between.

10

Masako and I spent most of the holiday in Kyoto. The weather was beautiful and the cherry blossom was in full bloom. We spent our time in the temples and shrines in the hills surrounding the city.

It was one of those situations which risks sounding like a cliché – it was as though we were merely resuming a very well-established and symbiotic relationship which had been interrupted for some reason or other, and that we were already in full knowledge of each other.

One night Masako told me that originally she had arranged to go to a university in New York, but that Osumi-sensei had told her that she should go to London to study, and that if she did so she would lead a very unusual life. Realizing that Osumi-sensei must have had good reason for saying this, Masako had gone to the British Council in Tokyo to find out how to apply to a university in London. There, she said, the woman behind the desk laughed at her and told her that she was far too late to apply for that year. Even so, Masako had gone ahead and applied. After having been asked to submit an essay of some kind, she had been accepted.

At the end of the week Masako returned to London, where it was arranged that I should join her in a month's time for our marriage, which we both felt was almost an unnecessary formality, but in our case a bureaucratic expedient. We were to remain in Britain for a holiday of three months before returning to Japan.

Meanwhile I went back to work and was beginning to feel some progress in my learning. Soon I was told by Osumi-sensei that they had advanced me a year in my training and she wanted to give me Seiki as soon as possible.

One evening when I was alone in the apartment with Sensei and her daughter she began to speak very seriously. 'It isn't easy to be given Seiki these days. There are very few people, maybe a handful in the world, who know how it's done and have the training and discipline to do so.' She was kneeling on the floor and shifted her position. 'Seiki means "vital life energy".' She picked up a ballpoint pen and drew two Chinese characters on the back of an envelope. 'I think in Europe it is called "life force". In Seiki-jutsu we can attract Seiki from the universe, all around.' She made broad sweeping movements around her with her arms. 'We can attract great amounts of it to us in order to transmit it into the body of the person who is to receive it.

'It's a very serious thing, to be given Seiki. To receive Seiki is a very precious thing. Once you've been given Seiki, you can't lose it. You have it for the rest of your life. Unless you develop it, though, it won't manifest properly. In order to develop it for self-healing, healing others and for your own spiritual growth, you must keep a strict discipline to concentrate your Seiki. Each day you must do your Seiki *taiso*. Seiki takes about three years to become properly active and maybe ten years for it to become fully mature.' She paused and looked at me. 'I will give you Seiki through the top of your head and it will come to rest at the base of your spine. It will always be with you, like your shadow.'

At this point I immediately thought of Kundalini[7] and wondered if a 'piece' of Seiki energy actually remained in the body or whether it woke or fired the regenerative energy that is already present and lying dormant at the base of the spine. I knew that as a *deshi* I was not really supposed to ask questions, but I tried to clarify this point. However, it became very complicated and I did not think she understood what I was trying to say, so instead I asked, 'Whereabouts does Seiki enter the head?'

'Seiki enters at the point of the hair whorl, though I actually cover the whole of that area with my hand,' she replied. 'We'll give you Seiki in the old house, in the room you slept in when you came to visit me there. That's where a Seiki line comes down. That is the place where the right volume of Seiki that a person needs will come together.'

I tried to ask what a Seiki line was, but she said I was getting tired and got up and went into the lavatory. My mind began to turn around ley lines, acupuncture meridians and Seiki lines, but she was right, I was suddenly feeling very tired and prepared my *futon*.

The next two or three days she said my body had too much tension in it to receive Seiki yet and I would have to wait. This depressed me as I had heard that, if a person's body rejects or is closed to receiving Seiki, then there is a kind of kick-back effect which can cause serious injury to those giving the Seiki. I had learned the reason for my receiving periodic treatment was to create a 'way' for Seiki to enter my body. However, at breakfast one morning Osumi-sensei unexpectedly announced that they would give me Seiki the following Saturday, in five day's time. She said that it was going to be a challenge for two reasons: one, that they had never given it so early to a *deshi* before and, two, she had never given Seiki on a Saturday, always on Sunday.

11

Three days before Seiki I began to see snakes. Of course, I was well aware of the symbolism of the snake or serpent in relation to life energy and healing but, curiously and almost absurdly to me now, during that period of three days I made no connection at all. I have since felt that if the symbolism of the snake had remained conscious, I probably would not have experienced the snake phenomenon as I did. It was as though my conscious knowledge concerning this subject had been supressed during that period.

It started one night when I was preparing for bed and had just removed my belt. As it fell to the *tatami* it suddenly began to twist and writhe across the floor, and as I looked down at it I saw a snake at my feet. I instinctively leaped out of the way and then, realizing my stupidity, I assumed it must have been due to my extreme tiredness.

The whole of the following day, out of the corner of my eye, I caught water pipes and electrical wiring transforming into snakes and slithering in and out of the walls around the apartment building. As soon as I looked directly at them they resumed their usual forms.

On the second day one of the patients brought a thin branch of a tree with bright red berries from her garden. It had been placed in a vase just in front of the *genkan*. That afternoon I was greeting a Japanese–American patient as she came through the door, when she suddenly stopped before removing her shoes and stared at the branch in the vase.

'Yes, isn't it beautiful. A patient brought it from her garden this morning,' I said.

'It's not that,' she replied. 'Snakes like that tree. They say that, wherever you see that tree, you will find snakes.'

That evening, after clearing the kitchen area of the day's debris, I gathered up the rubbish bags to take them down to the basement for collection. I left the apartment and rang for the lift. While I waited I looked over the balcony at the traffic below. It was dusk. Heavy clouds hung like unnatural smoke, decomposing over the city. It was raining drops so large that I could feel the displacement of air around them, like thousands of tiny wings against my face.

Suddenly the lift bell rang and the doors opened. I froze with horror. The whole of the floor of the lift was covered by a huge writhing pile of black snakes. In disbelief I stood paralysed for what seemed like minutes, but in reality must have only been a few seconds. Then slowly the snakes began to be flattened to the floor and finally resolved themselves into the black coat-of-arms printed on the floor mat. I stepped in and rested against the wall for a minute or so, pressed the button and descended.

The next morning was to be the day of Seiki. We were to finish work early that afternoon and proceed to the old house. I had been assisting with a treatment on a patient who was a friend and past colleague of Masako before she went to London. After her treatment I accompanied her in the lift down to the street level. As she was about to step out of the building, she stopped and, turning to me, said in English, 'Burt Foreman says you were talking to him some weeks ago about something called Kundalini.'

'Yes, it's sometimes called "serpent power",' I replied.

'He said he was surprised by how much you knew about it.'

'Well, I don't know that I know very much about it, but I once worked for someone who was interested in it and I read quite a bit about it at one time.'

Then she said, with an exaggerated shiver, 'I'm terrified of snakes.'

It was at this moment, when I had started to talk to her briefly about snake symbolism, that I began to realize how my mind, and certainly at one point the environment, had been responding to the situation. As she turned to go I noticed that while I had been speaking to her I had been lightly tapping her sacrum, quite unconsciously, with my left hand.

Ascending in the lift again, I was amazed at my not having made the connection between my snake hallucinations and what was about to happen to me that day. It seemed ridiculous, and, again, I thought how tired I must have become.

That afternoon at about four o'clock Osumi-sensei, Okajima-sensei, Sato-san and myself got into the car and drove the short distance to the old house. It was a warm, sunny day with an energetic breeze. I examined my feelings as we drove through the narrow, crowded streets. I was a little apprehensive, still worried about the condition of my body and wondering if I would be able to accept Seiki all right. The descriptions of receiving Seiki I had heard from patients who had received it came to mind. Each person's experience seemed to be different. I wondered what mine would be. After some of my experiences both in meditation and also during the times when I had been psychologically ill, I was expecting some kind of world-shattering apotheosis.

When we arrived, the carpenters were working on the ground floor. The house smelled of damp earth and raw wood, a smell that made me very relaxed and calm. We went upstairs to *san-jo* where Sato-san briefly swept the floor free of dust which had risen from below. Then they all took some minutes carefully placing a Seiki stool, like the one Masako had used for her *taiso*. One would place it and then Osumi-sensei would move it slightly; this procedure was repeated until it was in exactly the right spot.

I was asked to sit on the stool. I sat down and closed my eyes. They were making sounds of satisfaction and saying words which I knew meant 'good' and 'wonderful' and 'just right'. I later learned that, as soon as I sat on the stool, they could see that my body was in exactly the right condition for receiving Seiki.

Okajima-sensei began working on my spine, neck and shoulders, at first lightly and then with increasing pressure. Now and then he slapped my back all over and gently hit my spine, paying particular attention to the sacrum. Behind me, periodically, someone would hit the wall with what sounded like the palm of the hand and scream or shout. The noises behind me and Okajima-sensei's working on my body were building up into a faster and more intense rhythm. They were breathing very deeply great gouts of air, and hissing, screaming, clapping their hands and hitting the walls, working themselves up into a state of excited concentrated tension. I was to learn later that they did this in order to attract Seiki, and that while they did so it was essential to maintain a condition of emptiness or 'no-thought'.

Now Okajima-sensei was working on my head with a firm, almost painful pressure, then hissing and brushing down my spine with strong, sweeping movements. Suddenly the sounds and the movements reached a synchronous climax and I felt a hand or hands on top of my head. The room seemed filled by a mighty wind. I opened my eyes slightly and saw my trouser legs flapping. Then 'Hudtsss!' I hear Osumi-sensei give a loud *kiai* and felt her hand gently rocking my head back and forth. I followed the movement of her hand with my body and remembered Masako's *taiso*. After a minute or so her hand left the top of my head and she gently pushed my shoulders to continue the rocking motion. After a further two or three minutes I stopped and everyone prepared to leave. As we reached the bottom of the stairs I noticed that the carpenters had disappeared.

I was feeling disappointed. I had felt nothing at all in my body, nor had I seen anything. I thought that they must have made a mistake, that my body must have rejected Seiki. But they all seemed very pleased and were congratulating me in the car as we drove back to the apartment. I felt cheated somehow, although the only person, in reality, who was cheating me was myself through my absurd expectations and anticipation of an experience I had invented. I wanted to explain that nothing had happened, that I hadn't felt anything then and I didn't feel any different now.

On reaching the apartment Osumi-sensei disappeared into her room while everyone else set about preparing a huge meal. A woman *deshi*, who had recently arrived but who had remained behind, had already cooked seafood and vegetables. I was asked to rest until supper.

As we began to sit around the table, Masako Osumi suddenly arrived and I realized I would be able to explain that the celebrations were not in order. Before I could say anything. Osumi-sensei ordered a toast and they all hit their glasses against mine and shouted, '*Kampai!*' in unison.

'You had wonderful Seiki! Not just through your head, but it covered all over you,' Masako Osumi interpreted as her mother waved her hands about me. 'I felt Seiki come from all over. It was like a huge tide. Your head stuck to my hand, it wanted Seiki so much. It was like a baby at the breast. It stayed there until it had had enough.'

As she finished I saw that she looked very tired. She had difficulty sitting on the *tatami* and her left leg seemed to be giving her pain on what I later learned was a heart line. She kept rubbing it and grimacing. Then she turned to me again, holding out her upturned hands.

'This is the hand she gave you Seiki with,' said Masako, pointing at her mother's right hand. It was bright red and the palm looked puffy and raised like quilting. Her left hand looked completely different; it was an ordinary pinkish colour and flat.

'She says she's very happy that you all managed to meet the challenge. But she's exhausted now, as you can see.'

I began to tell them that I hadn't received Seiki, that I hadn't felt anything special, that I had made the rocking movement myself because I thought that was what they wanted me to do and that they had made a mistake.

They all laughed. 'Don't worry. You have Seiki,' they said. 'No mistake.'

I was not convinced, however, but I decided to enjoy the celebration supper anyway. It looked like a marriage feast.

12

All the next week, during which I arranged my flight to London, Osumi-sensei was still suffering from the effects of having given Seiki to me. The new woman *deshi* was looking exhausted and ill and complained that Osumi-sensei was too difficult a teacher for her. I was feeling less tired, or perhaps my exhaustion was now buoyed by the prospect of my journey to Britain and seeing Masako and my daughter Celine.

A few days before I was due to leave, Sensei taught me the Seiki exercises that I would need to do each day. I told her that I didn't have any spontaneous rocking, but she said that it didn't matter and that sometimes she had known a person wait for a year before moving spontaneously. She described how my Seiki was green at present; whereas 'hers was old Seiki', that mine was like a baby.

When the time came for my departure I was loaded up with gifts from Osumi-sensei for Masako and Celine. Sato-san was to drive me to the airport and Okajima-sensei came down to the street to see me off. As we drove away, and I bowed my head through the back window of the car to Okajima-sensei, who was bowing in the road, I suddenly saw the new woman *deshi* running into the street waving. I wondered if she would still be there on my return.

13

Masako and I were married in London and spent the following two months visiting friends in Scotland and Cornwall. In many ways it was a strange hiatus after the tension of the previous months, and somewhere I felt a deep unease at having begun something which I knew was going to demand all my strength, but of whose exact nature I was still virtually ignorant, and then interrupting it even for this important period.

Masako and Celine immediately formed a close relationship and ended my concern over what I thought might be a difficult prelude to friendship.

By the end of the three months I felt the need to resume my training, although there was a certain amount of anxiety attached to our return to Japan.

The two main concerns that occupied us were whether we would be able to afford to live in Tokyo on our fast dwindling resources, and exactly what kind of visa I was going to be able to obtain without having to travel to Hong Kong or Taiwan periodically in order to re-enter the country every six months, thereby obtaining a new visa each time. In Japan the fact that you are a foreign man married to a Japanese woman does not make any difference to your status in that country.

Miraculously, two weeks before we were due to return, Masako's mother wrote to say that they had found an old house which belonged to the family business, but which had been empty for seven years and was in a terrible state. She expressed her doubts about the desirability of anyone living in it, however. We learned later that my father-in-law had made up his mind that it would be ideal for us and had set about secretly repairing it and renewing the old *karakami* and *tatami*.

Masako vaguely remembered the house and wrote back to say that we would like it whatever condition it was in.

14

In October we returned to Tokyo and moved into our new home, a small traditional Japanese house standing in an oasis of trees and bamboo occupied by three similar houses and set back from a narrow street of restaurants and a few shops. The land the houses had been built on had originally been in the grounds of an old temple, whose main building, which was still standing, was three of four doors away and occupied by a very old monk.

The house was perfect for us. Its fresh *tatami* made it smell like a haystack. Its interior was built with wood of different types and grain. The ridgepoles upstairs were of sturdy bamboo, and here and there were unexpected features to a

Westerner, like a window high up under the ceiling and one set at floor level, with thin sticks of bamboo used as spacers between the ceiling panels in the bathroom. We spent a month, at Osumi-sensei's suggestion, just setting up house and acclimatizing ourselves.

There was one room, however, the main living room, about which I felt a little uneasy for some reason. I did not know why exactly, as aesthetically it was a very attractive room, but somehow it felt cold and uninviting for living in. Masako explained that it had been the room in which the old woman who had last occupied the house had spent most of her time. Her Buddha image had sat in one corner and every day she had been in the habit of practising her calligraphy on the floor in front of it. She had been related to the family and Masako remembered visiting her in the past.

Soon after we had moved in Osumi-sensei phoned to say that she and Sato-san were going to pay us a visit in order to congratulate us on our marriage and welcome us back to Japan.

They arrived about three o'clock one afternoon on their way to visit a patient. They brought with them a larged cooked red fish called a *tai*. This Osumi-sensei delivered in the *genkan* beneath a special cloth embroidered with a crane, a turtle, a pine tree, a Japanese plum tree and bamboo – all symbols of longevity, happiness and good luck. She greeted us and then withdrew from the *genkan* and stood outside the house, looking at it. As Sato-san, who had been parking the car, came up behind her, she asked him to look at the house with her. They both stood silent for a moment. Then Osumi-sensei said, 'Wonderful! It couldn't be better. Can you see, Sato-Kun?' (She used the dimunitive often reserved for someone younger or lower in status.) He replied that it looked like a very nice house to him.

'Yes, but can you see?' she said. 'Look more carefully.' Then, moving towards the front door, she turned and said, 'Very good. Excellent. But you must never place anything to the left of the doorway. It must always be free.'

She turned and looked at the house to the right of ours and said in a whisper, 'Something wrong there. The entrance is very bad.'

We later discovered that the mother and daughter who lived next door had a very difficult life and were not liked locally for some reason. The mother always seemed to be in very bad health.

Sensei carefully entered our house, now and then bowing and making noises of satisfaction to herself. When she came to the living room, however, she stopped at the threshold. 'This room needs warming up!' Masako and I looked at each other. Perhaps there was more to my feelings than imagination. 'The old woman lay here when she was sick,' she continued, pointing at exactly the place where Masako had said the old woman had practised her calligraphy on the floor. Sensei had no idea who had lived there before us or, I should say, no one had told her.

She looked around the room. 'Move that Buddha image.' She pointed at the shelf over the door leading to the kitchen where I had placed the Buddha image which I had brought from Thailand many years ago and always carried with me. 'That place is too busy for it. Too many comings and goings. It needs to be placed under that window, but not so that it receives direct sunlight.'

Now she pointed at a small window directly beneath the ceiling. 'That Buddha image is protecting you. It glows and I don't mean because it's covered in gold.'

This interested me, as there is a name on the formalized *naga* (or serpent) plinth on which the image sits in the position of meditation. A Thai friend of mine had told me that it is the name of the monk who made the image and 'put his energy into it'. At the time I took this to be a metaphorical expression, but now I began to realize that it must have been charged with the same energy that Osumi-sensei called Seiki.

After inspecting the rest of the house, which seemed to meet with her approval, we went upstairs to the large eight-mat room to have tea which we had prepared previously. The red *tai* fish was to be the most important central dish. As we sat eating, Sensei said that this was the room that we should use as a bedroom. We had in fact been sleeping in the smaller room next to it. She indicated where our *futon* should be, in front of the *tokonoma*.[8] Masako was to sleep on the right, looking out of the *tokonoma*, and I was to sleep on the left with my head close to the post of the *tokonoma*, which was covered in cherry bark.

As they were about to leave, Sensei said that she was thinking about the best way for me to continue my training and would phone us in a few days to invite us to dinner, when we could discuss the matter.

15

A few days later we arrived at Sensei's old house; the renovation work had now been completed. To my surprise and disappointment, many things about the house had been changed. No longer was there a wooden gate like a huge door that rolled back and forth, but a small metal garden gate, and beyond it, instead of steps made of great stones, there was a flight of concrete stairs.

Inside the house, on the ground floor, there was now a large kitchen, and next to it a new, but traditionally designed, room with a *kotatsu*[9]. This room now contained Sensei's shrines and all the assorted domestic objects which were not allowed to reside in any of the rooms used by patients.

We were shown upstairs to a large eight-mat room which served as a treatment room during the day and Sensei's bedroom at night. It had been remodelled with new plaster and the old wood replaced by new. I was pleased to discover that neither of the other two rooms had been altered; Sensei said she felt she shouldn't change anything in the room in which Seiki was given.

As usual the meal was enormous, and during our conversation I learned that the woman *deshi* had left and that a new *deshi*, Okajima-sensei's niece, who had just left school, would be coming in a few months' time. Sensei told us that Okajima-sensei was going to stay with Mr Kilcullen in America for a few months, so they were going to be very busy. She said that Okajima-sensei thought that I should come and work every other day in her house, resting on the days between, but returning on the evening of the rest day to spend the night at the house. This meant that I would spend every other night at home and most of every other day. I was to start work on the evening I arrived and start again very early the next morning. Masako and I were very pleased as we had imagined that we would see much less of each other. Sensei said that she thought this arrangement was best in order to prevent me from becoming too tired. This routine was to come into effect within a week. Masako in the meantime was going to search for a job. This would probably be difficult as an academic position in Japan requires a legally enforceable commitment of several years.

16

Soon I got used to saying goodbye to Masako after supper and travelling across Tokyo to Sensei's house, where I would begin work at about eight o'clock and finish at eleven. The next morning I would rise early and open up the house, do my training practice until breakfast and spend half the day waiting on patients and the other half in the treatment rooms with Osumi-sensei. I was allowed to work only on arms and legs and would at the same time try to watch Sensei's treatment on the patient.

One afternoon I was working with Osumi-sensei and Okajima-sensei, who was due to leave for America in a few days, on a patient who spoke fluent English and with whom they had been discussing something of which I could only understand the odd word. The patient suddenly said to me, 'They say that you're a natural for this therapy. They think you must have had something to do with Seiki-jutsu in a former life.' My teachers waited while I was informed of their remarks and then we all laughed. At first I felt pleased and flattered by their comments, but I realized, quite quickly, that I had to guard against any feelings of satisfaction when I thought about what I had to accomplish. Anyway, if that had been food for my ego, within a few weeks the plate was to be rudely snatched away!

On the nights that I stayed in Sensei's house, I slept in *san-jo*, where I had spent the night of my first visit and the room in which Seiki is given. Each night I would wake at about 2 a.m. to the sound of strange eerie, flute music. Somewhere close by a hypnotic tune was played over and over on some kind of instrument which I imagined must be an ancient ritual flute. I would lie awake listening to its unearthly tones as they seemed to orchestrate the strangeness of my new life. A few weeks later, when I inquired about this nocturnal music, I was to discover that the sacred flute was in fact the pipe of the late-night noodle seller!

17

The night before Okajima-sensei was due to depart for America, he treated Masako, myself and Burt Foreman to a meal at one of his favourite *sushi* bars. After the meal we went to a hotel bar and here Okajima-sensei left. As usual, as the three of us sat drinking we started to talk about Seiki.

Some time before, Burt had told me when talking about his own experience of receiving Seiki of three features concerning it which had interested me. One was that if the weather is overcast at the time that Seiki is transmitted, as it was in his own case, then almost immediately afterwards the sun breaks through regardless of weather conditions. The second was that his arms shot up into the air and he could not bring them down. And the third was that, at the point of receiving Seiki, he saw a bright flash of lightning. Being fascinated by what he had told me, I had checked with Osumi-sensei. She verified the first two statements, but on the last, however, with great laughter, she explained that, in the enthusiasm of giving Seiki, someone had inadvertently switched the light on and then quickly switched it off again! I told Burt about this and we all laughed so hilariously that some people entering the bar stopped in their tracks to turn and stare at us.

'Anyway, Burt,' I suggested, 'it probably helped to dramatize what was taking place for you, so had a beneficial effect on your acceptance of Seiki.' I explained to him my own disappointment over my experience of receiving Seiki and also how it had taken four months of doing my *taiso* before I experienced any spontaneous rocking. I told him how it was only a week or so ago that, after my usual *taiso*, I was about to get up from the stool when suddenly my body started to rock back and forth. It felt like a firm warm hand pushing from the sacrum. In order that he should not feel too bad about his 'lightning' having been supplied by Tokyo Electrical Company, I recounted how Masako and I had recently discovered that, when we came together in our *futon*, we experienced a Seiki-like electrical burring on the skin, particularly where bone came to the surface. I told him how, after two nights of wonder, awe and great excitement, at Sensei's suggestion I had unplugged the electric blanket we used to combat the extreme cold of a traditional wooden Japanese house in winter, and how, as miraculously as it had appeared, the 'Seiki' vanished!

18

Masako was still without a job and we were both worried as to how we were going to be able to survive; I still received no payment as a *deshi*. It happened that after Okajima-sensei had left a great many people became ill and were coming for treatment. We had become extremely busy and I was spending less time downstairs and more and more time in the treatment rooms. In fact, Sensei had started me working on patients' backs as well as on their arms and legs.

One evening Sensei said she wanted to speak to us both, so after the day's work and before Sensei and Sato-san went out to visit patients, Masako came to the house and we sat with Sensei in the waiting room. She told us that it was important for both of us that we should not be apart. She had decided that Masako should come and work at the house, serving tea and cooking for the patients, and she would pay us each a wage. She repeated again that we should grow together and become of one mind and one body with each other.

I was to move out of the kitchen area altogether and work upstairs on patients and, while domestic work was a far cry from the academic life Masako had trained for, she was very happy with the plan as it meant that we would both be receiving an income and spending all our time together.

This arrangement, we began to recognize, was actually initiating Masako as a *deshi*.

19

Now we were both working very hard and, instead of resting on our days off and regaining some energy, we spent most of our time wandering about Tokyo and even, now and then, taking train rides out of the city altogether. We had failed to understand a basic law of Seiki-jutsu training, that there is no space for anything other than just concentrating on Seiki.

Each alternate night I would return to sleep at Sensei's house, while Masako would remain at our home and arrive for work after breakfast the next day. I was fluctuating between feeling very tired and on occasions finding new energy, which, I was to learn later, I then squandered on our frequent expeditions.

I found in my treatments that I could not remain empty. I was caught up in thinking about what I was doing, how I was doing it and what I should do next. I was too attached to my technique. This was causing tension in my body and in my practice and creating one of the roots of my tiredness. I was having to move from one patient directly to another without any break between, until I felt as though I was working on an assembly line. I did not know what I was doing or why. I was just carrying out the instructions that I had been given. Sometimes I seemed to be working while sleeping, and it felt like dreaming someone else's dreams. Images began to appear while I was working and once or twice I realized that I had been listening to a voice without hearing what it was saying.

About this time poems started to arrive in my head without any intention or thought of poetry. While I was involved in sweeping the road outside or watering the garden, suddenly short epigrammatic poems would come complete. They had the feeling of *haiku*, though technically speaking they were not; they were more like a number of poems I had written several years earlier. I had not written anything for five or six years and the suddenness of this activity took me by surprise. The poems seemed to be speaking of the nature of 'above as below'; of reflection and echo; of reciprocation; of inner as outer. They began to arrive so regularly and with such apparent insistence that I began to carry a notebook in the garden and round the house in order to write them down. Although there was no thought or intention to write, I did not hinder the activity. The poems seemed born out of some simple experience – an action, something spotted in the road, a sudden memory. They seemed to arrive at the same time as the experience; there appeared to be no intervening thought or interpretation of any kind.

One night during this period of poetic activity I had a dream which seemed fuelled by the same energy. I dreamed of two Zen monks, one standing on the earth, the other in the sky. They are throwing a ball between them. As one throws it he listens to hear if the other has caught it and reacts with greater laughter at the knowledge.

20

I began to find that, while giving treatment to some patients, I developed very strong feelings about certain aspects of their lives. Usually afterwards I would find that these intuitions were correct.

On one occasion I started to discuss what I felt was a psychological problem which was expressing itself through the body of one of the patients, an elderly man, who spoke very good English. I began to describe his condition in the terms of a form of therapy that I had been involved in prior to coming to Japan. He seemed very interested in what I was saying, so I expounded the theory of this particular form of therapy at some length.

Two or three days later I received a very strong reprimand from Osumi-sensei. I was not to discuss other therapies with patients or lead them to believe I had intuited anything about their private lives. I was angry and confused. I felt that what I had experienced was genuine and I thought it might be of some help to the patient. I had not mentioned to the patient what I thought his problem was, however. But on reflection I later realized that Osumi-sensei was quite right. I had no right to introduce the theories of another therapy into the situation when I was only a *deshi* and the person concerned was not my patient. Sensei encourages patients to concentrate exclusively on the Seiki therapy they are receiving and, of course, I had unconsciously risked diverting or upsetting the patient's attention and openness to the treatment. I felt slightly ashamed and vowed to myself to keep my mouth shut should a similar situation occur.

21

After this I tried not to get into conversation with patients while giving treatment and referred any questions to Osumi-sensei, as all *deshi* are expected to. I realized that I should just concentrate on what I was doing, withhold my own observations and keep silent.

This decision received an upset one afternoon, however, when I was asked to start giving a treatment to a man in his seventies. He spoke very good English and kept asking me questions, which I answered briefly and simply as possible, trying to avoid any more complex conversation. He kept telling me that, although he was an old man, he wasn't made of porcelain and wouldn't break if I was to work on him harder. I ignored this for some time, until finally, when I was working on his spine and he had persisted in demanding that I use more strength, I slightly increased the weight behind my right hand.

Suddenly there was a dull crack like a stick breaking under a blanket. Accompanying it was the sickening sensation of a vertebra which had been out of alignment for a great number of years trying to go back in to a place that hardly recognized it any more. His face was contorted with pain. My own body seemed to register the same pain and for seconds we both seemed frozen by the one spasm. I fetched Sensei, and she and Sato-san entered the room while I remained outside.

When Sensei came out she told me not to worry as no harm had been done, and that I should go downstairs and have a cup of tea.

I knew that, with the crack of the old man's spine, something had cracked inside me – my confidence had fractured. I felt exhausted and depressed. Even the light in the house seemed to have dimmed. I was fed up with trying to give so many treatments without being allowed my own personal space and without knowing what I was doing. I felt I was never going to make a Seiki therapist.

Masako was in the kitchen. As I entered she turned brightly and then, seeing my face, her expression changed. 'What's wrong?' she asked.

'I've just broken someone in two!' I said. 'Some therapist I'm going to make!' I explained what had happened and went and sat in the room with the *kotatsu*. I knew too late that I should have followed my own instincts and ignored the old man's demands. I felt I could not possibly learn under these conditions. I realized an old pattern of flight was beginning to re-emerge. When things did not go right, my old way of dealing with them was to get out instead of facing up to the problem. But I could hardly drag Masako back to Britain to a certain uncertain future. Anyway, we could not even afford the fare to Yokohama, let alone halfway round the world!

Masako appeared at the door with a cup of tea. 'Don't worry, Sensei's with him.' As she spoke I heard Osumi-sensei at the foot of the staircase. She came into the kitchen.

'Don't worry Malcolm-san, it wasn't your fault. He shouldn't have told you to press harder. Don't worry. You have Seiki, it hasn't done any harm.' I doubted it, and the old man's contorted features appeared before me. 'Have a cup of tea and rest,' Sensei said again, touching my right shoulder.

Later the patient came down for tea. He was still in a little pain, but able to go home by himself without difficulty. Whether by design or not, I was not to see him again for some months.

22

On one of our days off Masako and I were exploring among the shelves of a small antique shop where we had previously bought some inexpensive pieces of pottery, when I came across what looked like a small shrine. It was made of plain, unadorned wood and the doors were tightly closed. Masako asked the dealer if he could open it for us. He took the shrine and carefully pulled back the doors. Inside there were several objects wrapped up in tissue paper. He extracted them one by one and began to unwrap them. Immediately the first object emerged from the paper, I recognized it as the image of a *tengu* – an anthropomorphic creature, roughly equivalent to the goblin of European folklore; in this case, it was in the common form of a crow, a crow *tengu*. I knew then that this must be a shrine belonging to a cult or spiritual Way called Shugendo or 'the Way of the Mountain', a sect that recognizes certain mountains as living mandalas and works with them accordingly in their rituals and initiations. It is a Buddhist–Shinto sect and these days usually under the protection of the Tendai or Shingon schools of Buddhism.

I expected that the next object to be unwrapped would be the image of the *kami*, numinon or manifestation of the sacred energy of whichever mountain this shrine belonged to. The *kami* was depicted as a ferocious-looking warrior brandishing a sword. The third object was another *tengu* which, with its companion, formed the guards for the *kami*. On the back of the shrine were some characters which described the mountain to which it belonged.

An idea was forming in my head, that we should buy it and try to locate the mountain it related to and discover if the cult was still extant and, if so, return the shrine to that area.

We brought the shrine and returned home with it. I unwrapped the three images and placed them in the shrine, putting it in an open cabinet of shelves.

Two nights later, on having returned late from Sensei's house, we were both very tired and decided to go straight to bed. As we went upstairs I told Masako that I was going to do my *taiso* in the small room next to our bedroom where we kept the Seiki stool.

It was just after midnight. I sat on the stool and relaxed. Outside the street was silent. A distant hum came from the main expressway. I started to breathe deeply and with each exhalation brushed down the sides of my body from the shoulders, down the chest and belly and across my thighs, my hands leaving my knees and circling high back towards my shoulders on inhalation, to repeat the cycle half a dozen times. Then I relaxed again, emptying my mind, just keeping awareness of the body feeling for a minute or so. Then I placed the tips of my fingers lightly against the inside corners of each of my eyeballs with a light pressure. My body began rocking gently backwards and forwards. I exhaled on the forward movement and inhaled on the backward one.

The rocking had been quietly continuing for about twenty minutes or so, when I suddenly felt a contraction in my lower belly. Slowly the contraction released and my lungs spontaneously inhaled violently and deeply and then released the air with a great explosion which brought my chest sharply down onto my thighs. Then what began as a low growl grew into a mighty roar and suddenly from me came a deep voice which spoke in a strangely modulated tone. Sometimes it spoke for a very long time without pausing to take breath, in a pitch far lower than my normal speaking voice. Occasionally it spoke very fast and at other times very slowly and deliberately. Some words I recognized as Japanese. It came with great energy and force, so much so that after a while my whole upper body was aching. I was perfectly conscious and just allowed it to speak as it needed. I was even able to worry whether Masako was frightened by it and what our neighbours would be thinking it was.

I became aware of Masako entering the room. She pushed something between my feet. As I happened to be doubled up at that point with an excruciating pressure in my belly, I was able to see she had placed a tiny tape recorder in front of me.

The voice or voices, as the tone and personality of the voice seemed to change at times, carried on. Now and then it paused and gave 'me' time to take a breather. Then it continued with renewed force, so that at times it felt as though my body might burst open. I was aware that I was becoming increasingly weaker and finally, when the speaking arrived at one of the pauses, I straightened up and, concentrating on the sound of the engine of a car that was slowly cruising the street outside, got up from the stool and went into the bedroom. Masako was sitting up in the *futon* with her knees to her chin.

'I'm sorry, I didn't have any chance but to allow it to happen. Did it frighten you?'

'Well at first it was a bit of a shock,' she said, laughing. 'I wondered what it was. I wasn't really so much frightened as interested. It sounded just like classical Japanese. It was exactly like Noh. That's why I thought you might like to listen to it afterwards.'

I explained to Masako that it was not the first time that this kind of thing had happened. It first happened when I started meditation. Very soon after I started to practise meditation I found that sometimes this kind of voice would begin speaking out. There was nothing extraordinary about this. It did not mean that I was a shaman or a medium or possessed any kind of strange power. I had known several people to whom similar things had happened during meditation. I told Masako about my misgivings and fear when I went on my first meditation retreat, because I knew I was liable to start speaking like this in the middle of a meditation period, but that my meditation teacher had actually encouraged me to allow it to happen. He had taught me not to interpret or label what came out, but merely to give it space without judging it or identifying with it. In my early days of experiencing this kind of thing I had often regressed and spoken with my voice as it was when I was seven or eight years old and whole pieces of 'forgotten' conversation had come out. At other times I seemed to speak in foreign languages that sounded like Arabic or Chinese, and I often sang incomprehensibly for long periods. Sometimes I thought of it as a kind of mediumship, but the 'spirits' were from my own mind. However, there were times when memories of other lives seemed to surface, often with attendant visual scenes of a particular period or geographical location, but I was careful not to identify them as such as they might also be repressed memories that my ego still could not face, so it clothed them in such a way as to keep them distanced.

Masako and I talked about the danger of people confusing the psychological for the spiritual and the fact that too many people assume spiritual powers when they are in fact just vomiting psychologically. We talked well into the next morning, missing the sleep that we both needed. We talked about glossolalia or speaking in tongues; about the connection between shamanism and Noh; the fact that in Shugendo a medium or mediums are trained in order that at certain times the *kami* of a particular mountain could speak through them and have dialogue with the villagers, who would relate to the *kami* as oracle and protector. I was well aware of this and wondered whether I had somehow unconsciously 'invented' these Japanese Noh-like voices.

Now and then, as we talked, my body shook slightly, as though it still was not free of the energy. We decided we should take the tape to Osumi-sensei the next day and see what her reaction to it was. Also it occurred to me that we should tell her about the shrine.

23

It was one of those laser-bright winter days that you get in Tokyo. I felt almost transparent as we walked in its light. It seemed to penetrate the habitat of even the smallest organism. Today we were working on what should have been a day off, which was why I had slept at home the previous night.

The *genkan* was filled with the smells of breakfast and incense as we took off our shoes. In the *kotatsu* room Osumi-sensei and Sato-san were still eating. Sensei always likes to drink a cup of freshly ground coffee in the morning and she offered us some. As we sat down with our coffees, I took out the tape recorder and placed it on the table, pressing the playback button as I did so. The voice boomed, hissed and roared into the room. They both looked briefly at the tape recorder and carried on eating. 'Ah yes, Noh,' said Sensei, nodding, and, at the same time, Sato-san reacted with 'Kabuki.'

'No, it's Malcolm,' said Masako, and added, 'during his *taiso* last night.' Sensei looked down at her plate and carried on eating. It was as though she had not heard Masako.

I began to tell Sensei about the shrine, but it was too complicated, so Masako took over for me. She had barely finished when Sensei said, 'That talking injured your lungs. You're exhausted. Now is not the time to speak about it.' She seemed agitated.

There were a great many patients that day, and we were kept very busy, so I thought no more about it.

Later that evening, at supper, Sensei told us how recently, when she had been exorcising an area of land, Sato-san had told her that she had jumped about and spoken with the voice of an animal. Then she became very serious and told us that the shrine we had bought had made a deep impression on me and that I was very tired and we must return it to the man from whom we had bought it. She stressed that we must make a clean break with it. We must also give the man a present, and we must not exchange the shrine for anything else of equivalent value but ask him to return our money fully.

This made me wonder whether there was some connection between my voices and the shrine apart from a psychological one. Or did she mean the strict instructions for returning the shrine to have the psychological effect of undoing or removing the 'impression' she said the shrine had made on me. It was quite obvious by her manner that now was not the time to go any deeper into the subject.

24

It seemed as though I had lost an enormous amount of energy. On the days and nights I spent in Sensei's house I felt trapped and depressed; and on my return to the house in the evenings a terrible blackness enveloped me as soon as I turned the corner into the road that led to it. I felt no contact now between myself and patients and decided I would never be able to become a Seiki therapist.

At the end of a particularly busy day, when I was feeling ill with tiredness, a dreadful feeling as though my marrow were exhausted, Osumi-sensei asked me to stay behind that night and entertain Burt Foreman and Pat Kilcullen, who had just arrived in Tokyo on one of his regular flights. Usually, as a *deshi* should, I obeyed whatever order I was given by Sensei, at whatever time, whether it entailed working on a particular patient, being told to eat or drink something she felt I needed at that moment, or whatever the situation. This time, however, a great anger surged through my body. I turned and stared at her. She was standing in the doorway between the kitchen and the waiting room. I could hear Burt and Pat Kilcullen talking in the room beyond. Then, before I was aware of its arrival, 'No!' exploded from me. 'No! No! No!' As though the energy of all the negatives of my life came flooding through my mouth at once. I was shaking, as much with shock as with the expending of energy that had just occurred.

I walked passed Sensei without looking at her and into the room with the *kotatsu* and sat on the floor. My body was jerking and shaking. I felt psychologically and physically numbed. Sato-san came in a bit later with a plate of food for me. I could not speak to him but, to indicate that I was not angry with him, I squeezed the arm that held out the plate. I felt as though I could not breathe. I got up and went through to the kitchen again. 'I'm sorry, love,' I said to Masako as I passed her and slammed out of the door.

The moon was dazzlingly bright. I was walking very fast. I knew this cadence. I knew this darkness inside and the sensation of strong moonlight that seemed almost to burn the skin. Many years ago it had been a fairly frequent nocturnal experience – an explosion of rage, the cadence of despair in burning moonlight – my anger at woman, mother–woman. For years I thought I had worked through this. For years I had not experienced any rages. Now here it was again, like revisiting a place in which you had been desperately unhappy. I thought, with a terrible fear, that I might be going crazy again.

By the time I had walked about half a mile some of the anger had burned off and was being replaced by the familiar feelings of shame, ridiculousness and hopelessness. Had I been through all the difficulties of working with myself all these years to find myself back at 'Go' – or was it 'Jail'? Just when I thought I could see a bit of the board it suddenly seemed to have been folded up again. I knew I had to return to the house. The house was quiet. Osumi-sensei and Sato-san had left to visit patients. Masako and I hugged each other. 'I'm sorry love. I can't take any more,' I said.

'I know,' she replied.

'I must apologize to Pat and Burt,' I said, going into the lounge. They both said they understood and Pat said he wouldn't last five minutes as a *deshi*. We talked a little and then Burt said that he must go home and correct papers. After I saw Burt off, I went back to tell Pat that, although I was supposed to remain in the house that night and look after him, I had to go home after what had happened. As I opened my mouth to explain this and apologize, I found that I had lost my voice. My throat seemed to have closed up, so I whispered my apologies and Masako and I gathered up our belongings and left.

25

For the next week I remained in bed inert, absorbed by a total desirelessness for any kind of action. I seemed to be in a condition of profound shock, like someone who has been exposed to a great explosion and whose whole being is deafened.

Masako was away from early morning till late in the evening, when she would return and cook for me, so I was alone most of the time in a limbo of self-disgust and despair.

It was at this time that I became aware of the depth of Masako's extraordinary spiritual quality, and my respect and love for her grew each day. Beside her, I felt like a reeking demon, still caught up in my petty self-theatricals. This contrast between us had the strange effect of making me feel hopeful on the one hand and utterly hopeless on the other. When I was able to think about my position objectively, I realized that in fact, although I was re-experiencing an old pattern of behaviour, my relationship to it and the quality of it were in fact quite different now. I knew that this was obviously a wound[10] that was very deep and had not totally healed. This time, perhaps, I was to crawl back into it, but deeper, and complete the work. I knew this, but the energy required to do so seemed to have deserted me. Each evening when Masako returned I would ask her if Sensei had inquired after me. Each evening the answer was always the same: no, she hadn't. This increased my depression and endorsed my own feeling of worthlessness.

By the end of the week I felt a bit stronger and was even experiencing a sense of relief at not having to go back to Sensei's house and not having to learn Seiki therapy. It gave me the physical sensation of feeling lighter and I even went out for short walks. Maybe I could learn Shiatsu here, and then Masako and I could return to Britain.

This fantasy was similar in nature to the fabric that composed the wings which early birdmen used to strap to their backs with the illusion that they would be endowed with the gift of flight, only to find themselves abducted by gravity as soon as they stepped off the edge of the cliff. I was indulging in the old familiar game of avoidance again, and deep down I knew this very well. I recognized that, for many reasons, it was no accident that had led me to Osumi-sensei's door and that I was probably avoiding the most important thing in my life. But this thought would immediately be balanced by the thought that, accident or no accident, it was quite evident that I had taken on too much in trying to be a *deshi* with Osumi-sensei – a task too difficult for most Japanese even, let alone a foreigner who could not even speak the language. This would then leave me with a feeling of satisfaction at having done my best in an impossible situation.

26

A few days later Masako came home in the early afternoon. She complained of suddenly developing dizzy spells similar to the ones she had suffered when she had been seriously ill and a patient of Osumi-sensei. Sensei had told her to come home and go to bed and to tell me to give her therapy each day. Masako

was exhausted and obviously worried that she might be
becoming seriously ill again. I was concerned that it was
probably my behaviour and state of mind that had produced
this condition in her.

Now it was my turn to nurse Masako. I did the cooking and
shopping and gave her a Seiki treatment each day as best I
could. Her condition strengthened my opinion that working at
Osumi-sensei's was far too difficult for any ordinary human
being, and we agreed that neither of us was strong enough.

During Masako's sickness a small parcel arrived for me
containing a novel by an old friend of mine who is a very gifted
poet. The novel was about a magical healing institute and was
set in Cornwall, where he lives and where I too had lived and
first met him when we were both patients of the psychotherapist John Layard.

The book acted on me like a hallucinogenic drug. The words
became a complete sensory trip, which released great arcs of
energy that illuminated and resurrected memories of our many
nocturnal alcoholic expeditions across the land of Cornwall. It
stimulated me so much that I began to write a series of long
rambling letters to my friend, whose name is Peter. However,
these letters were to become a source of suffering for me in the
months ahead.

One afternoon Osumi-sensei phoned to say that she was
coming to give Masako a treatment. This was marvellous
news, but I was feeling a bit awkward about seeing both Sensei
and Sato-san after my behaviour.

When they arrived, Sensei was very serious and did not say
anything throughout the treatment. Sato-san was friendly and
smiling as usual.

During the treatment Sensei gave a great deal of Seiki to
Masako with a loud dramatic *kiai*. Her right arm turned like a
windmill, sweeping down either side of Masako's body, her
left arm pointing slightly behind her. The sweeping became
more and more energetic and her breathing faster and faster,
until suddenly the movement and the breathing both stopped.
She was holding her breath under what seemed great tension
with her face contorted, as her right hand moved to a point
over Masako's right lung. With a spiralling motion it came to

settle with a loud explosive 'Hudtss$!' on her right breast and the tension relaxed.

Afterwards she explained that Masako's condition was not serious, that she was recovering but needed another week in bed. Then she gave me some instructions as to what kind of treatment I should give her. She did not mention my behaviour or anything about my position since I had left. She told me that, although I felt a little better, I was still sick. I went out to the car to see them off.

27

The following week, Masako and I talked about what we should do. I was still enthusiastic about finding out if I could learn Shiatsu. Masako in her wisdom, however, thought I should get treatment from Sensei. At this point, though, I still found it impossible to consider going back to the house even as a patient.

When Masako was up and about we began to make inquiries as to the possibilities of my studying Shiatsu by phoning each of the Shiatsu schools in Tokyo. After two or three days it was obvious that foreigners could only study part time and that meant I would learn very little.

I was still very weak and had lost a lot of weight. Unbeknown to me, Masako went out one afternoon and telephoned Osumi-sensei to ask if I could become a patient. When she returned she told me what she had done and that Osumi-sensei was going to visit us the following Sunday evening.

After our abortive attempts at finding a place in which to train in Shiatsu, I was beginning to understand that there was no alternative to my returning to train in Seiki-jutsu.

28

We were sitting upstairs in the eight-mat room, the one we used as a bedroom. Sensei was looking at me very seriously. She had been saying that when I collapsed they had expected me to ask them for treatment. I told her that it had been impossible for me even to consider it at the time as I had turned away from Seiki-jutsu and was feeling very tired and angry about the situation. I then explained that just the underlying tension day to day of not understanding what was being said around me or being able to express myself in the ordinary way had created tiredness on top of the exhaustion naturally created by working under such demanding conditions. I also complained that there was no time in which I could explain or ask anything of her, and that this too had created frustration, which had failed to be diffused as my situation became more desperate. I told her that, with the intensity of my position, I needed some space. I ended by saying that I realized that there was nowhere I could learn Seiki therapy and asked, somewhat shamefacedly, if I could be reinstated as a *deshi*.

She listened as Masako interpreted what I was saying, now and then nodding her head, never once relaxing the very serious expression on her face. Then, with a long sigh, she said she was going to give the whole situation deep thought, that at present Okajima-sensei was still in America and that she would wait until he returned. She would contact us in a month or so.

Sensei had come to the house on her own, so I walked with her to the main street and flagged down a taxi for her. She turned, smiled and bowed and climbed into the taxi. I stood in the gutter bowing as the taxi pulled out into the traffic.

29

During the next five or six weeks I found it difficult to remain in the house. There was still much of Tokyo I had not seen while working at Sensei's and, although our financial position was far from healthy, we managed to take a walk each day and have tea in a café.

On one of these walks we happened to discover a Soto Zen temple not far from our house. It turned out to be one of the main training temples for the Soto Zen priesthood and was a city branch of the great and ancient Eiheiji Temple where in the thirteenth century Dogen Zenji, after his return from China, had founded the Soto Zen sect in Japan.

I was eager to find somewhere where I could continue my meditation practice, as I had been sitting alone at home. Although I had trained in Vipassana, which is a form of meditation that belongs to the Theravada school of Buddhism, I had for some years been interested in Zen. In fact, although there are some fundamental differences in doctrine between the different Buddhist schools, there is basically little difference in the actual technique of meditation between Vipassana and *shikantaza* or 'themeless *zazen*' of the Soto Zen school.

As we entered the temple compound I noticed a monk washing a car. He did not look Japanese, but more like an Indian. We went across to him and he greeted us in both fluent Japanese and English. He said he was from Sri Lanka where he had been a Theravada monk, but that he was now training in this temple and at the same time taking a master's degree in an aspect of Buddhist doctrine at a Buddhist university in Tokyo.

We asked if it was possible to join some of the meditation periods or sittings. He said that there were times when lay people came and practised *zazen* with the monks and that he would accompany us to the office and arrange it. It turned out that there were to be two sessions of *zazen* to which lay people were invited on Monday evening.

That Monday, Masako decided to come as well, partly in case some interpretation was needed and partly out of curiosity. There was quite a large group of lay men and women, among them one or two foreigners like myself.

For the first half hour we were instructed on how to conduct ourselves within the temple grounds and buildings – how to walk, how and at which points we should bow (*gassho*) to particular Buddhist images, how to bow to monks when we passed them, and so forth. Each action in a Zen temple is accounted for, so to speak. Ordinary daily activities are ritualized, so there are very particular ways of doing everything, from the way in which you turn on your meditation cushion, to walking, going to the lavatory, cleaning your teeth, eating and so on. The mind's attention is always brought to bear on each and every action in order to create a natural, uninterrupted flow of mindfulness or absorption in everything that a monk is doing moment to moment.

As we waited to go into the *zendo*, the meditation hall, one of the foreigners suddenly turned to me and asked me in broken English if I was a Yugoslav. Immediately I looked at him to reply I knew he was very sick and emotionally disturbed. I told him I was British and he said he was an Italian and that he thought I was Yugoslavian because of my face.

Just then we filed into the *zendo*. Slippers were donned at the doorway, as we were bare-footed and the floor of the *zendo* was stone. Each of us bowed before entering and walked silently to a vacant cushion, bowing to the image of Manjusri (the guardian of *zazen* and Bodhisattva of Wisdom) as we passed it. One of the monks divided the two or three women, including Masako, from the main group, so that they sat together.

In the *zendo* the cushions (*zafu*) for *za-zen* are placed on a raised platform. We bowed to our cushions, turned in a clockwise direction, bowed to the monk or lay person on the wall opposite, then, in one action, slipping out of our slippers and sitting back on the cushion, propelling ourselves away from the edge of the platform and pulling up our legs at the same time, we bent over and placed our slippers, correctly facing out, beneath the platform. Then we turned on our cushions in a clockwise direction to face the wall, bringing our legs into the lotus or half-lotus position, rocking slightly back and forth and side to side, until in a comfortable and stable position with the centre of gravity low in the belly or *tanden* and the spine held straight but relaxed.

It was bitterly cold. The doors and the windows had been left open and it was the coldest time of the year. I took one or two deep breaths to try to still my mind and body and settle into meditation, but it was difficult in the strange and freezing surroundings.

In a Zen temple during *za-zen* the *zendo* is patrolled by a monk who carries a long flat piece of wood called a *kyosaku*. If a monk is not sitting properly or has fallen asleep, he is given a sharp slap on the right shoulder with it. This is not given as a punishment, but is used compassionately as a form of encouragement, to remind the monk of his purpose in sitting. Sometimes, if a monk is finding it difficult to stay awake or keep his practice, he may ask for the *kyosaku* by bowing as the monk passes.

It happened on this first night, as on most of my subsequent sittings, that I ended up sitting exactly where the monk with the *kyosaku* stood behind me at the end of each round of the *zendo*. I could hear the creak of his slippers as his body swayed back and forth and the sound of his breath whistling in unclean nostrils.

As the silence intensified I became aware of the Italian, who was sitting next to me. He frequently shifted his position and his breathing was irregular and punctuated by soft groans. When the monks began to chant, he suddenly exploded with what sounded like an aria. He sang at the top of his voice roughly in time with the breaks in the chanting, though its throbbing operatic passion was very audible against the celibate monotone of the Buddhist sutra. The opera and the chanting miraculously ended together.

There were two sittings with a short, ten-minute, break between them. Near the end of the second sitting I heard the *kyosaku* crack at the far end of the *zendo*. The sound of the *kyosaku* falling continued until I realized it was getting closer, that it was working its way up through all the monks and lay people. The next moment I felt it lightly settle on my right shoulder. I bowed with my palms together, bent my head towards my left shoulder and received it, bowed and continued sitting. Slowly the rhythmic sound of it clapping receded to the other end of the *zendo*. After everyone had been hit, the drum was sounded, then the bell and the sitting ended.

As we filed out slowly, I noticed the Italian suddenly run past me. He ran from the entrance of the *zendo* and through the Buddha hall. He paused in mid-flight like a goalie making a save, bowed to the Buddha image on the left and almost fell. I bowed and followed him into the *genkan*. Masako had caught up with me and, by the time we had retrieved our shoes, the Italian already had his on and had launched himself into the dark of the compound. We could see his shadow sprinting as he passed the hall dedicated to Kannon (the Bodhisattva of Compassion). He forgot to bow to it and we could hear his feet leaving the gravel as he jogged beyond the temple gate and into the night.

Masako and I shared our experiences of the evening's sitting. I had found it impossible to reach anything approaching a *samadhi* or absorption in my sitting and hoped I would find it less distracting in the future. Masako said that it was the first time she had ever tried to meditate and she was finding it very painful. She suggested I get a *hakama*, a kind of divided skirt worn for formal occasions and in the martial arts like *kendo*. It would be very comfortable for sitting in and would cover my bare feet in the winter time.

30

One evening during supper we received a phone call from Masako's eldest brother (whom we address in the traditional Japanese way, as Onisan – 'Elder Brother'). He said that he wanted to come and talk with us that evening about something important.

When he arrived he was slightly drunk and we shared what remained of our supper with him. Before he started to eat he began to tell us that their father had just undergone a medical examination at the local hospital. Later the doctor had phoned Onisan and told him that he wanted to discuss his father's case with him. The doctor had told him that his father was suffering from cancer of the liver. He said he should come into hospital immediately and that he probably only had about two months to live.

This naturally came as a terrible shock and there was a long silence. Masako began to weep and I put my arm around her. Onisan told us that for several days he had kept this news to himself, but that sitting beside his father every day at work and watching him with this knowledge was beginning to become unbearable. He said he then had 'an inspiration' – he thought of Osumi-sensei. He had remembered Masako being healed by her when she was so sick and thought that her father should become her patient if there was any hope. What did we think? He looked at us. We both agreed in unison. He said that the whole matter would have to be discussed with all the members of the family and that, obviously, he thought that their father should not know of his condition until we had worked out what to do. He also said that he wasn't going to tell their mother the true nature of her husband's sickness, just that he had a liver complaint.

A meeting was arranged for the whole family, apart from my father-in-law, the following week at our house. We all gathered around a table in our large room upstairs. Onisan had already phoned the other two brothers and given them the news, and now he set about telling everyone how he had suddenly thought of Osumi-sensei's treatment and how his feeling was that it would be better than a hospital. He asked me to explain Osumi-sensei's Seiki therapy, which I did as best I could while Masako interpreted for everyone. Afterwards, with very little discussion, everyone agreed that Seiki therapy would be better than medical treatment if the prognosis was as bleak as the hospital had said it was. Masako said that she would arrange it with Osumi-sensei the next day.

31

Osumi-sensei's prognosis for my father-in-law was good and she decided that he should receive a double treatment each day, seven days a week, for at least the first eighteen months. Masako was to 'attach' herself to him and accompany him to and from his treatment and sit next to him while his treatment was being given. This was to be her training, to be one with her father during this period. Very often during his treatment Masako would feel her own Seiki being drawn out by Sensei's own body to be given to her father.

During this time my father-in-law was allowed to carry on working as usual and there was also no prohibition on either smoking or drinking, because Sensei said that at that time she didn't want to make him change his life suddenly as he might think his condition was serious and worry about it.

I was also receiving treatment seven days a week for my own illness and usually our appointments coincided, so on most days we all travelled together in Onisan's car to Osumi-sensei's house.

I received one treatment a day which usually lasted for about an hour. I was given therapy by either Sato-san or Okajima-sensei and sometimes by both of them. Osumi-sensei said that she wouldn't be giving me therapy until later, when my body condition had changed. My treatment during this period was general and covered my whole body, the main purpose being, I was told, to get my blood, lymphatic system and hormones balanced and working properly before any specific treatment was applied. Usually, after an initial examination of my body, therapy commenced on my back, working particularly on the muscles that run down either side of the spine. This was followed by work on the backs of my legs and feet and sometimes on the back of my head and neck. Then, having turned over, they worked on the front of my legs and feet, then my arms and finally my head, which included the neck again and often the shoulder for a second time. Each day the actual treatment would vary very slightly according to the condition of my body that day, and it usually ended with a hand placed over the right side of my chest in order to put Seiki energy into my lungs.

I was very pleased to find that, far from acting as a kind of hiatus in my training, receiving treatment proved to be the most dynamic way of learning. During this time I learned very quickly things which would have taken me a year or so if my training had been confined to giving treatment. It also created a deep awareness of how exactly different conditions affect body and mind, and how the changes relating to these conditions manifest themselves and in turn are affected by Seiki therapy. Most of my questions about Seiki therapy at this time, though, were completely ignored.

After our treatment we would all return home with either Onisan or Masako's youngest brother in his car.

32

I was still sitting regularly at the temple and the head monk was arranging for me to join the early-morning sittings and chantings with the monks at 4.30 a.m. in order that, when I recommenced working at Sensei's house, it would not interfere with my formal *za-zen*. This was one of my many naive notions during this time. First, it was going to be a very long time before I was healthy enough to begin working as a *deshi* again; secondly, I was soon to have so little strength that it would have been physically impossible for me to attend morning *za-zen* anyway. And, thirdly, Osumi-sensei was soon to ban my visits to the temple altogether.

As my sittings had settled down in the *zendo*, I had become aware of an unnamable fear rising in me. This fear was nurtured by the presence of the monk with the *kyosaku* standing behind me, until it reached the point where I felt as though someone stood behind me with a sword that would strike me dead at any moment.

Suddenly images of death were beginning to arise and obsessed me for the next few weeks. Years before I had been interested in death and had written a great deal about it. Now, however, it was not an objective study. Something very frightening was beginning to happen.

It happened that the only way I could find any solace for my state of mind was by taking long walks through the large cemetery near our house. I found great peace just walking among the graves with their tiny gardens, often decorated with flowers and with incense burning in front of them. On top of a hill at the centre of the cemetery was a place where tramps camped out with rain-swollen *futon* and cardboard structures. They seemed like intermediaries between the world of the dead and the world of the living. They looked like human crows perched amongst the stone shrines and calligraphied boulders, croaking messages between the two realms.

It also happened that I became very attracted to certain kinds of 'shops' and would hang around their windows or point them out to Masako as we passed them in the car. It always turned out that these 'shops', with their fascinating displays of shrines and images, were undertakers.

Each day, for two or three weeks, on our journey to Osumi-sensei's I was confronted by images of death. They began with hearses, which in Japan are designed like very ornate and beautiful temples on wheels. It seemed that each day one of these would pull out in front of us so that we followed it for a mile or so. Then one day, as we stopped at some lights, I looked out to the left and there, lying beside me on the pavement, was a dead cat with a handful of wild flowers strewn across its body. Returning home the very next afternoon by taxi, we were passing between two of the fields that you often find on the outskirts of Tokyo, when I saw a cat's head sticking out of the long grass beside the road in front of us. I thought it would probably wait until we had passed before it crossed the road, but the rear wheels of the taxi bumped over something. We turned round and disappearing through the speed perspective of the back window was the cat running upside down. The driver was very upset and, for the next mile or so, we had to console him that it was not his fault, that there was nothing he could have done.

The last of these death images occurred when we were driving with my father-in-law to have dinner with him at his home. We were travelling down a street near his house, when we saw a car stopped by the roadside in front of us. It seemed to have broken down. There was a man lying underneath the front of it, apparently looking up at the radiator, with two or three people watching him. As we drew closer I suddenly noticed that the man underneath the car was dying or already dead. The windscreen of the car was broken and he had obviously been hit by the car and thrown up over the bonnet. I put my hand on the handle of the door to get out, but as I did so Onisan suddenly swerved down a side road. At first I was angry and felt that we should have stopped to help, but then I realized that he was protecting his father as the shock would undoubtedly have been very bad for his condition. By the manner of the people looking at the man, I reasoned afterwards, they were obviously waiting for an ambulance.

33

My condition seemed to be getting worse. I became very depressed and my belly was giving me problems with alternating diarrhoea and constipation. I felt that the major part of my sickness was psychosomatic, and although I tried to explain what I felt to Osumi-sensei, she always seemed to bring my attention back to my body.

'Sensei doesn't seem to understand psychology!' I complained to Masako, who as usual said nothing. I was becoming frustrated with the situation and felt that Sensei was really the cause of my sickness in the first place. I was still angry about this and decided I had to talk to Sensei and try to make some sense out of what was going on. This pattern of frustration and confrontation was to become very familiar to me over the next year, like a station where, no matter in which direction you travel, somehow the train always pulls in at this too familiar platform somewhere along the line.

Sensei agreed it was 'time we talked' and a meeting was arranged late one evening, after my treatment.

Osumi-sensei entered the room carrying her large black appointments book and her old gold man's wristwatch in her hand. She bowed, apologized for keeping us waiting and, squeezing between the table and an armchair, climbed into it, dropping her slippers to the floor and pulling up her legs beneath her so that she was kneeling in the chair. Tea was brought. She looked at me searchingly as though weighing my state of mind or the condition of my body, or both.

She began by saying that she knew it had all been very difficult for me, but that she had tried to warn me that it would be so. I agreed that she had. Then she looked at me carefully for what seemed like a long time.

'When you first visited me, I told you that your lungs were bad.' I nodded. 'Well, I also saw that you had only two years to live.'

Suddenly it was as if all sound had ceased, as if each object in the room had equal focus and I could see each object in its separateness, but as part of a homogenous texture at the same time. The silence in the house seemed to have expanded to the perimeters of the world. Somewhere in me, though, there was a thundering rush as if something was suddenly released. Then Sensei's voice again, it seemed to me, speaking from the moon. 'Every organ in your body is exhausted from too much of everything. You were burned out by the time you were thirty. In two years you would be dead from cancer of the lungs spreading to your intestines. Now I have to remove twenty years of tiredness from your body. Your body must be changed completely. Your body must be made completely white.'

I found my consciousness had registered each word like the objects of the room, hearing each one as though totally separate, but as part of the whole fabric of her telling at the same time. It had come to rest on 'white'. What did it mean? It sounded like purification. I asked her how she knew I was going to die.

'I saw your death face. I see it now. That first night you slept here, I came into *san-jo* and checked your breathing twice, but at that time it was all right.'

It seemed as though something in me wanted to say something, but that my speech centre was stunned. I felt my mouth opening and closing, expelling silence, a silence which seemed to have retracted now from the edges of the planet and concentrated inside me. The environment seemed normal again, but inside me I was dumb, as if each of my exhausted organs had paused and were listening intently to Sensei's voice. 'It will take three years for your body to be changed and for you to be strong again. In three years you will be a different person. I want to heal you from the root. Your way of learning now is through your own body. Your goal should be the top of Mount Fuji. At present you're lying broken in the bushes at the foot!'

As soon as we were in the road outside Masako and I fell into each other's arms and I briefly wept. My weeping was quickly replaced by a strange feeling of elation and silence again. We did not speak on the way home and, on entering the house, I went upstairs to do my *taiso*. One big question remained, though: why, if she knew I was so sick, did she work me so hard till I collapsed? I thought I knew the answer, but was frightened to ask.

34

Now at night my whole body spoke of the fear of death. I lay awake all night with the feeling I was encased in a cold bodice of slate, inside of which I would periodically feel one of my organs permeated with terror, my entire awareness taking on the shape of whichever organ it happened to be at that moment, like death's radar scanning my interior landscape and picking out features at random.

For weeks sleep seemed to avoid me, the nights sick with the cries of ambulances like two notes repeated on a mourning *shakuhachi*.[11] Some nights a dog's bark would be raised a few octaves by the walls of buildings till it sounded like a scream of terror or a man shouting in agony. I felt as though it expressed my condition for me, that it had divined it on the night air or been prompted by moonlight registering the pheromones of fear. At night my body began to jerk like a man on a jibbet.

35

Okajima-sensei complained during my treatment that my body was refusing his Seiki, that it was blocking it. I knew this was true and I knew the reason. Each time I waited for him to come into the treatment room, a tide of fear began to turn in me, and as soon as he put his hand on my body, my body would freeze. Over two or three weeks it slowly occurred to me that something in Okajima-sensei reminded me of my father I also felt that the very strong therapy that he had begun to give me was actually bringing repressed fear out of my body.

I explained this to Masako and told her not to worry if, from time to time, expressions of this fear happened spontaneously.

The fear I experienced during Okajima-sensei's treatment had a very different quality to my fear of death. It seemed as though a whole body of fears was accumulating and slowly becoming differentiated as the process evolved.

36

When I was feeling particularly depressed I began to wonder if somehow I had 'attracted' death through my interest and, at one time, near obsession with it – my collection of human bones and skulls; my coffin which I had used as a cupboard and an object of contemplation; my 'death suit' which had the bones of a human skeleton sewn on the outside; my death poems and love of cemeteries; and my job at one time of laying out corpses in a hospital. I had felt a need to learn about death in a culture whose allegiance seemed only to anaesthesia and living as an imitation death, but in which real life and death were taboo.

I knew that death is not some kind of cosmic hoodlum waiting around the corner for us with a hatchet. Death is not separate from us. It is the nature of conditioned life, conditioned consciousness – or self – that we die and are reborn, dissolve and re-form in each moment, and that each moment contains the potential for our making a leap away from the conditioned patterns, which reassemble as soon as they have dispersed because of our attachment and ignorance. I knew that death and life cannot be separated and that body death is not something that 'happens to us'.[12] Even so, to a frightened ego it felt sometimes that death was like an assassin waiting invisibly, and that we could signal either intentionally or accidentally for the bullet or the knife.

I went through a quiet panic that caused me to write 'I'm dying!' letters to a few close friends and then feel extremely ashamed about them afterwards. I also phoned one or two friends on one pretext or another; sometimes I was afraid for them and just needed to hear their voices to know they were all right. This was really a way of turning around my fear for myself.

In my mind the island I had been living on had become like the view in an angel's wing mirror. I seemed able to remember every nuance in the light over the sea, every surface of the landscape, in the same way one remembers the body of a lost lover. I knew it was partly idealized, fanned as it was by draughts from the pinions of a desired flight from what I knew I had to face.

One afternoon, after he had given me a treatment, Okajima-sensei said, 'If you don't go through with this training, you will disappear into the forest.' Whether he used 'forest' simply as a metaphor or whether he had drawn up this image from my body, I did not know, but going back to Scotland and living in a hut in the forest with Masako was exactly the fantasy I had been entertaining. 'Disappearing' had always seemed desirable, but I had understood for some time that my need to disappear in the past had always been for the wrong reasons.

During this period any equanimity that I may have attained in the past was now shot completely, and I seemed thrown into a state of centrifugal confusion. I had become so agitated that I found it impossible to meditate and was loosing all sense of time and occasionally, at night, of place. If it had not been for my previous experiences with my psychological processes and for my relationship with Masako, I would have found myself in a vortex of intolerable forces.

37

On our way to treatment a few days later, a van suddenly pulled out in front of us and led us for most of the way. It was painted white all over except for one word written in English in green paint across its two rear doors – 'LIFE'. (It seemed so ridiculous that I did not point it out to Masako at the time, and only told her about it when I came across the entry in my notebook while writing this part.)

At the end of one of Sato-san's treatments Osumi-sensei came in and started working on my head. As she worked she talked to me quietly but firmly. 'You don't concentrate on your own sickness and body. Your acceptance of this therapy is delayed and far behind your father-in-law's. Don't think of other people, just concentrate on yourself. And, during therapy, if you can concentrate on the place where I put my hand, you can take Seiki more easily.

154 THE SHAMANIC HEALER

'I want you to eat plenty of butter and one raw egg a day, for your lungs. I also want you to drink the juice from a freshly grated apple each day to clean between the pleats in your intestines. This will prevent any infection caused by the poor functioning of your intestines at the present time.'

She described how food moved through the intestines, explaining peristalsis by bunching the blanket on the *futon*, releasing it and bunching it again, repeating the movement until it looked like some kind of caterpillar among the bed-clothes.

It was true, my father-in-law's progress had seemed extraor-dinary, and everyone was commenting on how well he looked and how much weight he had put on. Added to this, he had suffered from a skin disease for many years and had been treated by one of the leading skin specialists in Japan. The specialist had told him that there was no way of healing his condition and that all he could do was apply an expensive ointment each day to reduce the irritation caused by the disease. In fact, his doctor had said that if anyone could discover a cure for this disease 'they should be awarded the Nobel Prize'. Well, the great purple-black patches were begin-ning to disappear. Sensei had ordered my father-in-law to stop using the ointment gradually as she considered it one of the reasons why his liver was sick, and, of course, it was the condition of his liver in the first place which had caused the skin disease – it was a vicious circle.

Most patients with serious illnesses seemed to suffer a roller-coaster effect on their paths to recovery – periods of apparent regression followed by further increases in energy and strength. My father-in-law's recovery seemed like a steadi-ly rising curve. Essential for this was his environment, which was kept very stable and supportive by those around him.

38

Sensei had at one point advised me to look at Sumo wrestlers to see how they used *kiai* – *kiai* in this case refers specifically to the concentration of energy, or *ki* power, and not to the expression or release of it. Both Osumi-sensei and Okajima-sensei had impressed upon me the importance of developing the belly or *hara* as the centre of this energy.

I studied Sumo on Masako's parents' television whenever we visited them and there was a tournament – that is, until I was banned from watching television.

I found to my amazement and everyone else's in the family, that I could predict the outcome of a bout with on average an incredible eighty per cent accuracy. I would look at the two wrestlers as they entered the ring and somehow was able to read the one with the better *kiai*. However, as I became familiar with each wrestler and his performance and more conscious of trying to make predictions, this average began to drop miserably, until I stopped trying even for myself.

39

Without my noticing it, spring had come. On the evenings when we took the train to visit Masako's parents, we found that it often carried butterflies and huge moths, and once a large mantis, down from the mountain area which was the start of its journey. These exotic passengers would alight in the centre of Tokyo and sit bewildered on the walls and the platform.

During the day all the windows in the house were open and the air that entered it seemed filled with the sweetness of the breath of insects. The *tatami* smelled green again with the rise in temperature, as though it had been secretly growing beneath us all winter.

We took frequent walks in the cemetery. Sometimes it was so still you could almost hear the clouds moving overhead. Old women were sweeping up the winter debris from the shrubs and trees and burning it. Their bonfires blew aromatic smoke which blended with the incense burning on the graves and perfumed our skin like the incense of our own bodies burning with the world.

Some days, though, it seemed different. I was aware of a subtle disturbance, presaged by a smell like the scent of some kind of electricity in the air, as though the earth's nervous system were overloaded – any moment clouds might stall, trees burst into flames, rocks fly apart, all earth's history play back in one orgasmic time flash and be gone, leaving just a small scorch wandering briefly in space, until that too be extinguished.

These feelings and the fantasies and images that informed them were, I recognized, projections of my own fears for my state of mind and the condition of my body.

By now, my letters to Peter had become prolific, rambling and very confused, filled with contradictions and misrepresentations of my own beliefs and feelings. While writing them I felt charged and inspired, but immediately on posting them I realized they were insane epistles to the void and I experienced great anxiety about them. On more than one occasion I immediately wrote another letter correcting or explaining what I meant to have said or clarifying what I had written; at one point I even made a telephone call to Britain to apologize!

At night the whole letter of that day would echo through my mind and each phrase or sentence would produce the most violent shocks in my body, as though each arrangement of words had set up a very powerful charge of energy. I had developed a terror of words, but, paradoxically, this fear seemed to drive me to write more and more, as though I were creating knives for some personal penance.

Only now did I begin to understand why Osumi-sensei had banned me from writing letters. I was amused to find in an old notebook, which I had brought to Japan with me, the following note: 'Old Saxon *writan* means 'to cut', 'to injure' and 'to write'.

40

Okajima-sensei's therapy was getting stronger than ever before; Osumi-sensei too was working much more firmly on my head each day. 'Even if you feel pain after treatment, don't worry about it,' she said. 'And I don't want you to wash your hair more than once a week or it will excite your blood, which will affect the nerves in your brain.'

My body had begun to jerk and shake at night and one morning a scream suddenly broke from me. I told Masako that the strong therapy seemed to be bringing something up.

The following day was a Sunday and my father-in-law and I were due to have our treatments at our house and then go on to my father-in-law's house for the afternoon and dinner afterwards.

When we arrived at their house, I lit two sticks of incense, rang the bell and bowed at the family Buddhist altar, as I did whenever I visited. Sometimes I used to get the feeling that I was bowing before all the invisible Hagiwara ancestors, stretching back in time like a dissolved rosary of individuals caught momentarily in the gestures of their professions, trades and passions, as they glanced forwards into a time which briefly appears to them like the face of a distant tree caught in sudden lightning. I sometimes felt as though we acknowledged each other like labourers, standing up to stretch from our toil and glancing at each other across time fields; that somehow, as I bowed, we were united in the same time – the one time.

I always enjoyed being at Masako's parents' house, but this time something was wrong. I knew from experience by the feeling of being filled up, of pressure in my belly and chest, that something needed to come out. I sat on the floor at the table and tried to make light, and necessarily limited, conversation, but it was no good. I knew I had to leave. 'I can't stay in the house. Let's go for a walk,' I said quietly to Masako. She nodded and with foresight picked up her bag. She explained that I needed a walk and we left the house. I intended that we should just walk around the block and see how I felt, but as I walked I became more angry and desperate.

'What can I do? I can't go back to Sensei's house, they don't understand my condition! Every time these psychological states come up, she says I have a cold! But I'm trapped. How can I leave if I'm supposed to die in two years? Well, it must be less than that now.' Then I told Masako that I was terrified I might be going crazy again and that I knew that if that happened I would never come out of it again.

'I've taken all these years working through my shit and here I am. I seem to have been thrown back in it again.'

We were passing my favourite house in the area, a wooden house surrounded by trees and built on top of a mound. Today it looked like a squat brown skull filled with darkness.

Masako reminded me that only a few days earlier I had been praising the therapy and saying how incredible it was at bringing up repressed emotions. She squeezed my hand. I knew she was right, but at this moment all I could do was conceal it behind the blind of panic that had descended.

Just then Masako's parents' house came into view and the pressure in my body told me that it was impossible to sit and have a convivial evening.

'Let's get a taxi home,' I said as one rounded a bend in the road. 'You can phone your mother and apologize when we get back.'

All the way home in the taxi I tried to control my body, which had begun to twitch and shake. On reaching the house I went straight upstairs and sat on my meditation cushion for an hour. Slowly my mind and body relaxed and became quiet, and later when I went downstairs I felt better. I felt like going out for a walk, so we strolled in a nearby park.

When we got home, we had dinner and afterwards I felt very sleepy, so I went upstairs to bed. I could not sleep, however, and after about half an hour I heard Masako answer the door to someone. I lay awake listening to the drone of voices below, then, realizing I was not going to sleep, I went downstairs to find Onisan, who had brought some *sushi* from Masako's mother.

We talked for a while and Masako heated up some *saké* on the stove for Onisan. Soon a feeling of uneasiness began to take hold of me. My heart began to feel bad and my appearance must have betrayed as much, because Masako suddenly asked Onisan to go home.

Soon after he left, I began to feel worse. I had the sensation of being threatened, by what or whom I had no idea. This feeling quickly increased till I felt I needed to scream. I knew suddenly and without any doubt that I was going to die at any moment. Afterwards, the only way that I could think of describing this terrifying state was to compare it with the time/space between the release of safety catches and the flash of ignition from the guns of a firing squad, or the smell of your own corpse on the breath of a judge who is sentencing you to death.

I was pacing the room. My mind seemed to be racing around like a trapped bird. Now and then I would say something to Masako, to report to her what was happening, my breath coming in gasps as if I had been running. 'I'm going to die at any minute! It's here, like some awful beast! Some indescribable thing! It's here, only I can't see it! It's the whole room! It's everything! Oh, my god! My god!'

Suddenly my mind seemed to freeze like a rabbit. Just the awareness of terrified body. Just pure animal fear. No thought. Hands tearing at clothes. Feet pounding the ground. The body backing against the wall. Pressing hard against it as though trying to enter it or become absorbed by its composition. Trying to climb the wall backwards. Feet and hands slipping. Sound of skin against wall surface. Air difficult to breath. It was there! It was here! It was me! I collapsed to the floor weeping.

I wept for some time. Then Masako touched me lightly, though at that time I could not bear to be touched even by her whom I loved dearly and trusted completely.

'Please bring me my *zafu* and blanket down,' I whispered to Masako, who went upstairs to fetch them. When she returned, she turned down the lamp. I sat on my cushion in the position for formal meditation. My body was shaking and I was crying or, rather, I should say that there was crying, as I now suddenly had a very clear space around what was happening and could watch it clearly.

The fear was still there but diminished, laughter alternating with crying. Then all the fears of my life began to parade through me, as though they were coming from some deep place inside me and were actually making passage through my body, as if it were a long avenue or tunnel. Memories of all the situations that had caused me anxiety or to be frightened;

some I could easily recall, others I had forgotten. Some came just as memory, others were accompanied by pieces of conversation which either I heard in my head or actually spoke aloud, some with just images and others with their whole physical and emotional surroundings. They seemed to begin with me as a baby, then progressed through my years of suffering at a boarding school in the remote wilds of Scotland, and I saw how these related to relationships with people and places in my past. Many convolutions and levels revealed themselves, which I had only glimpsed before at different periods of working with myself, but now I saw them in a very powerful and coherent way.

Endlessly it seemed, but in fact for only an hour, this drama unfolded. At the end I was left with my fear of death, which I recognized was also my fear of being, my fear of life.

I had never understood so clearly before how the continual background static to my life had been just this fear. I began to see how my maniacal rages in the past had hidden this small frightened child.

Fear had gone. I pulled the blanket around my shoulders. I noticed Masako sitting quietly to my left. I was exhausted. Masako said she would make some tea. I told her everything that had happened and she asked about one or two things she had heard me say.

'I feel too weak to go for a treatment tomorrow,' I said to Masako.

'Don't worry about it. Onisan will take you in the car.' Somehow I had forgotten that we usually travelled by car and I agreed that I would go, and we both went up to bed.

41

The next day we told Sensei about the previous night. She listened quietly and then simply said, 'That kind of wave will repeat. In this season the sky and the earth are unstable and human beings will be affected by this.'

After my treatment that day I recovered so well that Masako said the night before was like a dream. I knew that once the psychological eruption had occurred it would be followed by my physical energy being restored, and I felt much better.

Masako told Sensei that she was amazed at my recovery and Sensei replied, 'Malcolm-san should be immersed in a peaceful atmosphere at this time, from the top of his head to the tip of his toes.'

Poor Masako, I thought, stuck with both her father and me! But she was learning a great deal and her attention was essential for the recovery of both of us.

Fear still came at night and during Okajima-sensei's treatment. It seemed to come, as Sensei had said, in waves. I felt like a pool after a huge rock has fallen into it.

42

A few nights later I had a dream which was to transform my relationship with Okajima-sensei and his treatment.

I was standing with a group of people around a hospital bed in which someone was lying sick. I seemed to be describing some past experience to the people present and ended by saying, 'And then we all stood in a circle and held hands.' As I said this, suddenly everyone who was standing around the bed took hold of the hands of the person on either side. As I took hold of the hand of the person on my right, I realized the hand was very hot. I looked at the person to whom it belonged and saw that it was my father. I suddenly knew that my father's hand was the healing hand!

Two days later Okajima-sensei came in to give me a treatment and, soon after he had started and was working on my back, he said to me, 'Very good Malcolm-san. Your body has started to accept my Seiki.'

I tried to tell him about my dream, but in my inadequate Japanese it just left him with a puzzled expression on his face.

43

After one of my treatments, Masako and I decided to take a walk to visit the temple dedicated to Kannon, with which, many years ago, some of Osumi-sensei's patients had attempted to have her formally associated. She does have some connection with this temple now, but on what level exactly I am not sure.

The temple was very old and its architecture obviously influenced by Chinese temple architecture. As we entered the big ornate gateway a flock of pigeons rose up from the compound and turned back and forth in the sky above. Now black, now white and again black to white, negative to positive, leaving after-images stuttering against a dark cloud bank. I pointed out to Masako how the pigeons had echoed the yin—yang symbol of the complementary opposite forces in nature which was painted over one of the temple buildings. The atmosphere was peaceful and seemed far removed from the busy streets which surrounded us. We sat for some time by a large pond filled with carp and overlooked by a large image of Kannon. The temple interested me very much and I told Masako that we must return to it again.

That night I could not sleep and experienced some anxiety in my belly.

The next day Osumi-sensei gave me treatment. She explained that she felt I needed treatment from her when she heard my footsteps on the stairs. While she worked I told her how impressed I was by the Kannon temple. She got up and called Masako into the room.

Sensei told me it was much too early for me to visit temples. My nerves were in a very sensitive condition and I had become too excited and stimulated by the visit. This kind of excitement, she said, would delay my recovery and had produced my feelings of anxiety. 'Malcolm-san, you must keep a strict routine. You must stay within the triangle formed by this house, your own house and the house of Masako's parents. This is a dangerous period and there's a risk of your losing the recovery you are making. I don't even want you to go shopping. Masako must do that alone. I don't want you to take a walk for longer than ten minutes, it's too much for your lungs. Giving Masako Seiki treatment is much better for you than going for a walk, because it relates to Seiki. Getting sunshine is good for the nerves of the brain, but extremely bad for your lungs. So you must avoid sunshine.' She wore her most serious expression as she added, 'And don't break the triangle.'

The room was quiet for a while, then she said, 'One day I will take you to the temple and introduce you to the head monk. You will have an interesting conversation.'

I lay there pondering what she had said. While I was a little dismayed at the restrictions, I was actually glad of the structure, as I realized we had been living the exact antithesis of this discipline. Then, in face of these restrictions, the obvious question came to mind. 'What about sex, Sensei?'

She giggled, 'Sex is good for you at any time you feel like it.'

Masako and I looked at each other with relief in our smiles.

44

I felt very ill. Now and again there were pains in my chest. As I had noticed on many occasions before I felt sick, I became very sensitive to smells in the house. I could smell the walls and the wood, my own body and Masako's, and even believed I was beginning to sense the smells from the bodies of the spiders and cockroaches that had taken up residence with us. I was feeling depressed about my condition again.

At night my sleep was broken and filled by dreams. I dreamed I heard a voice telling me I must 'return to the original race'. On waking I immediately associated 'original race' with the famous Zen *koan*: 'What was your original face, the one before your parents were born', that is, your original, intuitive and unconditioned nature. Perhaps my dream meant aboriginal race in the sense of original instinctive nature. On returning to sleep I dreamed I was burying Zen monks.

I complained to Masako that I had felt better until Sensei had said that my lungs were tired after the visit to the temple, and that now I felt worse.

Okajima-sensei gave me treatment for my lungs, which he also said were very tired. It was obvious by his manner that he was displeased with my condition.

After treatment we had to go home by bus and subway. As we came out of the subway station there was a Zen monk standing before us with a begging bowl and ringing a small handbell. He wore a broken, dome-shaped, wicker hat and straw sandles, the traditional costume of a mendicant monk. He looked like a vision of old Edo,[13] sprung from the well of the city's past, a shadow spirit clinging to the wall of a ferro-concrete subway station. I thought of Ryokan[14] as I looked at his torn robes. His hat was pulled down, obscuring his face, but in a low, steady voice he recited a sutra as I dropped a coin into his bowl.

On the bus I told Masako that they made me feel guilty about my condition each time they told me it had got worse. Again I repeated to long-suffering Masako, 'They don't understand psychology! What can I do under these conditions?'

Before I could continue, Masako interrupted me. 'When your tiredness is accumulated, you start to diagnose your own condition. When it is different from Osumi-sensei's, you get angry about it and say she's wrong. You've repeated it these last few months and it's made you tired. You are her patient, so why don't you stop analysing yourself? I don't think you should compare your diagnosis with hers. Can you forget your diagnosis?'

'How can I forget it when all they repeat is, "Your lungs are tired! Your lungs are tired!"'

When we got home I was feeling ill. Masako said that she thought it was because she had cut off my flow of negative expression. I knew that it was partly that, but also it was due to a conflict in me between recognizing that what she said was true and not being able to let go of my anger at their seeming inability to understand the psychological conditions which I felt were at the root of my problem, and there being no space in which to discuss it.

That night my body shook a great deal and periodically screams broke from me for about three hours. Finally I could not bear to lie down any longer and leaped from the *futon* and, according to Masako afterwards, said, 'A hundred patients have slept on this *futon*! It is difficult to lie on.' We changed the *futon* and I went to sleep and dreamed.

It was the Middle Ages. There was to be a trial. I could see the prisoner standing in a doorway, but not his face, it was obscured by shadow. A voice said, 'The connection with God is broken. The judgement will come from a higher authority.' When I woke in the morning, my body was shaking and screaming. At breakfast I was complaining again. 'She shouldn't have told me that she saw my death face.' I wanted to avoid seeing Sensei. Instead I would write to her explaining my condition, but finally I did not.

That day Osumi-sensei gave me a treatment and, with Masako interpreting in order to make what I had to say clear, I complained. Sensei accepted everything that I said and I felt much better afterwards.

The next day I felt stable emotionally, but physically exhausted. The weather was beautiful and we lunched upstairs, half sitting on the tiny balcony and half in the room.

Masako talked about her own experiences as a patient some years before, ending with, 'The important thing is how we can accumulate energy from our treatment in order to recover completely. The need for support from all those around the patient is crucial. At last I am beginning to understand what Osumi-sensei meant by this treatment helping a person to heal themselves.'.

45

It was strange, but it was as though a trial, perhaps foreshadowed by the dream, had begun. For a period of three weeks I became obsessed with my past life. I had the absurd, but very real, sense of having committed crimes against the people with whom I had had relationships. Of having caused people unhappiness and suffering. Of having involved people in relationships that should never have been. I found myself indulging in the negative (and useless) emotion of regret. Regretting my past and its torturous, complicated path. Regretting so many relationships with women which seemed to have been nothing but crutches for the emotional pyrotechnics of a confused mind, and which seemed to cover the entire range of the sexual spectrum. A path that my relationship with Masako now seemed to illuminate like a beacon.

Each night this new level of my history flashed before me in minute detail. If a drowning man sees his past life passing in front of his eyes, then I was a man who seemed to be drowning in the waters held by the composition of his own body, the pool of his own past.

Although I knew there was no blame in all this, I felt blame. I felt blame for a son from a failed marriage whom I had not seen and a daughter to whom I was only a distant father. (There is perhaps no blame while one is blown by the winds of one's unconscious conditioning, but once one wakes up and gains some insight, then there comes a clear responsibility.) I felt the absurd need to go into the street and recite the sins of a useless life.

During this period fragments of my past life actually began to float back to me in external reality, from the environment around me, like objects washed up on a beach after a shipwreck. Pieces of my past appeared in unlikely places. One night, on television, an old film was shown in which a girl I had lived with for a few years appeared in a part in which she actually bears my surname. A week later, as I passed an optician's on my way home from Sensei's house, the face of the same girlfriend was hanging in the window modelling a pair of sunglasses. It was a very old picture of her and had yellowed and peeled. It hung like an icon from the event horizon of the black hole of my past. A week later the entire shop had been gutted and redesigned.

A few days after this Masako and I went to the bank to send some money to my daughter. As it was near our house I felt this breaking of bounds was permissible. I sat down on a couch while Masako read a notice on the wall beside the counter. Suddenly I saw a rack of magazines and as I approached it I had the overpowering feeling that there was a magazine with an article on an old friend whom I had not seen for a number of years. In the middle of the selection of magazines was a foreign publication. I picked it up and immediately opened it at the last page to find an article on my friend! It gave me a powerful shock and I stared at it, turning the pages, dumbfounded. I went across to Masako and, explaining what had happened, showed her the article, feeling a bit ridiculous after the event.

46

Now my confinement was complete. I had been told not to read, drink alcohol, coffee or tea, and not to eat sugar or potatoes. I was to go for no walks, watch no television, but remain at home. Apart from dining with Masako's parents and having my treatment, I was to do nothing, not even listen to music that would involve me in any way. I was only to look at the trees and the sky.

During this period I suffered fissures inside my nose which bled regularly and blocked my nostrils with dried blood, which, if it was removed, merely started the bleeding again. I also had a plague of boils on my arse which made sitting excruciatingly painful. These new afflictions lasted for about three months.

Even so Osumi-sensei said that my condition had improved and that the boils were due to my lymphatic system still not functioning properly. She said that my mind was less distracted now.

In fact, the only distraction from my confinement now was an occasional visit from an old close friend of Masako and our monk friend from the Soto Zen temple. He would often arrive with food which he seemed to have pilfered from the temple kitchen and with boxes of tea from Sri Lanka. He would stay for dinner and tell us amusing stories about his life at the temple and his family at home.

A rumour had long been circulating, and later apparently given more substance by a book written by a meteorologist who studied weather patterns in relation to seismic activity, that Mount Fuji was going to erupt in September. Not only erupt, but actually explode, so that one third of the mountain would be blown away, triggering the long-predicted Tokyo earthquake. We had been experiencing a great increase is seismic activity during this time and this had helped augment my general anxieties and fear. Up to then the odd earthquake had never worried me, but now, suddenly, I registered every terrestrial shiver, every flinch of the Pacific plates, often when no one else could and frequently when none existed! The quakes of my own body felt like the whole planet shifting.

After this activity had persisted for some time, with my seismic foreboding convincing me that the predictions were correct, I learned that the words for 'earthquake' and 'self' in Japanese, though their characters are different when they are romanized or spoken, are the same – *jishin*.

I noticed that everything affected my condition one way or another. My body seemed to act like a barometer and register every change in the weather, every nuance in atmospheric pressure. I noticed how different thoughts affected my body in different ways. And how, if I even so much as saw another person who was obviously sick and thought about his or her condition, I too became sick.

I first became aware of this when I was returning from my treatment by bus and my attention was drawn to a man suffering from muscular spasms. I sat and watched how his whole body was racked by each spasm, how his jaw clenched and his shoulder and arm became rigid. On reaching home I was so weak I had to go to bed.

The second time this kind of thing happened was when Masako's friend came to visit one evening. She has a slight deformation of her upper spine which is pulled over towards her right shoulder. As she stepped up from the *genkan*, I touched her back to guide her into the sitting room and at the same time wondered if one could heal such a condition. Immediately I became exhausted and had to excuse myself and go to bed for the rest of the evening.

During treatment one day I mentioned this to Sensei. She said very firmly, 'You are only half a human being at the present time and cannot think of others. You must avoid anyone who is sick and not even think about them. Even thinking about them, you lose your Seiki. You must look after yourself and only think about your own condition.'

47

We were now in the typhoon or rainy season, and the weather was very hot and humid. The small window near the ceiling, under which Sensei had advised us to place the Buddha image, now became a focal point for me – my window on the world.

The bamboo that crowded it provided a theatre for birds, huge butterflies and insects, a trellice for the moon and a bower for the sun. Even the odd helicopter strayed into its frame. Each morning, when I lit incense at the house altar beneath it, its flowing calligraphy often rose on a page of sunlight slipped in between the dark covers of storm clouds.

At night the air was restless, as though nervous. Bamboo tapped and scratched the house walls with storm warnings and threats from Fuji.

I still lacked energy and became exhausted by the simplest activity. Even thinking too hard or too long about something would result in my having to go to bed. I mentioned to Sensei that I did not understand why I seemed to be getting worse when I was doing all that I had been told to do. She asked me how I expected to recover immediately from a condition that had taken probably twenty years to create and that my worrying and depression were actually helping to undermine my recovery.

Just as she finished speaking to me, there was a fairly violent earthquake. All the windows and the *karakami* shook and the lights swung back and forth. I heard Okajima-sensei and Sato-san run out of the treatment rooms to check for damage and make sure the cooking stoves and gas appliances were safe.

'Ah,' said Sensei, 'this means the end of the rainy season.'

48

The heat seemed to have become even more intense, as though the primordial processes held within the earth were indeed working their way to the surface. The house suddenly smelled like a foreign country. Sitting in its rooms was like sitting within a grove of piping-hot trees. Now and then loud cracks reported that knots in the wood were loosening or doors which had been closed all winter were reopening.

Outside, the air was so hot and heavy that bird flight seemed almost arrested, as huge crows struggled across the sky from one part of the city to another.

At night, returning from Masako's parents' house, it felt as though my body were evaporating, its cells recruited by atoms of the greasy air. As though each breath or step became movement through a series of invisible but palpable moulds, like wings of hot fat closing and enfolding me, opening and releasing me, or rather an image of me, which was formed, dissolved and then re-formed out of the body of the air itself, so that space lifted me across its arena like mirage waves in a pulsating peristalsis down the street. Now and then this semi-carnal medium of air was shot through by the mind-flying scent of *chinchoge*[15] which hit the night almost visibly like olfactory lightning.

49

Two or three months had passed, September being one of them. Fuji was still in situ and I was feeling much stronger, but my mother-in-law had become sick. She complained of a heavy feeling in her chest and of a roughness, like something growing, on her tongue. She had been receiving treatment from some kind of therapist for a month or so, but was now about to make an appointment with a doctor.

The next day we told Osumi-sensei about her condition. Sensei looked very serious. 'She's in danger of developing cancer of the tongue,' she said. Then she turned to me. 'I want you to begin giving your mother-in-law regular treatment twice a week. Giving her therapy will delay your own recovery. Even so, I want you to do it.

'You are feeling that you don't have enough knowledge about Seiki and that your technique is not good enough, but as long as you have a strong enough belief that you can heal her, that is the most important thing.' She encouraged me to have confidence.

As we walked in the direction of the main road, neither of us spoke. We passed a garden that seemed almost erased by the shrilling of crickets. Passing it, the sound seemed to penetrate my bones as though the rhythm of the crickets' song resonated perfectly with the vibratory hymn of my marrow and the garden became an extension of my own subatomic structure, my bones briefly becoming a manifestation of cricketness. · I looked at Masako. She seemed deep in thought. I wondered if she was worrying about her mother and particularly the idea of my giving her treatment for her condition. 'Do you really think she is in danger of developing cancer of the tongue, or is Sensei just giving me something to bite on, so to speak?' I apologized for the terrible joke.

'I don't know,' she replied. 'But, anyway, you should do as she says and give my mother treatment.'

I felt a bit confused. Why, if there really was a danger of her developing tongue cancer, did not Osumi-sensei offer to give her therapy herself, instead of trusting me, an ignorant, half-human *deshi*, with what was obviously a potentially serious case? I could see that, if I dwelt on it for too long, any confidence I might have would very quickly dissolve. I decided to try to forget the possibility of any serious condition developing with my mother-in-law and just treat her as intuitively and spontaneously as possible. I concluded that Sensei must be just creating a wall for me to go through.

We were now walking beside the railway line and a crossing bell was clanging. A sudden breeze played with its sound-shape until it became a cowbell and then the tolling of a chapel bell. We caught the train that it was signalling.

On arriving home I discovered a letter in the postbox from the daughter of an old friend of mine, who had been a colleague and contemporary of John Layard. Her name was Winifred Rushforth and she had pioneered psychotherapy in Scotland, having founded the Davidson Clinic in Edinburgh and Glasgow. The letter told me of Winifred's death and was accompanied by a card from the service of thanksgiving held for her. Although I was not surprised by her death, as, though still practising and writing, she was ninety-five years old when I had last visited her, the news still nevertheless came as a shock.

The next day I gave my mother-in-law the first of her treatments. Before I started her therapy, she showed me her back. It was covered in red rings and blotches which I recognized were the result of a form of therapy that uses glass suction bowls. I instinctively felt that it was the wrong therapy for her and was not at all surprised that her condition had not improved.

That night my body began to shake violently in the bathtub and the shaking was to continue for the next three days. On the third day my shaking had become very violent, and, during treatment, Osumi-sensei told me that I had caught a cold and that I must stay in the *futon* and sweat it out. She instructed Masako to grate ginger root and make it into a tea with hot water and *shoyu* (soy sauce).

I woke several times in the night feeling bad, both physically and psychologically. In my mind, as usual, I was fighting with Osumi-sensei.

My position again seemed ridiculous to me. Why, when I was supposed to be half dead myself, was I giving treatment to someone who herself was supposed to be on the brink of developing a serious illness? Why did Sensei keep on telling me I had a cold when I saw the cause of my present condition as psychological? How was I ever going to recover properly? The possibility of becoming a Seiki therapist seemed utterly remote and hardly desirable!

At breakfast I complained to Masako, 'I must ask Osumi-sensei why she made me give treatment to your mother while I'm in this condition. Why is she always pushing me into corners that I can't get out of? And why did she tell me I was going to die in two years?' I asked Masako to accompany me during my treatment in order that she could interpret for me and get some sense out of the situation.

After breakfast I did my Seiki *taiso* as usual. My whole body shook violently for a long time as though something was trapped inside it and wanted to be free.

50

Osumi-sensei entered the treatment room, bowed and knelt down beside me, placing her watch and appointments book beside the head of the *futon* as she did so. After she took my pulse, I asked if Masako could come in and she called for her.

After Masako had settled on the other side of the *futon*, I explained to Sensei exactly how I felt. She listened, nodding her head slightly now and then. When I had finished and my last words had left Masako's lips, there was silence. Outside, a crow spoke from a roof somewhere. Downstairs someone was pouring water. By the quality of the sound I knew it was boiling water and that someone was making tea.

Sensei moved slightly in Masako's direction and began to speak. She seemed to be delivering what she had to say very firmly. Her words came to me via Masako's mouth. 'When I told you to begin treating your mother-in-law, I had already thought very deeply about it. In September your condition was not good enough and I advised you to rest without giving treatment to Masako. But now you have to continue giving therapy even if you have to crawl on your knees. This way you will begin to learn to look after your own body and be careful about your condition. Even if you told me you didn't feel well and that your condition was bad, I should say you could manage very well. You have to be aware of the level of your own condition. Being aware of that level, I think you will manage. You have already done very well with your learning and your sickness. Even if the state of your lungs is not very good, you mustn't miss giving your mother-in-law her treatment. This is very important.

'You complained that after such a long time your health isn't getting any better. When I said to you that you had to be a patient without doing anything, it was not for a very simple reason. I believe you definitely will recover. You have to look after yourself and take care of yourself, otherwise you will miss your chance.

'Before you came here you wandered around the world to learn and collect knowledge, but you could not find the truth of what you needed. Part of your tiredness came from that kind of life and so many things are coming up out of your body now. So don't worry about your condition. Your past life, which was scattered, will be the foundation for your future.'

As so often in the past, it was not so much the content of what she said but the energy which came with it that created the right breeze to turn me around. I felt much better as we sat drinking tea downstairs. Sensei also suggested we eat a bowl of noodles before we left, as it was by now rather late in the evening.

Outside it was already dark. In the garden, as we walked down the steps, a solitary cricket ticked in the dark, like a thin mechanism winching up the moon. Masako said that although I was still having difficulties and often didn't feel so good, she could see a definite improvement in my health. She said that Sensei had told her that I must give up worrying about the world outside, about which I could do nothing, and give priority to my own condition.

I had to concede that it was true. My health had improved. I now had colour in my face that I had never had in my life before. My complexion had always been the colour of moonlight. And my belly or *hara* was beginning to get larger. In the bath we joked about my 'pregnancy'.

51

I had received a letter from my old meditation teacher. He was going to travel from America to visit his parents' home in Thailand and wanted to come and stay with us on the way. I was delighted and looked forward to meeting him again; I was also happy that he and Masako would meet. We started to make plans as to how best to entertain him and show him the sights around Tokyo and perhaps farther afield. Then it occurred to us that we were going to have to ask Osumi-sensei for permission to do so. I did not expect that there would be much problem in this, as there is so much reverence bestowed on teachers in Japan that I imagined it would be a very natural thing to do. I had already, somewhat prematurely, replied to his letter to say how delighted we would be to receive him as our guest.

However, when we approached Osumi-sensei on the subject, she was very negative. 'I told you that you must concentrate on Seiki treatment and your own healing and not waste your energy. Seeing people at this time will break your resolve to master Seiki. I understand your wanting to see your teacher, but I feel that if he comes here he will become ill, if he isn't sick already. If that happens, he will have to remain in your house, and it will be too much for your present state of health. He can come next year if he wants to. Then I will personally show him something of Seiki myself.'

That evening I wrote a letter to my meditation teacher, apologizing and trying to explain the very difficult circumstances under which we lived. For some reason I found the letter very difficult to write and was completely exhausted after finishing it. On my way up to bed I looked out at the moon resting in a nearby tree, hanging by a hare's breath,[16] on its way up.

52

During the next two or three days I started to read some of my old poetry and writings from ten to fifteen years ago, with thoughts of reorganizing the best of it. I was aware that I should not be trying to do this at this point and became very tired afterwards, so that I could not sleep at night and my mind was filled with thoughts and images.

During therapy Okajima-sensei said that my brain was very tense. After he had finished his treatment and left the room, Osumi-sensei came in. Just before she entered I had heard her tell Okajima-sensei to send Masako into my room. While she waited for Masako, she sat looking at me very hard till neither of us could stop from laughing.

When Masako came in, Sensei said that although I couldn't sleep very well at night, I wasn't to worry because my tiredness was not a deep tiredness. Then she began to look at me again, this time with a strange expression on her face. 'You are emerging from the egg,' she said suddenly, not having changed her expression or averted her eyes from my face. 'Your head and shoulders are already out. Some time, probably at the end of January, you will emerge, but your left leg will be trapped by the shell. Your left leg will be trailing.' She got up and did an extraordinary imitation of a chick trailing its left leg, which sent Masako and me into hysterical laughter. Then she returned to where she was sitting beside me and her face settled back into its strange concentrated expression. 'You will feel frightened about coming out of the egg. Your mind will be away from your body again. Sometimes you will want to climb back in!' We laughed and she got up smiling, bowed '*Odaijini*' ('Good health') and left the room.

As we were drinking tea downstairs afterwards, Sensei came in and sat with us. 'One thing I meant to say was, don't mix up confidence and arrogance. I told you you are all right to give therapy to your mother-in-law, so do your best to concentrate on her treatment and in comparing the condition of her body from one treatment to the next.'

I was about to say that there was little chance of my confusing confidence and arrogance because, if there were such a thing as a personal coat-of-arms for one's *self*, mine would have as its motto beneath it: 'Self-doubt'. As I was about to say this, I suddenly realized that in fact all my disagreements and mind battles with Sensei were really based on a kind of conceit that I knew more about my condition than she did. So I kept quiet.

Osumi-sensei continued, 'To be a Seiki therapist it is necessary to practice *mu-shin*, emptiness. Not to have the mind filled with thoughts and ideas and things. We must be like the monk in *zazen* to give really good treatment. We must concentrate only on the patient. When you have patients, you have no time to think of anything else. That's why you see clearly. When I get a call from a patient, I begin to concentrate on that patient immediately. That is the starting point of healing. Concentrating on that patient is itself healing and it also makes me empty.'

53

I had had a cold for about a week and Osumi-sensei came in to give me a treatment on a day when it was particularly bad.

'You still have your cold. You have to recover from it as soon as possible.'

I asked her if it was all right to give my mother-in-law her treatment. 'Definitely you should. She can't catch your cold. Don't even think whether you can give her therapy or not. It is very important to have *ki* power. Definitely you should give her her treatment. Before you think about whether you should or not, you should think about how you can avoid having a cold.'

I explained that I knew why my cold had got worse. That it was because I had been reading some of my old writings. I knew that my lungs had become weakened by having too much attachment to what I was reading.

'That's good. It's very important to know your own body. That's how you begin to understand a patient's condition.'

She was quiet for a time while she worked on my head, then she said, 'What is happening to you is not exactly rebirth, because to be reborn we need to throw everything away and start anew. You don't need to throw everything away. There are a lot of things you should keep. For example, you shouldn't throw your writing away. You will write several books. I have a feeling that one day you're going to write a book about hands.'

Afterwards I lay in the *futon* thinking about what she had said. I was feeling happy about what she had said concerning writing. Some years previously I had abandoned writing as I had come to identify it with my old life and its attendant psychological problems, before I commenced training with my Thai meditation teacher. Recently, though, I had begun to feel like writing again; since the onset of the spontaneous poems the previous year I felt that my writing would be of a very different kind now.

54

Masako and her father had travelled ahead of me as our appointments were at different times. It was a bright clear day, with half a moon on its back, like a bowl with half a hare stuck in it.

As I entered the waiting room I found Osumi-sensei and an elderly woman patient sitting at the table talking very seriously together. They were obviously discussing some problem or other that the elderly patient was having. In front of Sensei was a sheet of paper which she glanced at now and then as they talked.

I sat down on an upright chair against the wall to the left of the door. As I did so they both noticed my presence and we bowed 'Konnichiwa' ('Good day') to each other. Then they resumed their discussion. It appeared, by the little that I could understand, that there was some kind of presence or ghost in the woman's house. The genkan was the area most affected and as Sensei studied the piece of paper in her hand I could see that it was a plan of the house. Suddenly Sensei's back straightened and her whole body tensed. She extended her left hand, holding the plan in front of her, while her right hand began to spin in a rapid circling movement, her palm open and the fingers pointing directly at the paper. The circling movement suddenly began to contact its circumference into a spiralling motion that diminished to a point, the closer it approached a place on the paper plan. 'Hudtsss! Hudtsss! Hudtsss!' she fired Seiki at it. I imagined at the place representing the genkan.

Her body had relaxed now and her right hand was waving back and forth across the paper with an increasingly relaxed movement until it left the paper altogether and came to rest on the table. Sensei sighed with a sound of satisfaction. The elderly woman bowed her head and thanked Sensei profusely. Sensei got up from her chair, bowed to her, said, 'Odaijini,' and left the room. Sato-san called me upstairs for my treatment.

When I came downstairs again Masako was sitting at the table. She said that Sensei wanted to speak to me. We sat drinking roast tea while we waited for her.

After she had settled, Sensei looked at me. Before she said anything, I told her that my mother-in-law had recovered and that the symptoms she had been suffering had disappeared. She looked pleased and smiled. 'You have done well. The last several months have been very difficult for you, but at last you are on the path as a human being.' She paused and looked at me again, her head nodding slightly.

'You are beginning to return to your self, which has a good grounding. In the past you have never really been on any path before. You've been attracted by one thing and then another. You've gone in this direction and found it wasn't what you thought it was. You've gone in that direction and found it wasn't what you thought it was. You've been attracted to things and places because of how they've looked. You've wondered why one thing stunk and another thing didn't. You've been curious. For the past twenty years you've repeated this kind of life because you were not on any path.'

'We are surrounded by many beautiful things, but few real things. Real things are truth. Now you are on the path, so when you see something beautiful you can pass it, just saying, "Beautiful." You must do that. Now you are in the Way of Seiki, you mustn't look to left or right any more.' Then she added softly. 'It's been hard for you, I know.'

All the years of chaos and unhappiness, and the strain of the last year or so, seemed to arrive in me at once and then flow out as though a door had opened. Tears streamed down my face.

'At the end of the month we are all going to Ito to celebrate I-san's[17] taking over the directorship of his father's business. So I want you to take good care of your condition. Ito is on the coast and it will be good for you to see the sea after such a long time. 'We will stay in a *ryokan*[18] overnight and return here the next morning. We are taking I-san with us in the car, so, with Sato, Okajima and myself, there won't be any room for the two of you, so you will have to come by train. But take it easy, don't rush. You won't have to leave early the next morning. You can take your time.' Then she told us that Okajima-sensei had made all the arrangements as the manager of the *ryokan* was a friend of his.

The idea sounded wonderful after a year's incarceration with its attendant prohibitions, and the thought of seeing the sea and being able to walk on the shore was exactly what I felt both Masako and I needed.

55

Ito was very different from what I dreamed, imagined or felt I needed! Masako and I had a very pleasant trip from Tokyo along the coast to Ito. After checking in at the *ryokan* and finding that the others had not arrived, we went for a walk along the shore. However, when we returned and everyone else had arrived, we all changed into *yukata*[19] and embarked on an orgy of drinking, eating and *enka*[20] singing. After my year's abstention I soon became very drunk and exhausted. Finally, after four hours, I knew I could go no farther and we told Osumi-sensei that we had to go to our room. She said she quite understood and that it wasn't her way of relaxing either.

No sooner was the door closed behind us in our room than I rushed to the lavatory and vomited violently. Afterwards I sat against the wall in the main room where the *futon* was laid out and tried to relax. As soon as I did, though, my body went into convulsions, my spine arching forwards and backwards so that my body flipped around the room like a freshly landed fish. Voices were coming out of my mouth in what seemed like many tongues. I just let my body go and do what it needed to do. I was aware of Masako moving briskly around the room throwing cushions against the wall wherever my head was in danger of striking it. The voices and the violent movement continued for about an hour. When they finally subsided I was left with just enough energy to roll into the *futon*.

The next morning it was some time before I could do anything. I lay half conscious, vaguely aware of Masako speaking on the telephone. I remember thinking that it sounded as though she was receiving some kind of directions. Finally she came over and told me that Osumi-sensei and the others had left for Tokyo and that we were to take our time. 'She says that she asked the manager of the *ryokan* to give you salt and water to drink,' Masako reported.

'Salt and water!' Why weren't they more careful with what they prescribed last night!' I said angrily. 'What on earth was all that about? At the beginning of this month she told me that I was in the Way of Seiki, I was "on the path". What are they trying to do, blow me off it?' I was angry and confused again, and certainly didn't want to go and drink salty water with the manager or even see him. I just wanted to get out of the place as fast as possible.

As I finished speaking there came a knock at the door and the manager poked his head round. Seeing us, he came in. 'How is he?' he asked Masako.

'Not bad. Osumi-sensei says he should drink salt and water.'

'Yes,' he replied. 'I know. Please come downstairs and I'll have it prepared.'

After he left I turned to Masako. 'I don't want it. I just want to get out of here!' I tried to move too fast and almost passed out. I went slowly over to the window and, shielding my eyes against the bright light of the sky, looked out at the trees and the mountainside. 'That's where we should have been. Walking among those trees. Not in a nightclub! Just when I was beginning to feel stronger. Now I feel like death!'

In the foyer half the staff had gathered and we were encircled by their concern and well-meaningness. I tried to explain that I was really all right, while at the same time wondering what the acoustics were like in the building and also catching sight of what looked like a refugee from Edvard Munch's *The Scream* in a mirror behind the reception desk.

We ended up in the coffee lounge which was set apart from the main building and approached over a small bridge. It was newly built and resembled a Las Vegas church complete with what looked like plastic stained glass.

56

It took me a week to recover from the experience of Ito, and after a further week I was amazed to find that my health had suddenly improved dramatically. This reminded me that I must stop judging situations from the usual criteria based on 'common sense' and remember that life with Osumi-sensei was operating on a completely different level of understanding and experience. I felt that the 'disaster' of Ito had in fact unlocked or released a new energy within me.

There was a card in the mail from Peter. It was in reply to a letter of mine upbraiding him for his declared 'envy' of my training. I had said something to the effect that 'If only you knew what hell this is, envy would be the farthest emotion from your mind!' His card simply bore the words 'COURAGE, MON BRAVE'. In my now elevated state of mind I was able to look at it and smile as I stuck it up on the wall. There were to be many more occasions, however, when I would need to remind myself of the words on that card.

57

One afternoon I had been lying for some time waiting for my treatment in *san-jo*, when I suddenly became aware that I had been listening to a story. The story was being told inside me and I had no idea how long it had been going on for. All that I managed to remember about it afterwards was that it concerned a master swordmaker. This swordmaker's art was so pure and he was so skilled that he never had to use his hands at all: a perfect sword would simply materialize without any physical labour. The master swordmaker was giving advice to his *deshi* who I somehow knew was also his nephew. He was advising him not to hurry, but to take his time and practise patience. By the time I had received my treatment, the actual words of advice and the details of the story were lost.

58

As my condition had improved so much, Sensei decided it was time for us to read her daughter Masako's translation of the book on Seiki-jutsu. She wanted to give it to us on 4 December, which, she said, she knew was my birthday. It happened that it was also a Sunday and she would be free in the evening. She said she would phone us around eight o'clock when she returned from visiting her last patient.

There was a cat in the waiting room. It must have crept in through the kitchen door. It was trying out its claws on the carpet with its ears back and a wary expression on its face, as if it knew that it was out of bounds and would be expelled at any moment. Were a cat able to anticipate such, then it would have found its fears justified, as Osumi-sensei flashed into the room

in her white coat, picked up the cat and, crooning '*Neko-chan!*
Neko-chan!' ('Little cat! Little cat!'), carried it to the kitchen
and out of the door. She came back laughing and settled into
her chair. I noticed there was no sign of the manuscript and
wondered if she had forgotten.

'How do you feel like giving therapy to F-san?' she asked,
looking at me. 'I think with your improved condition now, it's
time you had another patient.'

F-san often brought a member of his family to Osumi-sensei
for treatment and on the occasions that I had seen him I
thought he looked tense and exhausted. His body gave me the
impression that there was a great deal of pressure inside it, as
though it was about to burst. I agreed enthusiastically and
thanked her.

'If he doesn't receive treatment he will die in three years,' she
added. I experienced the sensation you get when you are
travelling in a lift that is ascending at speed and then unexpectedly stops. This was a floor I wasn't sure that I wanted to
get out at.

'Writing, your own treatment and your three patients are
how you will learn to master Seiki. Some people need to work
on a thousand patients and then perhaps a thousand more, but
you will be able to learn on only three. But you must look after
your patients and keep them away from Osumi-sensei!' She
laughed and looked at me, and a strange feeling of nervousness
invaded my belly. 'You must have that kind of strong will,' she
said slowly, looking straight into my face.

Sensei called into the kitchen for tea and then went off to the
lavatory.

When she returned and sat down, she said, 'Last month
Masako my daughter, Sato and myself went to visit Toyokawa
Inari Shrine near Nagoya. It's a very large shrine and in the
grounds of the main shrine are several small ones. Well, we
had just entered one of the shrines when I suddenly saw an
enormous white cat bigger than myself looking at me. It was
just sitting there with its right paw raised, and as I looked at it,
it smiled, a lovely smile that made me think, Everything's all
right. I said to Sato, "Can you see the white cat?" But he
looked and he couldn't see it. "Just over there," I said. But it

was no good, he couldn't see it. Then my daughter, hearing me, said, "Don't be silly mother, you know this is the shrine of the white fox!" But I didn't say fox. Suddenly I heard Masako say, "Mother, the ceremony is finished," but I hadn't been aware of what was going on around me!'

She then told us of two important cases in which ghosts had appeared while she was working on patients. In the second case the ghost was always watching the treatment whenever she visited the patient's house. Just the previous night, Sensei said, not only was the mother' ghost watching the treatment, but she had also seen a vision which described the patient's condition in a very beautiful and dramatic way. It indicated to her that, although the patient's condition was critical, there was going to be full recovery.[21]

During the evening none of us had mentioned the book and I was just wondering whether I should remind Sensei, when she disappeared into the back room and returned with something wrapped in a *furoshiki*.[22] It was the manuscript of the book. She held it out to me ceremoniously, bowing. I bowed and received it, and Masako and I went out to our waiting taxi.

Soon after the taxi had turned out into the main road, the driver, a young man in his twenties, started to speak excitedly to Masako. I could not understand what he was saying so nudged her to interpret for me. 'He says that last week he picked up a ghost!'

'A ghost?' I said in disbelief, then began to laugh, trying to avoid being seen by the driver in his mirror. 'A ghost?'

'Yes, he says several of the drivers at the firm where he works have picked up the same ghost and always at the same place. He didn't really believe it till last week.'

The driver was talking again, his white gloved hands moving excitedly like two birds flying within the circle of the wheel as he recounted his story.

'He says the ghost is of an elderly man with a beard. He stands on the pavement just in front of the magazine shop at Nishiazabu crossing and flags down a taxi. He tells the driver the destination he wants, but when the taxi arrives and the driver turns around for the fare, there's no one there. This is exactly what happened to him last week.'

I had moved to the edge to watch the driver's hands as he talked about his ghost, but now I sat back in the seat. 'Why so many ghosts this evening?'

'I know, it's odd isn't it,' Masako answered as we searched ourselves for the fare.

We got out of the taxi a short distance from our house and walked the last few yards. It was bright moonlight, so bright that as we entered the house I half expected to find a translucence to the walls and ceilings.

59

Although it was only the end of January, the morning was surprisingly mild and bright, like a spring day. I was travelling to Sensei's house alone. Business men were practising golf strokes with invisible clubs as they walked to their offices from the main railway station at Shibuya.

When I arrived at the house I found a man I had not seen before sitting in the waiting room. He looked terribly ill, as though his whole being had imploded. As I sat down he nodded his head to me. '*Konnichiwa*. My name is Mr S,' he said very slowly in good English, but with a hesitation behind it that suggested a doubt concerning his own identity. I introduced myself and there was silence for a while.

'I live in Korea,' he said suddenly, as though answering an unasked question, with a long-distance voice that sounded as though he was speaking from the other side of the East China Sea. 'I came here on business, but got sick and ended up in hospital. I'm dying. The doctors have given me only a few months. They've taken most of this away.' He indicated his stomach and his intestines. 'Cancer. I haven't eaten for six months. I have to be fed intravenously twice a day.' The words fell slowly from his mouth as though it was already registering redundancy.

For some time there was silence again. Then, pointing at the ceiling, he said, 'She says she can heal me, but I must come and live here in Japan. I can't do that. I have a big house near Seoul.

It would mean I would have to sell everything and lose my business. I can't do that.'

I looked at his face for a minute or so in the silence that followed, while he seemed to be gathering strength to speak again. 'If you're going to die in a few months, you're going to lose it anyway,' I said quietly.

'But I can't lose my business!' he said with a surprising firmness. I said nothing and looked out of the window. In the parking space there was a large car which he indicated was his. I wondered how he managed to drive, particularly in Tokyo, in his condition. It was as though I had wondered it aloud, because he explained that it was fully automatic and that he didn't really have to do much to drive it.

There was another silence and I could hear the floor creaking upstairs as someone moved a *futon* while working on a patient. Then he began speaking again, with the compulsion of someone who has to tell all his secrets. 'I used to have a terrible temper. If someone overtook me in my car, I would go after them. I would want to kill them!' Then he said very faintly, as if he were informing himself, 'I don't care now.'

There was another silence, this time slightly longer. It was broken by the sound of someone's back being firmly and rhythmically patted upstairs.

'I'm going to come here every day now and they'll give me two treatments a day while I sit here in between times. She told me not to waste my energy reading anything, but just to sit here and look at the trees through the window. Y'know, I never looked at trees before.'

'It's good to look at trees,' I said, putting my hand on his arm. Just then Sato-san came downstairs and told me a room was free for my treatment. Before I went upstairs I went into the lavatory, and while I was pissing I suddenly started to weep. Something in Mr. S had resonated deep inside me.

At the end of my treatment from Sato-san, Osumi-sensei came in and worked on my head for a while. She said that she noticed when I came up the stairs that my body was tired. I told her that I had been having more of the voices over the last week. All she said was, 'You'll probably have those all your life.' Then she asked me when I was going to give F-san his treatment. I explained that he had been very busy for the last fortnight or so and that he had now made an appointment for the second week in February. She said enigmatically, 'Giving treatment to F-san will give you another page for the book.'

I was just going to ask her what she meant when she started to speak again. 'I have the feeling that when you read the newspaper, you read every part of it. Your body is tired. Your lungs and heart are tired from using your eyes too much. Don't read any books you think you might need in order to write the book on Seiki, you don't need to. Don't look at the outside world or get lost or involved in listening to music. You have three patients now. You must stay in good condition for them and the book only. Make space in your mind and body in case an emergency arises with them or in the outside world. You don't need to worry about how things will be when you return to Britain. Britain, Tokyo, they won't fall over. It takes a long time for change.'

When she spoke like this I always had the strange feeling that she had been watching me, both my external behaviour and my mind. When she spoke like this, she was always perfectly correct.

60

The next day I found Mr S sitting in the same chair, staring out of the window and wearing the same clothes as he had had on the previous day. It was as though he had never moved.

Masako and her father went upstairs and I sat down next to Mr S 'How are you, Malcolm. What are you doing here anyway? You look so healthy!'

I explained that when I had begun having treatment I apparently had only two years to live and that I had actually been very ill.

'Well, you certainly don't look it now,' he said. He looked down at his hands and slowly put them together on the table. They looked like two sick animals crawling towards each other for comfort. After a time he slowly put his left hand inside his jacket and extracted a clear plastic wallet from which he withdrew some photographs. 'This is how I used to look,' he said with a smile of resignation. All the photographs seemed to have been taken during some kind of dinner or reception. A man who vaguely resembled Mr S was at the centre of most of the pictures. He wore a tuxedo and was mostly surrounded by beautiful women in evening gowns, but in one picture he was surrounded by a group of Western men who, were either bald or by their haircuts, looked as though they belonged to the military.

'I was a very different man in those days. I always had beautiful women and expensive cars. I was a real man-about-town, isn't that what you say?' I nodded, but he was not looking a me. While he had been speaking, he had been looking at the table and addressing it rather than me, as though he thought that it might accept the image more readily, or maybe half of him already identified with the inanimate world and was finding it easier to relate to.

I said nothing. When anyone passed the doorway he would look up, slowly moving his head as though it were independent of his body, as if it were swimming with the movements of a tanked fish that is suddenly aware that its ocean has shrunk intolerably. I could feel his dying like an invisible burning. I saw and smelled something of my own death in Mr S. I wanted somehow to give him some kind of strength, the kind that allows you the miracle of that weakness with which to give yourself totally and unconditionally to both life and death at once. The weakness that is the strength of a baby that allows itself to be born. But I knew that it wouldn't be possible for him.

'I'm giving my wife a divorce,' he continued, this time looking at me. 'Every time she looked at me, I could see the disgust in her eyes. I can't expect her to be tied to this!' Now the disgust was in his own eyes.

To change the subject, I asked him how he was feeling. 'This morning the doctor came to give me my IV.' He must have seen the question in my face, because he paused. 'Intravenous injection. He said he was giving a double dose so that he wouldn't need to come back again that day. Well, it made me very ill.'

Sato-san called me for my treatment, so I shook hands with Mr S and went upstairs.

When Osumi-sensei came into the room I told her that, when I had returned home after my treatment the day before, I had felt very tired and again when I woke up that morning. 'You were sitting with Mr S yesterday. He took your energy. You probably thought about him when you got home. Try not to think about him, you'll lose your energy that way too.' She was right, of course; I had been thinking about him and discussing him with Masako the previous night. I noticed that I did not see him for the next few days. He always seemed to be in a treatment room when I was in the house. I did not know whether this was by arrangement or coincidence.

61

One evening F-san arrived at our house for his third treatment. He sat and drank a glass of water before going upstairs, and told us that that morning he had had a sudden nosebleed. I asked him why he thought it had happened and if he had had any trouble with his nose lately. He said that he hadn't and had no idea why it suddenly started bleeding. As his blood pressure was high, I immediately felt that it might be connected with that, but didn't say so in order not to worry him in case I was wrong. I thought that I had better check with Osumi-sensei if it recurred. After talking about continuing difficulties in his family and in his business, he went upstairs, and after a few minutes I heard bumps on the ceiling as he got into the *futon*.

Two days later F-san's wife phoned us to say that her husband's nose had started to bleed badly in the night and that they couldn't stop it, so he had gone to the hospital that morning. She said that the doctor couldn't stop the bleeding either and had given her husband a plug for his nose. He was now in his *futon*, but the blood was now running down the back of his throat and he was extremely uncomfortable and worried about it. Could we do anything?

Masako told her we would ring back in half an hour. We sat and talked about it for a few minutes. 'Keep your patients

away from Osumi-sensei!' kept echoing in my mind.
'I think we're going to have to phone Osumi-sensei,' Masako said, looking very serious.
'I'm afraid you're right. It's an emergency and I can't think
what else we can do,' I replied. I felt rather unhappy about the
situation. I had given my patient only three treatments and I
was already giving him up to Osumi-sensei.
Masako phoned Sensei and explained the situation. They
arranged a time for us all to meet at F-san's house that evening.
Masako then phoned F-san's wife and told her to expect us all
at seven o'clock that evening.
Masako and I were a few minutes early and we sat in the
sitting room with F-san's wife, drinking tea. Soon Sensei
arrived with Okajima-sensei and Mineko-san, Okajima-
sensei's niece, and we all went upstairs to F-san's bedroom.
The room was small, very warm, and almost in darkness
except for a dim light by F-san's head that illuminated his face.
When I looked at him I received quite a shock. I hardly
recognized him. His face seemed sunken and he looked like a
corpse. I remembered Sensei telling us that he had only three
years to live unless he received treatment.
Osumi-sensei moved to the right of the *futon*, while I knelt
behind her, and Okajima-sensei knelt at the left side of the
futon, with Masako directly behind him (that is to say, the
patient's left and right). Mineko-san sat at the foot.
After removing her scarf, studying F-san's face as she did so,
Sensei immediately gave Seiki to his heart with two loud *kiai*.
Then Okajima-sensei placed his hand over F-san's heart and
Sensei lightly touched the left side of F-san's nose, over the
place from where it was bleeding in the left nostril. After some
time Osumi-sensei started to work on the left side of F-san's
head, while Okajima-sensei worked on his left arm at a point
¹ ch relates directly to the heart. About fifteen minutes
⌐apsed and Sensei moved to F-san's right again and began to
work on his right arm. She was working on an area that relates
directly to the brain. She also worked on a place relating to the
lungs. Okajima-sensei meanwhile was alternately working on
the left arm and sitting with his hand placed directly over the
heart.

Suddenly Osumi-sensei stiffened and raised her head. At the same instant I felt violently nauseous and thought I was going to vomit. For a minute or so I tried to control it while I watched Sensei. Her right hand had left F-san's body and was pointing up at the ceiling. Her right hand swept right across the room, still pointing somewhere near the ceiling while she gave out three explosive *kiai*. Her hand traced a huge arc until it was pointing directly behind her, in fact directly at where I was sitting. I had never seen her give Seiki in quite this way before.

Again I thought I was going to vomit, so I turned round in the direction of the door, where I could see a crack of light coming from the landing. In front of me was Mineko-san, who was sitting motionless, her face misty pale in the light coming from the head of the *futon*. I realized that I was not going to vomit after all and turned back to the *futon*.

Osumi-sensei was still breathing heavily. Her right hand was now placed over F-san's right lung. After some time she began to talk to him. 'The left side of your brain is extremely tired. You have been worrying and thinking a great deal about your family and business, so a lot of that worrying has been emotional. You are very lucky that vein broke in your nose and not in the left side of your brain. If it had broken in your brain, it would obviously have been very serious.

'We can stop the bleeding in your nose, but it will take a few treatments. I'm going to ask you to be patient. We will come back tomorrow again.' Then she bowed '*Odaijini*,' and F-san thanked them. We slowly filed out and down to the *genkan*.

In the *genkan* Sensei was speaking very seriously with F-san's wife. She had a very grim expression on her face and I thought that she was looking at F-san's wife in a strange way.

As we went out to the car to see them off, Sensei told me that I should keep away from F-san or I would lose my strength and my recovery would suffer badly. She told Masako that she should go and hold the left side of F-san's head three times a day for fifteen minutes each time. She demonstrated by touching her own head. She cautioned her that she must not hold it for any longer or she would become very tired. She told us that, usually, if a woman's nose bleeds it is not very serious, but in the case of a man's nose bleeding, we should be very careful.

Walking home, I told Masako how helpless I felt in the situation and how I felt I had suddenly been cut off from 'my patient'. Also, how bad I felt having to bring in Sensei so early. I had the sense of having failed some kind of test. We both then wondered about the extraordinary Seiki *kiai* Sensei had given.

On returning to the house after visiting F-san the next morning, Masako reported that his bleeding had stopped that night, but had begun slightly again that morning. Part of the trouble, she thought, was that he kept snorting violently because of the uncomfortable feeling in his nostril.

Osumi-sensei and Okajima-sensei gave him one more treatment, but F-san was unable to put up with the discomfort any more. He was worrying about his business and could not summon the patience necessary for recovery with Seiki treatment. He went back to the hospital. There he found the doctor's diagnosis identical to Osumi-sensei's and this time he had a new plug fitted which checked the bleeding. After a few days' rest he returned to his office. I briefly saw him two or three times; he had lost a great deal of weight and looked very ill. I thought it best not to mention Seiki treatment, but to wait for any movement in that direction to come from him.

62

One star and piece of a moon, as though pinned by it. Rest of the sky empty and luminous with a breeze that seemed filled with the smell of space.

It was early evening and we were on our way to Sensei's house as she had phoned to say she wanted to tell us something about F-san's case.

When we arrived she was already sitting at the table in the waiting room. She rose and bowed as we entered, and we returned her bow before we sat down. Mineko-san brought in tea and, after sipping hers for a minute, Sensei started to speak. 'I wanted to tell you what happened when Okajima and I visited F-san for the first time.' She lifted up her watch and checked the time and then arranged it with a cloth on top of her appointments book.

'Just after I had finished working on his head, the ghost of an old woman in a white kimono flew into the room. She was very angry and told me that she was hungry. She wanted to eat F-san! Then she demanded bananas.' She started to laugh. 'She looked across at you, Masako and Okajima, and complained that you were both too solid to eat!' We all laughed and sipped our tea for a few minutes.

Then she continued, 'When I saw F-san's wife's face I realized that it must have been her grandmother. I had to give that very strong *kiai* to get rid of her. She floated away like smoke.' She leaned towards Masako. 'I want you to take three *ohagi*²³ or bananas, and place them on the F-san's family shrine for the old woman.'

Masako agreed to do this and Sensei got up to answer the telephone. When she returned, her face bore a different expression and she turned to me. 'Your experience of learning is like mountaineering. Nowadays people can go up mountains by cable car. They have no experience of the way up from the foot to the top. You could have gone to Shiatsu school instead of learning Seiki, but that might have been like going up the mountain by cable car. On the other hand, if we have to climb up, we sometimes have to negotiate upward climbs and then sometimes downward slopes on our way to the top. Sometimes we might see a waterfall or a stream, or come across some beautiful flowers or empty windswept places or snakes. This kind of experience changes us by the time we have reached the top of the mountain. Step by step is most important.

Then she referred to my experience with F-san. 'You were like the hub at the centre of the wheel. I was glad to see that you could keep space and not be too attached. It's just this kind of experience that makes a therapist.'

Just then Okajima-sensei, who had just returned from visiting a patient, appeared in the doorway. I explained how depressed I had been at the time and how hopeless I had felt about the situation with F-san.

Okajima-sensei laughed. 'Don't worry,' he said. 'I went through many such experiences. Ten years of tears! I ran away from here two or three times, but I always came back. There's nowhere else you can learn this.' He patted my shoulder and laughed again. His gold tooth twinkled from the darkness of his mouth. Then he took my hand, turned it palm upwards and placed his hand quickly over it, like someone performing a sleight of hand. 'Don't worry. There's Seiki there.' He turned and went into the back room.

Masako said that, although we were living in Nishiazabu, she felt we were very close to Osumi-sensei's house.

Sensei said, 'I never feel distance, even though our houses are physically apart. The relationship between master and *deshi* is of one mind, one body. Whenever you both leave here, to me "Goodbye" is meaningless, just convention. I feel you are always in this house.'

When we were putting on our shoes in the *genkan*, Sensei suddenly said, 'On second thoughts, Masako, I don't want you to take anything to F-san's family shrine.'

On our way home I thought about the ghost of the old woman and realized that the way in which Sensei had described it reflected my intuition concerning the psychological dynamics within the family. Masako and I discussed, with reference to one mind, one body, how many times each of us had gone to Sensei's house with a question or something we wanted to discuss with her, and how, so many times, before we could say anything, she herself initiated a discussion on the relevant subject or gave the answer to the unasked question. She had a knack of anticipating a great many of our problems this way.

We should not have been surprised that evening when Masako's mother phoned to tell us she had just visited F-san's house as she was friends of the family, and had taken *ohagi* for the family shrine, as it was the spring equinox; nevertheless we were.

63

A few days later on my way to Sensei's house I was passing F-san's office when he suddenly came out after me. 'Mr

Malcolm,' he said in English as we bowed to each other, 'please, I would like to have your treatment.'

'*Dozo! Denwa onegaishimasu*' ('Please! Phone me if you would be so kind'), I said.

'*Domo!*' ('Thank you'). We bowed and I continued on my way feeling happy.

When I arrived at the house, I found Mr. S sitting in the chair facing the window. We greeted each other like long-lost friends. After I had sat down, he said, 'You know, I really think I'm getting better! Yesterday Dr Osumi got me to eat a little bit and later I had my first shit in six months! I actually broke down and cried in the toilet.'

'I understand,' I said. 'That's marvellous news!'

'If she can make me eat, that's incredible! I really want to eat again. To taste something.' He seemed very animated today, as though the energy of hope was running through him.

I was called upstairs for my treatment, during which Sensei told me that Mr S's body had become very weak after his visit to the lavatory, and that she had told him that, after he had rested for a while downstairs, he must go home and lie down.

After my treatment I returned to the waiting room and found Masako waiting for me. She was watching something through the window and I followed her gaze to see Mr. S very slowly getting into his car. We watched him turn the car round and drive off in the direction of his office. It was obvious that he could not follow Sensei's instructions.

64

For the next few months we were very busy. Apart from giving Masako her treatment, I was also treating my mother-in-law and F-san twice a week, as well as spending two or three hours a day at Sensei's house receiving my own treatment and just being there. Also, now we had begun to look at and think about Sensei's manuscript, which had turned out to be a rather confused mixture of autobiography and fragments of case histories, and which entailed a completely fresh series of recording sessions with her, which were to be spread over the following year. Two evenings a week we spent at Masako's parents' home providing psychological and energetic support to her father.

The skin disease which had plagued my father-in-law for five years had now miraculously almost entirely vanished. The only areas where it now remained were over each lung, the liver and small patch over his stomach. These were all located on his back and provided an excellent pathological map of his condition.

It was during these frequent visits to Masako's parents' home that her youngest brother expressed the desire to receive Seiki. He had for some time now been asking a great many questions about it and was also very aware of the effect it had had on his sister's life, of the fact that it was steadily creating a state of recovery in their father, and of the enthusiasm that their mother had developed for her treatment.

After approaching Osumi-sensei, it was arranged that, after a short series of treatments in order to prepare his body, he should receive Seiki. On the day that Seiki was to be given to him Masako and I were at her parents' house. The day itself was overcast and it was raining. The forecast was for the rain to last all day. Both Masako and I were sitting reading newspapers at the table. Suddenly Masako kicked me. I looked up and she nodded at the floor. A thin veneer of sunlight had slipped across it. We both looked at the clock. It was 1.15 p.m. Sunlight flooded the room. We both let out yells. So the stories we had heard about the sun always shining when Seiki is given, no matter what the prevailing weather conditions are, were true! I looked up at the sky. It was still dark and overcast and a thin drizzle persisted, but a ragged hole had appeared through which the sun was shining. It continued to shine for a further ten minutes or so before the clouds mended the fracture.

When both Masako and I had received Seiki the sky had been clear and sunny, so we had never witnessed this phenomenon ourselves.

On my brother-in-law's return later that afternoon, we asked him what time he had been given Seiki. He told us that they started at one o'clock and that the whole business had

only taken about fifteen minutes. We laughed and told him
what had happened. 'Yes,' he said, 'they mentioned something
about the sun.'

65

Osumi-sensei was giving me one of the talks that took place
frequently during this time. I felt that she did this because she
knew I needed a shake of the tether every so often, so that I
didn't stray off the path or become too attracted by what was
growing in the hedgerow on either side.

'I have been thinking about you since some time in February.
Your condition got a little worse. I do really want you to
recover totally, from the root now, because I feel this is the best
time for you. You must bring your condition to complete
recovery in one leap. You have to reach another level.
Obviously your health is important to yourself, but also to
your patients. To look after your patients you need a very
strong will and you must retain it. Without caring for yourself,
you cannot keep your will.

'I want you to accomplish what you have determined. That
is, to master Seiki-jutsu as well as finishing the book, because
those are the two things that channel all your energies, all you
have learned and experienced and brought to this point.
Learning Seiki-jutsu should be the last thing you will learn in
your life. If you think only of Seiki-jutsu, definitely you will
think only of the condition of your body. Concentration of
Seiki is very important. You must think of yourself as if you are
in the mountains like Daruma,[24] without watching the outside
world or society, which scatters Seiki. This is how you should
be.'

She stopped talking and looked at me sideways for a long
time, until I began to feel uncomfortable. Slowly the sensation
began to develop that my head was a tunnel and she was
peering through it. Suddenly she said, 'Your Way is opening
up.'

Then, after a silence in which she continued to look at me
and nod, she relaxed her penetrating gaze and turned to

Masako. 'When I stopped to greet you and your father in the waiting room today, you may have thought I acted rather strangely. I apologize, but what happened was that as I looked into the room I saw a samurai in full armour standing next to your father. I could only see him from the waist up. That's why I paused for such a long time and kept saying "*Konnichiwa*." Actually I wasn't looking at your father at all!

'I've already explained this to your father, though, because when I was giving him his treatment the samurai was sitting beside the *futon* the whole time. He was so thirsty he could hardly speak, even so he kept begging me to save your father's life.

'When I described him to your father, he knew exactly who he was. He was your father's grandfather and he loved your father very much. He taught your father Kendo because he wanted to give him the samurai spirit.'

Masako asked why the samurai was so thirsty.

'Spirits who are supporting us get very thirsty. You must tell your mother to put an extra glass of water on the family shrine from tomorrow morning.'

As Sensei got up from the table, Mr S appeared in the doorway. As she made her way upstairs to the treatment rooms, he came in and sat in the chair which Sensei had just vacated. I introduced him to Masako, whom he had not previously met. 'You're lucky to have such a good wife,' he said, after I had told him she was probably the main factor in saving my life.

'How are you doing?' I asked him.

'Well, I don't know how long I can stay here. Dr Osumi wants me to stop working, but if I stop working I can't afford to stay here, you see?'

'Why don't you sell your house in Seoul?'

I looked at him. He was hopelessly chained to the things he thought were supporting him. In fact, they were now, in a sense, becoming the very agents of his death. I tried to tell him that for some of us it becomes very clear that we have to change our road. Everything about us is speaking of a need for change in the way in which we are relating to life. There comes a call for change and transformation, and, if the call is not heard or is ignored, then sometimes the only way the need for transformation can be manifested is through physical death. But it is not too late to hear the call even if one is in the terminal stage of an illness, for that in itself can become the gateway to a new and wonderful life, if we have the will and the guts to go through it and are fortunate enough to find ourselves in a situation in which we can receive guidance and support. In order to pass through the gate, however, it is necessary to learn to surrender and let go of all those things which we identify with as 'ourselves', both our attitudes and opinions as well as the objects of our external lifestyles. This was the only way that physical death from a sickness like his could be changed into psychological death and the emergence of a new life.

I told him I knew this wasn't easy; it was the most difficult thing any human being could undertake, but when you reach the point he had reached as I had earlier, there was no other way but to trust and let go.

Even as I spoke I could see that my words were being stopped at the barrier and searched. That they were found to be carrying weapons and manifestos which contravened the laws of the land they were trying to enter. He mumbled something which sounded as though it was meant to signify agreement or acceptance, but which did not bear any authentic stamp of authority.

It was time for Masako and me to leave and it was to be the last time that we saw Mr. S.

66

The following evening the phone rang. It was Masako's mother. It appeared that the previous morning she had placed an extra glass of water on the family shrine, as Sensei had suggested. But when she had come to replace the old water with fresh that morning she discovered that the water in the new glass had disappeared.

I said that she had probably made a mistake and forgotten to fill it. Masako had already suggested this to her mother, but her mother had insisted that she was always most careful in making sure that the glasses were filled each morning, and, anyway, to carry a full glass of water from the kitchen to the room where the shrine is takes a great deal of care and attention, and she would certainly have noticed if she had been carrying an empty glass. She was adamant that the glass had been filled with water when it was placed on the shrine.

We decided to ask Osumi-sensei about it. She confirmed that it was not an uncommon occurrence.

67

It was hot again. Inside our house the light seemed to be a yellowy brown, as though the wood and ochre wall plaster were bleeding into the air. It was like living inside a fruit that was ready to fall.

Sometimes the heat and humidity were so intense that I felt as though my body was subjected to extreme atmospheric pressure. I felt as though the air, in its need to expand, was threatening to occupy my body space. I watched a spider to see if it was affected by the heat, but it did not seem to be. It just carried on as usual with whatever it was engaged in – running and stopping, running and stopping.

One night I woke up and felt that I was lying in a large spacious house in India. I could feel the Ganges flowing just beyond the window at the foot of our *futon*. I glanced across at the curtain Masako had hung in front of the open *karakami*. It seemed to gather in its fabric what little light there was and glowed dimly. It looked like a waterfall arrested by sleep.

I felt very empty and peaceful, though it seemed the air about me was itself delirious and hallucinating, and that, as I breathed it in, so it transmitted to my blood the ambience of its vision.

I got up and went quietly downstairs. The night was silent, but I became aware of a strange tension in the house. It was as though there was a great din which was inaudible to my ordinary sense of hearing but which was nevertheless registered by some part of me. It was as if the whole house were roaring like a mighty waterfall but could only be heard somewhere else, in some other dimension. The more I 'listened', the more I realized the roar was coming from myself or, more correctly, the roar was me!

I took a drink of water. I had to let the water flow for a time before it became cool. Then I went back upstairs. I lay for some time in that hypnogogic state between waking and sleeping, when I suddenly saw the left half of my body naked. I had my eyes closed and saw it as though it were illuminated in the darkness of my head. This was immediately followed by a blue flash like lightning which struck right through my body, from my head to somewhere near my feet. In its light I saw the inside and the outside of my body simultaneously. At that same instant my whole body jerked violently as though kicked by heavy voltage.

The next morning on my way out I happened to pick up a book of Masako's by an author whose work had never interested me. I opened the book up at a section of diaries recording a period spent in India! I noted with amusement that the author's christian name was also Malcolm.

68

I had a dream one night that I was escaping from 'Russia'. I was accompanied by some other people, it seemed they were families with children. We were travelling through a series of subterranean passages that opened at intervals or were connected by egg-shaped caves or cells. It was like travelling through a hollow rosary. Sometimes we seemed to come close to the surface where there were often holes through which I could glimpse people moving above, but generally we avoided these areas.

Quite suddenly I was alone and knew that I was travelling to a place where I would be reunited with my 'brother'. The passage I was travelling through opened out into one of the caves or cell-like places and there was my 'brother' standing before me. I ran up to embrace him and found myself staring at myself! I broke down weeping and woke up sobbing.

69

For three days the left side of my body felt tense and painful. The left side of the body is the lunar side, psychologically relating to the 'feminine' side of our nature, while physiologically relating to the heart. Each morning when I got up I felt very ill. I could not help Masako with making breakfast. Instead I would sit on a chair with my body shaking so violently that I was eventually thrown to the floor. The shaking would last for about half an hour, when it would finally stop and I would feel well enough to eat breakfast.

On the third morning, however, the shaking suddenly turned into birthing[25] as I lay on the floor.

This was my fifth birthing, and whereas the first three had been very difficult and partial, and the fourth a long labour, this time it happened very quickly and easily and ended with a baby's crying coming from my throat.

That day I learned that what I had felt on the two days prior to and immediately before the birthing was the great anxiety and fear I had experienced in the womb before being born. My mother has told me that I took a very long time to be born and they had just brought in the instruments for a forceps delivery when I decided to emerge. (This was in 1940 in the middle of an air raid.)

Afterwards I felt wonderful and my condition seemed to have reached another level.

70

I was so excited by what had happened that I instantly wanted to tell Sensei about it. I felt that it was the strong Seiki therapy that I had been receiving that had caused this birthing to surface.

The opportunity to speak to Osumi-sensei came on a Sunday. I began by giving her a report on the condition of my patients. My mother-in-law had told me she felt so well now that she could 'run up and down the stairs carrying a *futon*', which, she said, was something she hadn't been able to do for two or three years. And that she went to the lavatory once a day instead of only twice a week. F-san, whom I had seen the day before, had just received the results of his regular check-up at the hospital and the doctor had said that his condition was now excellent. His blood pressure was normal and the sugar content of his blood at a healthy level, whereas before it had become alarmingly high. He looked very well now and said that he slept easily and could relax.

Next I eagerly told Sensei about my birthing. She listened quietly, but did not seem particularly interested. When I had finished she simply said, 'Yes, I've heard that in Western psychotherapy you can go back to your birth.'

'But what I mean . . .' I began, but she cut me short.

'A young monk makes a lot of noise reading sutras loudly and such. The old monk does like this –' She closed her eyes and nodded her head slightly, almost imperceptibly. 'We all have ways of changing. Some quietly inside. This therapy is for pushing out both physical and psychological illness.'

I felt as though I had been firmly put down. I sat back in the chair. At first I felt angry. Then, as Sensei and Masako were talking, I realized I had become too excited about it and perhaps made too much of it. Maybe I had used the experience like air to pump up my ego. Too much attachment, too much identifying with it.

The next thing Sensei said brought me out from the depth of my chair and from the brief darkness of my mood.

'You are supported by your ancestor,' she said to me.

'My ancestor! Which ancestor, Sensei?'

'Your grandfather on your father's side,' she replied, seeming to look past me.

I sat back in my chair again, Grandpa! At one time I had been closer to him than perhaps anyone in the family. It was he who, when I was young, had fertilized an interest in poetry in me. He would recite poetry, mostly Burns, and sing strange little songs, sometimes in Gaelic, while we worked together in his orchard. He had moved south to England in order to take up the post of headmaster at a school near Plymouth. He was short and very dark, a true Celt with a strong streak of Calvinism.*

---

*I asked my Father to send me a photograph of my grandfather. In it he happens to be wearing a snake-skin jacket, as quite uncharacteristically, he had asked me to exchange jackets with him that afternoon.

Sensei's voice snatched me back from my memories of my grandfather. 'You are also supported by the Hagiwara ancestor. It's an unusual situation.' There was a pause while we drank our tea and I mused upon what strange bedfellows a Calvanistic Scot and a samurai made. Then, turning to me, Sensei said, 'Your experience was very good.' She took hold of my right hand and held it between both of hers. She was looking at me or, it seemed again, just to one side of me with one of her strange expressions, as though she was looking into a landscape somewhere behind me, like the view behind the head in a Renaissance portrait. 'You'll have more of this kind of experience,' she said.

71

My father-in-law, whose state of health had improved so dramatically over the year that even his doctor had expressed incredulity at his condition, had over a period of three months become embroiled in very difficult negotiations over some property which he had been under pressure to sell for some time. The property had originally been bought jointly with his wife just after they married. More recently it had been under lease to a firm who repeatedly asked my father-in-law to sell it to them in order that they could develop it. His decision to do so now had resulted in a series of rather bitter court hearings in order to try to come to some agreement over a price that would be equitable to both sides. It had caused my father-in-law great anguish. Apart from the psychological strain caused by the financial side of the affair, there was also the emotional aspect involved in selling a property which he and his wife had bought together at the beginning of their married life. The final price decided by the court was far below my father-in-law's expectations and he had become depressed about it.

Osumi-sensei had tried to advise him against undertaking any business transactions during this period of his recovery, as keeping a physical and psychological equilibrium in his life was essential to his continued progress.

He began to lose the weight that he had put on over the previous year and was also beginning to lose his appetite. During this time he had a dream which, uncharacteristically, he told us. The dream worried me very much although at the time I did not mention to Masako what I thought the obvious meaning of the dream was.

He dreamed that he was watching a doctor talking to a patient. The doctor was holding a piece of red-hot iron and said to the patient, 'I'm going to throw this at you with *kiai* and you will have to catch it.' The doctor threw the piece of red-hot iron at the patient, but the patient could not catch it.

72

Still at the back of my mind during the past year and a half or so was the one question that I needed to have answered. Up to now I had kept it to myself for reasons I was not too clear about. I wanted to know why, if I was as sick as Sensei had said I was when I first came to Japan, did she work me to the point where it was obvious I was going to collapse?

Now that she was sitting opposite me and the question was on my lips, I felt a little apprehensive about asking it. I had always thought that I knew the answer and perhaps my reason for holding back from asking it was the fear that maybe her answer would be different from what I had thought it should be.

After the words of the question had left me, there was a pause. Then she said slowly, 'Yes,' as though she had repeated the question to herself after me, because my keeping the question so long inside myself had somehow caused its transmission to be impaired in some way. 'It was necessary for you to break down completely in order for you to learn.' The answer inside me saw its own reflection and bowed.

Sensei got up from the table and went into the kitchen. When she returned she was carrying three glasses and a bottle of Scotch whisky. After she had poured Masako and me a measure each and I had poured her one, she sat down again. 'I can't tell the difference any more between you,' she said putting her glass down. 'Except that you're obviously of different sexes, I can't tell the difference. I can say that you are both of one mind, one body now. You have both changed your fates.'

By this last I understood her to mean the difference between fate and destiny. On the one side, we unconsciously live life without any awareness or insight into our own conditioned patterns of behaviour, and on the other, we work with that conditioning and develop some insight into and awareness of our true nature. We slowly let go the description we have been given of ourselves and develop of a trust in life. Instead of trying to live life, we let life live us, so to speak.

I asked her about my death face and she said that she could no longer see it. Then she said, 'How you came here and have managed to remain here is a kind of miracle. You must have had some connection with Seiki-jutsu, Masako or Japan in a former life.' We laughed, and Sensei poured us another glass of whisky. I remembered her having said something similar not long after I had arrived in Japan.

'I have something to tell you tonight that is very important.' She looked very serious. 'Next year is going to be a dark year. A black year. For both of you, myself, my daughter Masako and for I-san. The planets of the four of you are supporting mine.' I did not know exactly what she meant by this, but guessed it must have to do with astrological planetary conjunctions.

'If this is the day,' she continued, 'next year is going to be like the night!'

Oh no! I thought. If this last year or so has been day, what the hell is night going to be like?

Sensei's face was still fixed like a Noh mask in its expression of seriousness. 'I want you to stay strictly within the triangle formed by this house, your parents' house and your own house at Nishiazabu. Everything will be all right if you stay within this triangle. I'm thinking that in September we may all go and visit Eizon Shrine and ask the priest there to purify us.'

I could already sense the 'night' creeping up behind us like a thick black cowl. I picked up my glass and, throwing my head back, dropped the remaining whisky to the back of my throat.

As we got up to leave, Sensei told us not to start worrying about what she had just said. Maybe nothing would happen. We mustn't make the whole thing too heavy. I was already thinking of my father-in-law's dream. We walked to the end of the road where Masako's youngest brother was to pick us up. As we stood by the roadside we talked about what Sensei had just said. Not being too heavy about it was not easy, though.

After he had turned the car round, Masako's brother suddenly said, 'You know, it's extraordinary, but the distance between our house [his parent's house], Osumi-sensei's and your house is exactly the same. I noticed it on Sunday when I drove father between the three houses. Isn't that strange?'

I turned to look at Masako, who was sitting in the back seat, as the car pulled out into heavy traffic.

As we walked past our neighbours' gardens to our front door, the night was choired by crickets, like the voices of stars singing back to themselves from the earth – the laughter of aeons echoing in the hearts of grasses.

EPILOGUE

The 'black year' predicted by Osumi-sensei, duly manifested itself, not merely one year, but two. Each of us was to experience a 'black year', apart from being drawn into each other's and affected by Osumi-sensei's. Masako's commenced a year before mine with the death of her father.

After his involvement with the legal problems concerning the selling of his land and subsequent appearances in court, his condition rapidly deteriorated until he finally took to his bed. At this point Masako was told by Osumi-sensei once more to 'attach' herself to him. For the next forty days and nights, she spent every moment with him, even sleeping on a *futon* next to his, feeding him, talking with him, and holding his body when he was in pain. During this period he continued to receive treatment at home several times a day.

At the end of the forty days and nights Masako and her mother were both exhausted, and it was also obvious that he had noticed this and was beginning to worry about it. Suddenly, one afternoon, my father-in-law decided to terminate his treatment with the words, 'Everyone has a right to choose,' and, having made this decision, he prepared himself for death. That night he summoned the whole family around the dining table in order to share his last supper of ice cream, the only food he felt able to eat at the time. The next day, while a glass of water was being fetched for him, he crawled out of his *futon* to go to the lavatory and collapsed in the hallway. As we lifted him back to his bed, we found he had haemorrhaged. Blood flowed from him like his shadow stealing away, with his light secreted beneath a dark kimono. Finally he died in a hospital at his own request as he knew the legal difficulties that would result for the family if he died at home without conventional

208

medical supervision. He died without drugs and without pain, in a hospital opposite his factory. Each of us had held him in turn, our hands never leaving his body, until he left us.

That night we spent in a room that was set deep in the ground beneath the hospital, cut into the rock, guarding his body with a small altar set up before it. We had gone into the ground with him to pray and burn incense in preparation for the start of his long journey. Even in this deep silent place the omnipresent mosquitoes had assembled like static charges of attendant spirits dancing in the dim candlelight. Now and then one or two tried to graze my father-in-law's face and were brushed away by one of his devoted guardians.

Throughout the night we remained sitting or lying on the *tatami*, exhausted, each joined with the others by shared grief, and separated also, each from the other, by his or her own personal thoughts and memories. Each face looked drained and vacant, like the faces of people whom events have carried too swiftly and uncomprehendingly to a place of time-lagged emptiness within their own lives. Now and then one of us would shuffle forward on our knees to burn fresh incense, bow and return to our place.

Sitting with my back against a wall, I thought about how central my father-in-law's presence had been in my recent life. And how, without him, our continued sojourn in Japan would have been impossible. He had not only provided a house for us and created a situation which allowed me, as a foreigner, to remain in Japan with a legal visa, but he had fully supported the idea of our training in Seiki-jutsu, and had supplemented our earnings in order to allow us to live comparatively free of financial worries during this period. Apart from this, he had shown intense interest and concern during the early stages of the writing of this book, even to the extent of inquiring daily from his sickbed as to its progress, and on two occasions waking in the night to tell Masako of dreams he had had concerning it. Then, with a strange shock, I realized that this night, his death night, was 5 December in Japan, which meant that it was 4 December in Britain – my birthday!

Just as I was about to whisper this to Masako, there was a dull rumbling and the whole room began to shake violently.

After about thirty seconds, we began to look inquiringly at each other. '*Jishin*' ('Earthquake'), people began murmuring as the rumbling and shaking continued. Like the West Coast of America, the east coast of Japan is waiting a predicted major earthquake, which may happen at any time. This one sounded major and felt as though the entire city above was collapsing. After a full minute of seismic convulsion, Onisan got up and went out of the room. He returned looking briefly relaxed. 'It's the furnaces. The furnaces are starting up!' Faint grins were shared among us. But there *had* been an earthquake. The ground of the family and its tree had been shaken violently, and the aftershocks were to be felt for the whole of the following year.

The next day we returned to the family home with my father-in-law's corpse. Here we dressed him according to the rites of the Jodo sect, in the costume of a mendicant monk. Each member of the immediate family assisted in dressing him in a white kimono, with straw hat and straw sandals. In one hand he held a wooden staff, and in the other a Buddhist rosary, and on his chest lay a small sword for protection against evil spirits. In this way he was prepared for the long journey to the Pure Land. The coffin was then set up on a bier surrounded by flowers, and candles and incense lighted. Later a monk arrived and held a short service which was attended by the family and close relations.

The following morning we travelled with the coffin to the family temple, an ancient Jodo-shu temple which has been designated as a national treasure. Here five hundred mourners came to burn incense, pay their respects and say their last farewells. At one point a pale young man appeared before the censer in front of the altar. As he bowed he burst into loud sobbing, his body shaking uncontrollably. The sound of his grief added counterpoint to the emotionless chanting of the monks, as the heavy smoke from the incense steeped the bodies of mourners and monks alike, infusing us all with a common fragrance. (I later learned that the young man was one of countless young people my father-in-law had taken under his wing and assisted over the years, often welcoming them into his home as members of an extended family.)

After the service we travelled to the crematorium. It was here, as the coffin was taken from us to the fire, that I looked up and saw a row of square, plain wooden boxes, high on a shelf. These were the simplest, and therefore the cheapest, containers for the ashes of the dead. It was just such a box that I had seen in my dream before leaving Arran and coming to Japan. As the bier was borne back to us, the family stood quietly in a semicircle. The husband, the father, the father-in-law had been returned – bones laid out in the form of a skeleton,[1] as though by a chance tide, randomly arranged. A skeleton bleached by a subterranean sun. A stark geology purified by chthonic winds. A tree of lunar debris. What had been intimately recognizable and loveable in its form a moment ago had now been transformed into something strange and impersonal that lay like a calcified path leading in the direction of a place it was not yet time for us to enter, though something had already been set down upon that path and made its entry without our noticing it.

The monk remarked in a detached, almost academic, tone on how unblemished the bones were, and then instructed us on how to place them in a large white ceramic urn, which was held by a uniformed attendant. We were each given a pair of chopsticks with which to lift the bones one by one, in turn and place them in the urn. Sometimes a bone would be passed between several of us, from one person's chopsticks to another, before being placed in the urn. (This is the only occasion on which etiquette allows something to be passed from one person's chopsticks to another's. At mealtimes it would be considered most improper.)

The last bone to be placed in the urn, apart from the skull, which caps the rest, was the atlas, the cervical vertebra that supports the skull. The reason for this, the monk explained, was that it is shaped like someone in *zazen*, that is, sitting in the lotus position.

The remains of my father-in-law were then taken back to the house and an altar erected. For a hundred days people came with offerings and to pay their respects, and on the fifth of each month a monk came to hold a short service to guide my father-in-law's spirit at each stage of its journey to the Pure Land. Finally after a hundred days, the remains were interred in the family grave at the temple and another service held. The emotionally and physically gruelling mourning period had had a psychologically purifying and creative effect on everyone. Slowly and perhaps hesitantly at times the family's life began to change and a new order with a new rhythm began to exert itself.

It is to the memory of Masako's father, my father-in-law, a man of honour, humour and compassion – known by his associates in Tokyo as 'the last samurai' – that 'A *Deshi*'s Tale' is dedicated.

It seemed that as soon as Masako's 'black year' had terminated, my own commenced. The book by this time was in what I considered only a half-finished state. Osumi-sensei, however, having 'seen' that it was going to be published, sent us off to London with it.

Our visit to Britain was like a nightmare for me. I felt that my own country had become a foreign land and my old friends and loved ones seemed like strangers, when it was I who had become both a foreigner and a stranger. The manuscript was understandably rejected, but interested the publishers enough for them to ask to see it again at a later stage.

On returning to Japan we commenced further interviews with Osumi-sensei and I continued with my training patients. All the while my Seiki exercises were becoming more and more wild. The voices had returned and my body adopted a strange ritual of *gassho* (bowing with palms together) and calling on Buddha each time I sat on the stool.

It was during this period that one day, when I had just finished retyping the story of Eizon Hoin and was sitting staring blankly at the typing in front of me, something strange happened. My right hand, holding a pencil, was resting on a sheet of paper beside the typewriter. Suddenly it began to move in an agitated manner across the paper. I looked down at it and to my astonishment realized it was drawing something. As I watched, the head and shoulders of a man began to appear. After a minute or so the drawing ceased and I picked up the paper. In a style which was totally unlike my own drawing style was the head and shoulders of a rather wild-looking Japanese man. His eyes seemed closed or possibly half-closed as though sleeping or meditating. We immediately wondered if it was Eizon Hoin.

Two or three days later we showed the drawing to Osumi-sensei and explained to her what had happened. She stared at the drawing for a very long time. Then she placed it back on the table in front of me. As with the tape of the voices three years earlier, she said nothing and, though it may seem strange, we knew not to ask any questions about it at that time.

Soon I stopped being able to sleep and my body experienced violent convulsions day and night. On several occasions, while I was standing up, my body began to spin spontaneously, and one afternoon, while I was seated at the table, my body stood up and spun violently in a clockwise direction the full length of the house and dumped me heavily against the end wall, exhausted and very frightened.

A few nights later, attempting to rest but filled by a consuming fear, I went to get up from the *futon*. As I reached an upright sitting position, I suddenly saw the man in my automatic drawing kneeling in front of me. His image appeared very powerfully in what seemed like a sudden flash. He was sitting slightly at an angle to me, looking to my left.

Soon I was too weak to get up from my *futon* and my body went into convulsions hourly, accompanied by voices. Sato-san, who came to give me daily treatments, said they sounded like the chanting of an old monk.

Osumi-sensei called this my 'last illness', by which I understood her to mean 'last' in the sense of the end of a period of psycho-energetic readjustment, rather than an end to experiencing sickness in the ordinary sense. This 'illness' was worse than anything I had suffered in the period covered by 'A *Deshi*'s Tale', and made those experiences seem more like a trailer or a mere synopsis of what now took place. Death again seemed to accompany me like my own breath.

One night I had become particularly weak and it seemed that my body would never cease its convulsive seizures and babblings. Osumi-sensei phoned and said she was going to come and give me treatment at about midnight. During the course of her treatment she suddenly worked herself up into a state that took her beyond herself. Her hands moved powerfully and swiftly back and forth across my upper back, her breathing, which had previously been loud and violent, now became that of an excited animal. Simultaneously with her giving several loud *kiai*, the room filled with an almost overpoweringly heavy smell that seemed at once both unearthly, but at the same time of the deepest earth. Afterwards Masako said that it was like the 'smell of animals'; certainly one of the first images that came to my mind was that of wild goats. My body immediately became passive and I slept well that night for the first time.

A few days later, Osumi-sensei said she had seen Eizon Hoin standing up in his shrine like a *Nio* (one of the fierce warrior figures that stand guard on either side of temple gates). She said she heard him say, "I won't lie in the earth any longer!" She said, "He is guarding this book".

A few weeks after my recovery we left for Britain again. It had been a year since our last visit and this time our main object was to finish the book and to find ourselves somewhere to live when we eventually returned to Britain at the end of our training. Masako's father had left her just enough money to purchase a small cottage or flat. We based ourselves at my sister's cottage in Cornwall and, after three months, work on the book was complete and the manuscript had been sent to the publishers.

After a few weeks spent searching for a cottage, we decided to travel up to Scotland to visit friends, but prior to leaving we spent two nights with an old friend who lives in a nearby village.

Bill is an antique dealer, tall and spare, with a mild, eighteenth-century-squirish face. He lives in a large eighteenth-century rectory of weathered stone that one might expect to find in the middle of an open moor rather than in the centre of a tranquil Cornish village. Its walled garden, however, is protective and fecund, and bears evidence of a very different and more local climate.

After greeting us and picking up one of our bags, Bill led us up the staircase to the landing. We followed him across the landing and down three steps into a corridor which led to two rooms. He opened the door of the first. It was a large, light room overlooking the garden. 'I've put you in here,' he said. 'I've moved out and into the room at the end. Sometimes I sleep in here, just to keep it aired.' He placed the bag he was carrying beside the bed. 'I call this the snake room,' he said with a laugh. 'The snake room?' I said, returning his laugh. 'Why?' He pointed at the carpet. 'Look. You see that snake there? And here? It's a Meshed. It's rather nice really.' As we looked down at the richly designed carpet at our feet, more and more snakes seemed to disentangle themselves from the design, until the carpet seemed filled by them.

'I've always called this the snake room,' he said as he left to go downstairs.

The next day a strange cat entered the house from the garden through the kitchen door, and installed herself as though she were in her own residence and in full knowledge of its topography and occupants. She made a great fuss of each of us in turn, as though we had only recently returned from a long absence. On returning from a short walk to visit a cottage I had once lived in at the foot of the village, Masako and I discovered her sleeping on our bed in the 'snake room'.

By the evening Bill was in a quandary as to what to do about the cat, which showed no signs of leaving voluntarily. We suggested that as she had obviously chosen his house, he should keep her, as her appearance seemed auspicious. This resulted in the sudden appearance of saucers of milk and tuna fish.

As we were to leave early for Scotland the following morning, I tried to arrange for an alarm call. To our dismay, we discovered that the phone was not working properly and the operator had difficulty phoning back. I moved the phone, at her suggestion, to another point on the landing, but this did not seem to improve matters.

On returning to the sitting room, we opened a bottle of whisky and sat talking for an hour or so. Just as we were closing the house for the night, the telephone on the landing suddenly rang. Thinking it was the operator checking the number again, I ran up to answer it. It was Oliver Caldecott, the publisher, who had traced us through friends, ringing from his home to tell us that the book had been accepted. We sat up for a further hour or so and finished the rest of the bottle.

The next morning we left for Glasow and Arran.

It is difficult to present a concise summary of the last few years while still in the midst of a process which is by no means completed as yet, the contours and structure of which seem hardly defined. I had started out with the simplistic notion that I was to learn a method of healing and return to Britain in order to practice what I had been taught. 'A *Deshi*'s Tale' is clearly a testimony to my stupidity in this respect. What I in fact embarked upon was not only the continuation of a path or quest for knowledge which now resumed on a far more intense level than I had formerly experienced under any other teacher, but also a resumption of self-healing and personal revelation. It is a path, which, while it is often excruciatingly difficult and engenders a strong desire to flee, I find myself incapable of leaving.

Death — psychological and physical — seems to have been a persistently recurring motif in my life and training during the past four years. Death with all its positive energies of transformation and regeneration.

In the West death has become taboo and closeted by a fearful averting of our attention. But ignoring death has resulted in ignorance and a denial of our responsibility towards our need both to learn to 'die' within life as well as to understand life itself as a process by which we learn and prepare for actual physical death. This is a result of and has resulted in our loss of a way of dying. Through our misunderstanding of death in the West and our wont of disassociating it from life — seeing it as in opposition to life — we have misunderstood life itself and dangerously restricted our capacity and energy for living. This particular severing has contributed one of the major ingredients to a form of existence that we erroneously call our 'culture', which is nothing better than an existential coffin – by denying death we have created a not-living as a 'way of life'.

In retrospect the last years have seemed like some kind of dream, though they have in fact been an awakening for me. Awakenings of this kind are by their nature at times frightening and painful, and lead to the need for continuing awakenings before we can become fully awake. It is a process that may take many lifetimes.

My experience of learning with Osumi-sensei is due partly to what I have brought to it, to 'who I am' at this space in time. Another's experience might be quite different. Masako's way of learning is very different from mine and only she would be able to describe it, which is why there is no description of it here in this book.

Again, it is very difficult to be objective about the changes that I have noticed taking place in myself. Certainly the shape of my body has entirely altered, from a thinness that was becoming thinner with the years, to a body that has thickened in every area, particularly the *hara*, which has grown huge! With this increase in size has come a corresponding increase of over two stones in weight. This has taken place during periods of intense mental and physical suffering, when the opposite effect might well have been expected. On a psychological level, many hitherto habitual patterns of behaviour and thinking have either entirely disappeared or been altered.

Osumi-sensei said to me recently that I will not be aware of the real changes until after this book is completely out of my system. More than this I cannot say, and it would certainly be presumptuous of me to try to go farther at this time.

Osumi-sensei, while keeping time with the 'old world', also lives very much in the world of the technological present. She balances the 'old way' and the new skilfully, without seeing anything anachronistic or bizarre in the juxtapositions that sometimes result. For her the 'old way' and the 'new way' are simply integrated aspects of a life that she is perfectly comfortable with in the reality of her day-to-day living: the world of mass communications on the one hand and dialogue with the 'other world' of elemental energies and spirits on the other offer no contradictions or difficulties.

It is such an understanding that we need to develop within our own lives on this planet, in order to create a true balance between the spiritual and the material – a 'middle way', one of the effects of which would be the development of benign technologies in place of those which express the destructive, selfish and fearful attitudes of conditioned ego. This is also echoed in our need to return to the true 'centre' of the body, away from the head – domain of intellectual, conceptual thinking, of ego – to the belly or *hara*, the home of our natural, intuitive being. It is by returning to our 'home' in this sense that we will restore the balance between the spiritual and the material, intuition and intellect, and become one once again with the healing world.

NOTES

1. It is doubtful if consumer societies can be truly said to qualify for the description of 'culture'. In fact, if we look at the history and development of industrial, technological *man*, I believe that we see the morphology of sickness.
2. I am not suggesting that people of *all* early cultures lived profoundly.
3. This 'turning point' is in direct contrast to the 'last frontier' mentality which considers space as the last great tract of wilderness to be 'conquered' and used for commercial and military purposes. It is this same mentality that experiences the body as a kind of technology which can be serviced by technology. (This attitude should cause no surprise, as most of us have grown up with our bodies described to us in terms of mechanical functioning. It is reflected in the pop media and children's toys, with the obsession for cyborgs and androids – humans that are part machine and machines that are designed to resemble human beings and to perform human tasks.)

Part I   The Healing World of Ikuko Osumi

CHAPTER 1

1. See Fritjof Capra's *The Tao of Physics* (Fontana, 1983).
2. Buddhist doctrine states this situation very succinctly as: 'Form is emptiness, emptiness is form.' This is the doctrine of *sunyata* – 'Void', 'nothingness' or 'emptiness' – which does not deny existence, but recognizes that all that is manifest exists

219

through or because of causation. These causal factors are constantly in flux, always changing; there is no fixed, static or permanent existence – all existence is relative and inter-dependent. Emptiness is the ground of existence.

3. Ice and water have long been used in Zen as a metaphor describing the difference between 'small mind' (or the conditioned self), and 'big mind' (unconditioned or true nature). Ice is rigid and inflexible, while water flows and accommodates any situation, but both are different states of the same thing.

4. Even the concepts or perceptions of 'manifesting from' or 'returning to' are ultimately illusory.

5. The electrical resistance is different at these points, compared with any other parts of the body.

6. See research carried out by Dr Hiroshi Motoyama at the Institute of Religious Psychology, Tokyo.

7. This energy can be stored in a variety of materials and Ikuko Osumi regularly impregnates wads or raw silk – *mawata* – with Seiki. This is done in strict privacy and she has never shown or divulged the manner in which she does this to any *deshi* to date. All she will say on the subject is, When I'm putting Seiki into the *mawata*, it flies up and sticks to my hands.' These raw pads of silk are then worn by patients under their clothes and next to any part of the body which is giving pain or discomfort.

CHAPTER 2

1. In the Jōdō sect or Pure Land school of Buddhism, of which the Amida Buddha is the central figure, it is believed that one can gain entry to the Pure Land or Western Paradise through the repetition of a formula called the *Nembutsu* – *Namu Amida Butsu*. The Jōdō-shin sect of Pure Land Buddhism was founded in Japan by the monk Shinran (1173–1262), and remains one of the most popular schools of Buddhism in Japan, particularly in relation to funerary rites. While the Pure Land school is often denigrated by other schools of Buddhism, it is possible to gain a profound meditative state through concentration on reciting this formula.

2. There are two main schools of Buddhism. The earlier school of Hinayana (or Lesser Vehicle, now generally referred to as Theravada or The Teaching of the Elders), and Mahayana (or Greater Vehicle). The Hinayana or Theravada school is narrower and less flexible in its interpretation of Buddhist teaching. It stresses individual salvation through gradual enlightenment and recognizes that there is no essential ego--nature in human beings. The Mahayana school, on the other hand, is much more open and broad in its understanding of Buddhist doctrine, and had been influenced and coloured by the indigenous religious practices of many of the countries into which it has been introduced: for example, in Tibet the shamanic religion of Bon; in China Ch'an (Zen has been influenced by Taoism); in Japan Shinto has influenced Buddhism, and shamanic practices have influenced the Tantric schools.

Mahayana Buddhism recognizes that not only is there no existing ego-nature in human beings, but that this is true of all existence. Instead of emphasizing individual liberation, central to its teaching is the concept of the Bodhisattva ideal, by which an individual who attains enlightenment postpones Nirvana, or deliverence from all karmic involvement, until all sentient beings have been helped to attain complete liberation.

It should be noted that modern Theravada teaching recognizes *sunyata* as the underlying condition of all phenomena.

3. Originally called *honji-suijaku-setsu* to explain *kami* as manifestations of the Cosmic Buddha and Buddhist deities. Later reversed by Shintoists and called *han-honji-suijaku-setsu*.

4. Dharma means the teaching of the Buddha and also the Law of the Universe.

5. Strictly speaking, the word 'karma' refers to 'cause', whereas 'effect' is described as 'the fruits of karma'.

6. These heavens and hells are also reflected in the nature of our moment-to-moment existence as we transmigrate from one condition to another, according to the fluctuations in our psychological and physical states. The reality of our moment-to-moment existence is one of life, death and rebirth. This is not merely the larger or more obvious rhythm of existence, but

222 THE SHAMANIC HEALER

the essential rhythm of the discontinuous nature of conditioned consciousnes.

CHAPTER 3

1. There is a maxim, which I think comes from Sufism, that says, 'It is not the path that is difficult, but the difficulty that is the path.'
2. It is difficult to determine whether this was in fact her mother's own choice or a decision reached under pressure from her own family.
3. A place for training of a spiritual nature.
4. It is obvious that the white snake is either a messenger of Eizon Hoin or a manifestation of Eizon Hoin himself.
5. It is common in Japan for 'new religions' to be formed around individuals who display supranormal or spiritual powers.
6. A title that denotes an ordained Buddhist priest who is connected with the Shugendo sect.
7. Ikuko Osumi believes that only Eizon Hoin's skull is buried here.

CHAPTER 4

1. The sash of a kimono.
2. Japanese sleeping mattress filled with raw cotton.
3. Ikuko Osumi often refers to the head or brain as the 'sun', and the sacrum, because it reflects the condition of the head, as the 'moon'.
4. Very sour preserved apricots.
   This is a way of concentrating *ki* or Seiki energy in the lower belly and then suddenly releasing it, often with a loud cry, grunt or hissing sound. At the moment of *kiai*, mind and body are brought to a state of 'empty' synthesis, so that the energy that is expressed is free from any emotional content or intention; it is egoless and therefore of a powerful spiritual nature. It is this concentration of energy and its egoless release that enables exponents of the martial arts to perform feats that would otherwise be impossible.
   Kiai also refers to a high concentration of this energy in the

body through a state of undistracted mindfulness.

6. There may be some connection here between the way in which Seiki is attracted and the way in which a *kami* or a spirit is invoked or attracted by banging stones or pieces of wood together, or ringing bells, and so on.

7. A ceramic or metal-lined wooden tub or box containing a bed of ash on which charcoal is burned for heating.

8. Compare my own account on pp. 92–94.

9. A meat and vegetable stew, nowadays cooked on a gas ring at the centre of the table, from which one helps oneself.

CHAPTER 5

1. White socks, worn with a kimono, in which there is a division between the big toe and the rest of the foot to accommodate the thong of a small sandle (*zori*) or wooden block sandle (*geta*).

2. Rectangular pallets of straw to which reed mats are firmly attached. These are laid tightly together to form a dry, comfortable flooring.

3. Sliding screens of wooden lattice covered on one side with strong white paper and used for screening windows or dividing rooms.

4. A Buddhist deity, frequently depicted in ferocious aspect, surrounded by flames. He is connected with healing and employs a retinue of boy helpers and messengers.

CHAPTER 6

1. 'One mind' describes the undivided, undistracted and concentrated condition of mind.

2. Formal sitting, with the legs folded under the body and the buttocks resting on the heels.

3. Animals, young babies and sages, manifest their being through their actions, although there is a profound difference in the way of manifesting between the first two and the latter. When a baby screams, it is manifesting its being through its scream; the whole universe is 'aaaaaawhaaaaaa' because there is no conscious ego formed – there is no dualistic split between a 'me' crying 'aaaaaawhaaaaaa' because 'I'm unhappy due to

such and such and the actual cry, that is, no conceptualizing about conditions, just an instinctual response. There is nothing withheld or separate; nothing that is not the scream.

When a tea master or a Zen monk is making a mindful or meditative action, *being* is expressed through the action; it is the action. But, in this case there is a state of total awareness and a heightened state of consciousness as a result of transcending the conditioned state of self.

4. In his forties his business became bankrupt and he had to sell everything he owned, but within ten years he had built it up again.

5. For years he had suffered a skin disease of itchy purple blotches all over his body, and had been using very strong ointments, but to no effect.

CHAPTER 7

1. It is possible that this type of ghost is a premonitory vision.
2. A short coat worn over a kimono by both men and women.
3. He had dark, swarthy skin and jet black hair.
4. A special red fish served on occasions of congratulations.
5. It is interesting to note that in the Japanese language there existed no word for 'nature' until the Meiji era (1867–1912), when the concepts of man and nature were imported from the West and the word for 'nature' – *shizen* – appeared.
6. My experiences with Ikuko Osumi in this chapter postdate those events recorded in Part II 'A *Deshi*'s Tale'.
7. 'No good! No good!'
8. Exterior sliding window shutters.
9. A six-mat room.
10. It is said in Japan that some swords are filled with *sakki*, the *ki* of murder and killing.
11. Roughly thirty days after a Japanese baby is born it is taken to the local shrine and presented to the *kami*. The baby then becomes a *ujiko* or a 'child of the *kami*'. For the rest of its life it remains a parishioner of that shrine and is thereafter protected by that particular *kami*.
12. A ninth-century scholar with extraordinary gifts, who later came to be regarded as a *kami* and guardian of scholars and poets.

13. A recess or alcove reserved for the display of a prized or valuable scroll painting or a special religious object or flower arrangement.

CHAPTER 8

1. An experience of sudden enlightenment.
2. A place directly behind the front door in a Japanese house where outdoor shoes are left and slippers donned before entering the house.

Part II A Deshi's Tale

1. Tibet's most famous Buddhist saint.
2. Western psychology and Buddhist practice actually move in different directions, although there are crossroads where they meet. My own meditation teacher showed me how meditation can be useful as a psychotherapeutic tool for certain types of people in special training situations.
3. A period of existential hiatus, described in Tibetan Buddhism as experienced shortly after death and before rebirth. It also refers to those psychological states of insecurity which we all suffer, including doubt, disorientation, problems of identity, and so on.
4. See chapter 8, note 2, above.
5. This was extended to five years.
6. The paper-covered sliding door.
7. Kundalini yoga is a Hindu form of meditative practice designed to awaken the regenerative energy that lies dormant at the root of the spine in human beings. Through regular practice this energy is caused to rise up the spine through three main subtle nerves (nadi): a central one, which is located in the centre of the spine and is called the sushumna, around which a lunar nadi (called the ida) and a solar nadi (called the pingala) rise in a spiral. These two – the lunar and the solar – merge with the central nadi at certain critical centres of energy (chakra) on their path, causing the energies related to these centres to become activated. Successful practice results in the practitioners achieving a state of cosmic union.

Kundalini is often referred to as Serpent Power, and the more I become acquainted with Seiki-jutsu, the more I am convinced that part of being given Seiki is the awakening of this energy.

8. See chapter 7, note 12, above.

9. Traditionally, a table placed over a pit in the floor at the bottom of which, and guarded by a grid, is a charcoal fire. While sitting at the table, one dangles one's legs in the pit. A heavy quilted cover overlaps the sides of the table to prevent any loss of heat.

10. The image of a wound is common in Western psychology in relation to the concept of the psyche, but it is no longer a way of working that I find helpful in my own case. The fact that I was thinking in these terms during this time indicates, to me, my generally confused state.

11. A traditional five-holed bamboo flute.

12. As the human ego or conditioned self is illusory, in reality there is no one to die – the real or unconditioned self is unborn and undying. From this point of view death is not something that 'happens to us'. Death is not something 'outside' or 'inside', so to speak, that acts upon us. There is no such separation. Knowing this conceptually is of course, very different from *realizing* it!

13. The old name of what is now modern Tokyo.

14. The eighteenth-century Zen priest and poet.

15. A flowering shrub with a powerful scent.

16. In Asia it is a hare rather than a man that is seen in the moon's face.

17. I-san had been a patient of Osumi-sensei for three years. He had been suffering from a heart condition and his family and neighbours expected him to die. After three years of daily treatment and resting at home, he was now returning to work, having inherited his father's business.

18. A traditional Japanese inn. Here the term refers more to the style of management than to the architecture, however.

19. A light cotton kimono.

20. A type of popular Japanese song.

21. Unfortunately this story cannot be told as permission was not obtained from the patient.

22. A piece of material not unlike a headscarf, often brightly

decorated and used for wrapping objects, either to carry them conveniently or when presenting them as gifts.

23. Rice balls covered in paste made from red beans.

24. Bodhidarma, the monk who brought Ch'an (Zen) to China from India. He is reputed to have sat in meditation facing a wall for nine years, until his legs withered away. He is regarded as the first Patriarch of Zen.

25. The body remembers everything that it has experienced, and its own birth is no exception. Usually most of these memories, which are 'forgotten', remain unconscious. However, certain experiences can trigger them in such a way that the mind/body re-experiences them. The trauma of our own birth and the circumstances surrounding it, and our intrauterine experience prior to it, often result in psychological and psysical problems in later life, and by re-experiencing these traumas we can gain insight into the ways in which we are conditioned by them and can thus resolve them. There are therapies designed to work in exactly this way.

Epilogue

1. In Japan the corpse is cremated in such a way that only the soft body is burned and the entire skeleton is preserved. It is perhaps due to our need to sanitize death in the West that we reduce the skeleton to a formless ash.

Due to circumstances surrounding, and my own condition during, the period of writing this book, several inaccuracies remained in the text. I have taken the opportunity of this edition to try to remedy those that I was aware of.

POSTSCRIPT

Just before the galleyproofs of this book were due to be printed, I asked Osumi-sensei again about the drawing of the man I had shown her a year previously and who, I explained to her, I had later seen. I also told her that we thought that he might be Eizon Hoin.

'No,' she replied. 'He was younger than Eizon Hoin when he died. Bring me the drawing again.'

When we produced the drawing a few days later, she stared intently at it for some time. She had an expression on her face that I had seen on several previous occasions. An expression of extreme seriousness and concentration.

Suddenly, without looking up from the drawing, she said, 'He died of heart disease. He was a man of very strong faith, very intelligent and of a very high rank.' She indicated his heart and his head with her forefinger as she spoke.

'He's Japanese isn't he?' I asked, as when I had seen him he had a dark swarthy complexion, jet black hair and appeared to be wearing a kimono-like robe.

Osumi-sensei shook her head. 'No. He's an ancient ancestor of yours. He's like your grandfather. He's from his line, but he lived many generations before him.'

I immediately wondered if he was an ancient Celt or even earlier and the memory of some extraordinary experiences I had had in a stone circle on the West coast of Scotland came into my mind. I wondered if there was any connection.

'The reason he was looking to your left,' she continued, 'was that he wanted to take you with him. The left side is the side of death. That means that your life was in great danger at that time. Spirits have emotions and at times he gets very lonely, but he gave up because he realised that you have a good job to do and that you are living happily. He is guarding you, but at the same time, when he's lonely, he wants to take you.

'Just now I thought that you should burn the drawing, but then I felt that you might be too emotionally attached, so I don't think it's a good idea. Let me do it. I will show you the ashes afterwards and then I will bury them beside my gate.' She paused and the expression on

229

her face changed to what looked like controlled shock. 'We shouldn't do it,' she suddenly said very firmly. 'Just now I saw flames. That means that if I burn the drawing, your house might be destroyed by fire. Anyway, even if I do try to burn the drawing, he might not allow me to do it.' She paused again.

'He just told me that he wants to go to Eizon Shrine.' She turned and called to Mineko-san to bring the large picture of Eizon Shrine that she keeps beside her house shrine to Eizon Hoin. Mineko-san came in carrying the large wooden framed colour photograph of the shrine. Osumi-sensei very carefully folded the blank edges of the paper around the drawing so that it formed a square which accommodated just the drawing itself. Then she carefully removed the photograph from its frame and placed the drawing behind it, returning the picture of the shrine with the drawing beneath it, to the frame.

'I can see him,' she said staring at an area of the photograph. 'He is standing with Eizon Hoin. He is on the right hand side of Eizon Hoin, which means that he is of a higher rank than Eizon Hoin. He is like a kami. He is even more holy and stronger than Eizon Hoin and he lived long before him.'

She set the picture before us. 'Now he is alright. Every morning I will light a candle in front of the photograph. I'll keep my eye on him. Usually I ask people to provide water for spirits in this kind of situation, but if I did in this case, he might remain with you. That might be dangerous for you at times.' She instructed us to clap our hands three times and gassho, and then Mineko-san carried the picture back to Eizon Hoin's house shrine.

As we were putting on our shoes in the genkan, Osumi-sensei said to me, 'When you stayed here during your sickness (I had stayed for a few days due to my critical condition), he came to take you. At that time I banished him and purified the house.' She turned to Mineko-san, 'You remember don't you?' Mineko-san, who was carrying one of the cats that had just come into the house, nodded and said she remembered.

Osumi-sensei turned back to me. 'I felt that your voices and your gassho was you unconsciously talking to him, apologizing for not being able to go with him. When your energy is low, talking with spirits will exhaust you, it could even kill you. But at that time if you remember, you had an enormous appetite and could eat very well, in spite of your illness.

'He will visit you from time to time and one more time he will try and take you. At that same time you must not talk to him. You must cut off.' She looked at Masako. 'If he talks to him, you must stop him somehow.'

Just then Nagase-san, a recent addition to the household, came in through the front door and said that the car was waiting. We bowed and said goodnight.